I have waited for just this book on internal communication for a long time. Both Stemmle and Dollins are highly experienced professional communicators who also embrace research and theory development in strategic communication. Readers will immediately recognize the command of these authors over the employee communication function informed by their positive and upright emphasis on strategic goal setting and execution. And when the authors get down to brass tacks in their case studies as well as their elucidation of tools and tactics, readers will reimagine how to DO employee communication. All this comes together in a most readable book! I encourage every practitioner and teacher of employee communication to get and to use this book in their work.
—**Glen T. Cameron**, *Emeritus Gregory Chair of Journalism Research, Missouri School of Journalism, USA*

Finally, a book that directly links business success to effective employee engagement. Through personal experience and case studies, Mark Dollins and Jon Stemmle connect the dots between employee communications and business results. Important reading for future leaders in business and communications.
—**Ron Culp**, *Professional Director, Public Relations and Advertising Program, DePaul University, USA*

During more than two decades as a chief human resources officer for three iconic companies, employee communication has played a prominent role, and continues to be one of my top priorities today at GE. From ensuring the effectiveness of change leadership efforts—to strengthening the employee experience—employee communication is one of the most critical levers for companies and leaders alike. In this book, [Dollins and Stemmle] go well beyond the fundamentals of communications and illustrate the need for stronger and more strategic employee communications, particularly as organizations navigate a world in which the only constant seems to be rapid change.
—**Kevin Cox**, *Chief Human Resources Officer, General Electric Company, USA*

In *Engaging Employees through Strategic Communication*, Dollins and Stemmle provide grounded insights into the often-overlooked but inescapably essential skill of communicating to engage and influence teams. Their approach offers the rare combination of imparting learning through a compelling good read. Equally valuable for aspiring students and experienced professionals.
—**Tod J. MacKenzie**, *Retired Chief Communications Officer, PepsiCo, Dine Brands, Aramark, USA*

It's about time that we have such a terrific textbook on employee engagement—and who better to do it than Mark Dollins and Jon Stemmle! The authors masterfully provide us with context, tips and case studies based on research and validated by decades of experience—theirs and that of other experts.

—**Maril MacDonald**,
Founder and Chief Executive Officer, Gagen MacDonald, USA

Good communication skills are imperative for good leadership, and good, clear communication is more important than ever. Yet the topic of communications is often ignored in business school curricula. Mark Dollins and Jon Stemmle understand this and have now addressed this gap. As they state in the first chapter of this groundbreaking new textbook, communication is a critical enabler of business performance. An award-winning communications executive, Dollins has led some of the largest and most important employee and leadership communications initiatives in the world. This, combined with Stemmle's experience as a professor of strategic communication, results in a valuable and important new resource that combines academic rigor with real-world experience and practical advice for every business leader or student who aspires to be a leader one day.

—**Jen McClure**, *CEO, JEM & Distinguished Principal Fellow,*
Marketing & Communications Center, The Conference Board, USA

Employee communications and engagement have always been critical disciplines, but the pace of organization change and the impact of the global pandemic have literally exploded the need for communication professionals who understand how it works—with real-world strategies, skills and tactics. Mark Dollins and Jon Stemmle have nailed it with *Engaging Employees through Strategic Communication*. From students to communications professionals and chief communication officers, this a must-have, must-read new bible of employee communications. It's a clear and compelling road map to unlocking discretionary effort from internal stakeholders to drive tangible business results.

—**Colleen J. Rooney**, *Chief Communications & CSR Officer,*
Board of Advisors Signet Jewelers
Kay Jewelers, Zales, Jared, H. Samuel, Ernest Jones,
Peoples, Piercing Pagoda, JamesAllen.com, USA

ENGAGING EMPLOYEES THROUGH STRATEGIC COMMUNICATION

Engaging Employees through Strategic Communication provides a detailed overview of employee communication and its evolution as a tool to drive employee engagement and successful change management.

Approaching the subject with the philosophy that internal audiences are essential to the success of any strategic communication plan and business strategy—particularly as they relate to driving change. Mark Dollins and Jon Stemmle give readers a working knowledge of employee communication strategies, skills and tactics in ways that prepare students for careers in this rapidly expanding field. Providing the tools necessary to evaluate the impact of successful employee communication campaigns, they put theory and cutting-edge research into action with practical examples and case studies sourced from award-winning entries judged as best-in-class by the International Association of Business Communicators (IABC), the Public Relations Society of America (PRSA), *PR Week* and PRNews.

The book is ideal for undergraduate and graduate students in internal, corporate or employee communication courses and will be a useful reference for practitioners who want to understand how to carry out effective employee communication engagement and change-management campaigns.

Mark Dollins is president of North Star Communications Consulting, a consultancy with core capabilities in employee/change communication strategy, and has led global employee and change communications for organizations such as PepsiCo, DuPont, Accenture and The Quaker Oats Company, among others.

Jon Stemmle is the chair and professional practice professor of Strategic Communication at the School of Journalism and a core faculty member of the Master of Public Health Program at the University of Missouri, USA.

ENGAGING EMPLOYEES THROUGH STRATEGIC COMMUNICATION

Skills, Strategies and Tactics

Mark Dollins and Jon Stemmle

Routledge
Taylor & Francis Group

NEW YORK AND LONDON

First published 2022
by Routledge
605 Third Avenue, New York, NY 10158

and by Routledge
2 Park Square, Milton Park, Abingdon, Oxon, OX14 4RN

Routledge is an imprint of the Taylor & Francis Group, an informa business

Library of Congress Cataloging-in-Publication Data
Names: Dollins, Mark, author. | Stemmle, Jon, author.
Title: Engaging employees through strategic communication : skills, strategies, and tactics / Mark Dollins and Jon Stemmle.
Description: New York, NY : Routledge, 2022. | Includes bibliographical references and index.
Subjects: LCSH: Communication in personnel management. | Employee motivation. | Organizational change.
Classification: LCC HF5549.5.C6 D55 2022 (print) | LCC HF5549.5.C6 (ebook) | DDC 658.4/5—dc23
LC record available at https://lccn.loc.gov/2021018969
LC ebook record available at https://lccn.loc.gov/2021018970

ISBN: 978-0-367-90391-6 (hbk)
ISBN: 978-0-367-90390-9 (pbk)
ISBN: 978-1-003-02411-8 (ebk)

DOI: 10.4324/9781003024118

Typeset in Bembo
by Apex CoVantage, LLC

Access the Support Material: www.routledge.com/9780367903909

CONTENTS

ABOUT THE AUTHORS

Mark Dollins is president of North Star Communications Consulting, a consultancy with core capabilities in employee communication strategy and communications talent development. His previous corporate experience spans more than 30 years with Fortune 500 companies. As head of Executive and Global Employee Communication for DuPont, he created and executed communication strategies that engaged 35,000 employees in the company's growth initiatives and empowered 8,000 people leaders to measurably engage their teams during the company's $130B merger with Dow. In 2018, *PR Week* awarded DuPont its highest honors for employee communication in North America, as did both the International Association of Business Communicators (IABC) and the Public Relations Society of America (PRSA).

Dollins previously spent 17 years in executive communication leadership roles with PepsiCo, where he was SVP and Chief Communications Officer at Pepsi Beverages and PepsiCo Americas Foods, and SVP of Global Internal Communication. He led corporate communication and brand communication for The Quaker Oats Company, with responsibilities for corporate public relations, internal communication, government affairs, philanthropy and community relations. He also led corporate communication for Northern Indiana Public Service Company, and employee communication for Indiana Michigan Power, after several years with ABC News and local newspaper reporting.

As a consultant, he has provided communication services to clients that include Raytheon, United Technologies, Visa, Toyota, Louis Vuitton, Xerox, Signet Jewelers and Keep America Beautiful, among others. He holds a BA in Radio/TV from The George Washington University and an MA in Communications from Purdue University. He is also a silver-level-certified USA Wrestling coach and three-time national masters folk style wrestling titleholder.

 **Jon Stemmle** is the chair and professor of Strategic Communication at the University of Missouri School of Journalism, where he teaches classes in public relations, health and science communication and integrated marketing campaigns. Additionally, he is also a core faculty member of the Master of Public Health Program at Missouri and the former director of the Health Communication Research Center. His primary research interests involve health-related community-based participatory research, and tailored health communication and messaging through storytelling and narrative. His co-authored research has been published in a wide array of journals including the *Journal of Health Communication*, the *Journal of Management & Marketing in Healthcare* and the *Journal of Interactive Advertising* and presented to the CDC, NCI and various health literacy groups around the nation.

In his career, he has led a variety of projects on topics such as health and science literacy, cancer prevention communication and photovoice. These projects were conducted on a variety of levels—from local to international and everything in between—and totaled more than $30 million. Since stepping down from his director role in the summer 2014, he now serves the HCRC in an advisory capacity.

His career began in journalism with the *Asbury Park Press* in New Jersey and continued at newspapers around the country for nearly a decade. He has been involved with public relations and strategic communication for more than 20 years.

He has an MA in journalism from The University of Arizona (1997) and undergraduate degrees in history and communications from Virginia Wesleyan College (1993).

ACKNOWLEDGMENTS

Mark Dollins

This labor of love came with tremendous support from family and friends—starting with my beautiful wife, Princess Angie, who served as a great first editor and proofer, and constant supporter of a career-long ambition. My gratitude also goes to my partner on this project, Jon Stemmle, for his wisdom, vision and never-ending skill sets, making this process not just educational for me, but also fun.

Thanks as well to Mary Barton and Shel Holtz for lending their voices and expertise to important chapters in this book, and a special thanks to Sharon McIntosh for her employee communication brilliance, support and partnership. My son and daughter, Eric and Claire Dollins, also gave steadfast support, for which I'm truly grateful.

Four amazing bosses and mentors during the course of my corporate communication career gave me the space, guidance and freedom to innovate in the world of employee engagement and communication. I'm eternally grateful to Margaret Eichman, Tod MacKenzie, Julie Hamp and AnnaMaria DeSalva; each contributed to my growth as a communicator and ultimately the content in this book.

Thanks as well to my mom, Jane Dollins, who passed before this went to print but showed tremendous excitement and encouragement for her youngest son's first book.

And finally, thanks to every employee communicator across the globe, for driving greater results and gaining influence in their organizations as they strategically engage their employees. Yes, my friends, you're now working in the "sexy" part of communications. Keep going.

Jon Stemmle

This 18+ month process was an incredibly daunting yet energizing experience and wouldn't have been possible without a multitude of individuals who made this possible—first and foremost among those, my wife and partner, Shelly Rodgers, who taught me the ropes of writing a textbook, provided constant encouragement and guidance, as well as time and support. Once she gave the thumbs up on the first few chapters, I knew we were in business! I would also be remiss not to thank my children—Brianna and Brandon—for putting up with me working nights and weekends (and during breaks from school) to complete this manuscript.

Professionally, none of this would have happened without my co-author and friend, Mark Dollins (and a shout out to Dean David Kurpius for introducing us). Mark was the force and the voice behind this book that elevated the material into something that's conversational, informative and uplifting. I'd never heard of anyone enjoying writing a book like this, but with a partner like Mark, I'm ready to do this again anytime!

I also want to acknowledge my parents, June and Joe, for instilling a love of writing and teaching into me from the time I was a child, as well as my academic mentor, Glen T. Cameron, who helped show me how to blaze a path in this field.

Finally, I'd like to thank a quartet of students who assisted with various parts of this book—Jihwan Aum, Jalyn Byrd and Maya Patel on research and Abby Walden on the design of all of our charts, graphs and models as well as Ron Kelley, executive director of Student Development, Diversity and Inclusion for the School of Journalism and graduate student Brandon Eigenman for their help on a final review of the manuscript.

This book truly was a labor of love (as cliché as that is!) and I hope all of the teachers who use this and students who read it can sense the joy and excitement that's possible in this profession in the same way Mark and I do!

FOREWORD

Employee communication has always been a bit of a mystery for practitioners and an almost invisible career path for students of communication. While there have been many well-written stories about engaging internal stakeholders, most professional communicators have been learning on the job (often by trial and error) and applying some of what they know from the world of PR to the discipline. Students tend to get a single chapter, or perhaps a case study about the topic, in a book or broader curriculum about PR or strategic communication.

Even before Covid, we saw the need for a deeper, more comprehensive and integrated look not only at communicating with employees but also with engaging them strategically for the purpose of accelerating performance for the enterprises that employ them.

In the meantime, C-suite executives have been developing a functional understanding of the role and importance of internal communication for decades. As they've led their organizations through significant change agendas, begun digital transformations or initiated cultural change, they've come to realize the critical strategic importance of the discipline.

With growing numbers of employee communication jobs, a need for greater education and a growing awareness of how the discipline could enable performance, the stage was already set for something big.

And the lightning rod turned out to be a global pandemic.

The year 2020 changed everything for employee communication. It puts the importance of strategic employee communication at the top of the priority list: internal communication on steroids. As organizations sent employees home overnight as a measure of protection from the global pandemic, the issues of connectivity, engagement and culture became far greater business issues than simply deploying new technologies to help more remote workforces communicate or broadcasting email messages to employees to tell them what the organization wanted them to know.

Employee communication moved squarely into the spotlight as a strategic tool that could enable enterprises to survive, or better yet, thrive in the most disruptive environment ever to hit a digital, global economy.

There could be no better time to take a step back, chronicle and methodically organize a text that could orient students and professionals alike to what the best of employee engagement looks like, strategically, through the eyes of the communicators who are among the best across the globe.

They've spent decades transitioning their discipline from tactical and one-directional to strategic, omni-directional and results driven. These are their stories, and we're pleased and proud to share them—helping create a new generation of strategic employee communication and engagement professionals.

1

DEFINING EMPLOYEE COMMUNICATION AND ITS HISTORY

Employee communication is a lot like giving a traveler a map that has 1,000 different paths to get to a destination. It can tell you the shortest and longest routes to get there but won't tell you where a bridge is out, where there is civil unrest or where there's road construction—all insights that can impact the journey and what happens when you get there. There are clear pathways to getting there, but the decisions about which path to take, and when, are akin to the multitude of choices that the modern-day employee communicator must make.

Before we dive deep into what employee communication is, we need to define it and discern what makes it different from other forms of communication. Since it's often included in the broader definition of *public relations*, we can start there. Glen T. Cameron in the book *Public Relations*, co-authored with Dennis Wilcox and Bryan H. Reber, defines public relations as "strategic management of competition and conflict for the benefit of one's own organization—and when possible—also for the benefit of the organization and its various stakeholders or publics." Similarly, in the book *Excellence in Public Relations and Communication Management*, James Grunig defines public relations (as well as communication management) as the "management of communication between an organization and its publics."

Although these concepts fit within employee communication, the goals of employee communication are more specific in nature, in both audience and practice, than these overarching concepts. Once considered the sleepy, "unsexy" stepchild of public relations, employee communication increasingly is viewed as a critical enabler of communicator career growth and of business performance. To that end, *employee communication*—often also called *internal communication*—is defined by Carole M. Howard in *Public Relations Quarterly* as "a tool to help achieve your business goals and these days, in many organizations, cultural change

DOI: 10.4324/9781003024118-1

goals. After all, changing behavior, or preserving the behavior you want, is what employee communications is all about."

Future executive and employee communication leaders, and future Chief Communication Officers, will be well served to take note of, and invest in, people, processes and innovation in this rapidly burgeoning discipline. Without it, any communicator is operating without a significant required tool to drive results for any enterprise.

Importantly, employee communication is not a stand-alone communication discipline. It is integrally tied to external-facing communication disciplines such as reputation management, crisis communication and even media relations. In fact, some global companies such as PepsiCo and General Motors, have used the expression "outside in—inside out" to clearly articulate the symbiotic connection between what's communicated inside and outside any enterprise. Advertising about an organizations' values—when they don't reflect employees' experiences—can lead to internal discord and external embarrassment. Communicating an internal change without assessing impacts on external stakeholders can result in everything from bad press coverage to regulatory or legislative issues.

While the disciplines and sophistication of employee communication practices can vary widely for organizations and practitioners, the function most commonly produces and delivers messages and campaigns on behalf of management, facilitates multi-directional dialogue, develops the communication skills of the organization's participants and measures the impact of its efforts. For some enterprises, "internal communication" could include not only employees but also contractors, tenants and government or municipal professionals—such as police, security and fire-fighters. Although not on the direct payroll as employees, those workers can play critical roles in supporting the organization's mission and business objectives and are considered to be important internal stakeholders.

The stakes are high for any organization to attract, retain and develop employees who can be the best problem solvers, innovators and executors of any organization's agenda. And, just as important, organizations are recognizing that keeping hundreds, thousands or hundreds of thousands of employees engaged in their work and connected to the mission and vision of the enterprise can make or break their success.

The floodgates have opened, both for the need for strategic workforce communication and for the training of people who have the communication skills to do that work.

Based on this, we can view the world of employee communication as an ecosystem. In this book, this ecosystem model (see Figure 1.1) will be used to explore the facets and provide the resources needed to understand and succeed in this field.

We begin in Chapter 1 with a dive into the definition of employee communication as well as the origins and history of the profession. This includes articulating the value it delivers to organizations (for-profit, not-for-profit) and providing an overview of the skills or competencies required to be effective with

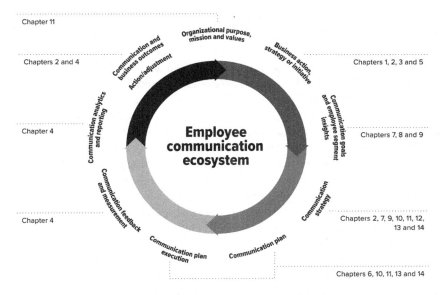

FIGURE 1.1 The employee communication ecosystem and how each chapter in this book fits within the model.

this communication discipline. We'll also broadly introduce perspectives about the influence and interdependency of other communication disciplines on how it is deployed in an organization and how other influences (such as reporting relationship, budget and other resources and team structure) drive its influence in any organization. These elements are all part of the ecosystem related to business actions, strategies or initiatives employee communicators pursue as they assess the state of their organization and begin the path to determine what should be done moving forward.

Chapter 2 goes into the critical idea of what makes employee communication strategic. Apart from the tools and skills required for effective employee communication, making those efforts truly strategic demands unique, relevant insights from stakeholders, clarity on success measures, creative ideas and clear messaging that sticks. The idea of strategy weaves its way into various parts of the ecosystem, from the business actions, strategies or initiatives to the communication strategy to the communication and business outcomes. This chapter also will acknowledge the importance of flexibility and creativity in addressing internal and external influences that invariably drive the ability to execute a strategy and still deliver intended results.

While some skill sets for employee communication are consistent with other externally focused disciplines, in Chapter 3 we also explore competencies that are unique to employee communication professionals and provide insights into how internal and external communication skill sets ultimately produce the most effective employee communicators. Within the ecosystem, this fits under business actions, strategies and initiatives as the need for some skill sets, particularly those with social media, are evolving quickly with internal stakeholders. Additionally, this chapter will highlight how those skill sets, and an increasing knowledge of technology platforms, will be a key enabler of career growth in this space.

Whether an organization is for profit or not, it's critical that any communication effort to "internal stakeholders" deliver on expected results for the enterprise. In Chapter 4, we answer the question of how to measure the impact of employee communication. Measurement comes up toward the end of the ecosystem cycle, related to communication feedback, analytics and reporting, and communication and business outcomes, related to actions and adjustments. This includes metrics such as awareness, understanding and belief as content-based metrics; digital metrics that, in many cases, mirror external social media metrics; and human resources (HR)-based metrics that reflect how internal communication efforts move the dial on performance.

Picking up from the broad-brush introduction in the first chapter, Chapter 5 goes more in-depth about what influences the discipline and how. This includes where the employee communication group reports and how that influences how it is managed, and how it interacts with other communication disciplines should be more than a check-the-box activity. This chapter will present insights on the influences of functions such as HR, Marketing and Legal can have on how employee communication is managed and relates to the business actions, strategies or initiatives in the ecosystem. The interactivity and interdependencies with other communication functions are equally critical, and we will introduce the concept of the increasingly invisible wall between internal and external communication and the opportunities and risks that this particular dynamic can make available.

Communicating internally in an ethical way, and in compliance with laws across the globe, isn't negotiable—it's table stakes. In Chapter 6, we will cover the increasing need for ethical practices in transparency and candor when communicating with employees. More recent examples of employee activism (such as Google's global employee walk out over management's handling of sexual misconduct in the management ranks) highlight why doing the business the right way—and communicating effectively—has significant consequences for internal stakeholders as well as customers and shareholders. Ethics plays a significant role in the ecosystem with how a communication plan is created and executed.

In Chapter 7, we discuss how one size doesn't fit all when it comes to employee engagement. Empowering middle and senior leaders, and other key influencers, to drive change with communications increasingly is a strategy that must be deployed for effective engagement strategies. In this chapter, we will provide an overview of how to segment internal stakeholders, how to assess the unique needs of each cohort and how to build measurement and reporting that will drive effective execution. This step looms large early in the ecosystem model related to the communication goals and employee segment insights as well as the overall communication strategy.

The best-laid plans and best-prepared content won't work if they don't reach their intended internal audiences. In Chapter 8, we'll explore the critical partnership needed between communicators, information technology (IT) function leaders, HR and Legal to examine everything from technology limitations to governance and capital investments to reach increasingly mobile and diverse employee bases. This focus on working together as an organization factors strongly into the ecosystem related to the communication goals and employee segment insights. This is because assumptions about hitting the "send" or "post" button—when it comes to reaching employees—often are met with the harsh reality of issues with technology or policies that needed to be reviewed. We introduce ways of auditing existing channels, assessing needs for new channels—before a crisis emerges, and a critical capability is not available.

The C-Suite's influence through communications with internal stakeholders is among the strongest that any enterprise has and it is explored in Chapter 9. While Chief Executive Officers (CEOs) clearly must address a wide range of external and internal stakeholders in running their organizations, the responsibility for advising on strategy, messaging, tone, feedback and channel delivery falls most often with the employee communication leader. In the ecosystem model, we explore how employee communication professionals shape the CEO and C-Suite's internal communication agenda related to the communication goals and employee segment insights, as well as the communication strategy overall. We'll also look at how employee communicators can earn the role of trusted advisor while representing the voice—and communication needs—of the employee.

The rapid explosion of Change Management Officers (CMOs) in organizations across the globe is proof positive that the discipline of managing change is here to stay. That's why change management communication is the focus of Chapter 10. Often housed in the HR function, HR leaders are tasked with enabling management to drive large-scale change agendas, including the ecosystem elements related to the communication strategy, planning and plan execution. The key enabler of success is a comprehensive change management communication discipline. HR increasingly is looking to Communication functions to supply that expertise. Understanding change management models such as Prosci's ADKAR (Awareness, Desire, Knowledge, Ability, Reinforcement) presents communicators with unique opportunities to build strategies, channels and content, and this chapter will provide a clear view of how to align communications with change strategies.

Although change management may sound uninspiring to many, through effective storytelling—a core communications competency—it can make the difference between broadcasting an idea and empowering employees to live its promise. In Chapter 11, we introduce the critical purpose of a master narrative, the importance of proof points/smaller stories to continue moving the organization and help it see progress in the story, and the skill base that leaders must develop to translate a corporate journey credibly and transparently into motivation. Storytelling factors into various phases of the ecosystem, from the very start with the organizational purpose, mission and values to the communication strategy, planning and plan execution.

Unlike the early days of employee communication—which deployed static/broadcast media and methodologies—contemporary employee communication work has evolved to much more dynamic models. In Chapter 12, we explore why, and how, today's successful employee communication capabilities are reliant on constant feedback loops, multi-directional communication models, measurement, analytics and reporting. At the same time, we introduce the importance of traditional communication competencies in helping communicators balance both the art and science of communication to internal stakeholders. We illustrate how this evolving discipline is more directly being deployed to business drivers such as organizational health and employee engagement, as well as how it fits into the ecosystem segment related to communication strategy.

While change management and general employee engagement in business priorities are big focus areas for employee communicators, there are several more areas that are increasingly engaging professionals in this space that are explored in Chapter 13. From diversity, equity and inclusion, to focused roles with functional areas such as HR, IT and Finance, employee communicators deployed to these areas are driving significant new capabilities. Like change management, HR support-related priorities, including recruiting, onboarding and various process-driven activities, fit into the ecosystem in the areas of communication strategy, planning and plan execution.

Finally, like any communication discipline, marketplace forces are driving new, complex issues and problems to solve. In Chapter 14, we'll gaze into the future to explore a number of those issues, including emerging communication and business technologies, the Gig economy, employee activism and implications for how organizations need to better serve a more diverse workforce of full time and contract employees, and remote workers.

Employee Communication Solutions

Now that we've explored the ecosystem of employee communication and the lineup of chapters, we need to look at solutions to employee communication problems, which are often as unique as a fingerprint. The right solution is akin to the outcome of a chemistry experiment that delivers a meaningful result. The communication tools and processes selected, the messaging and supporting stories, the cadence, sequence and creative components that can be deployed—when combined in the right way—can deliver a measurable impact on employee understanding, belief or, in the best of cases, behaviors. Whether it's for a not-for-profit, an educational institution, a Fortune 100 corporation or anywhere in between, the

Employee communication solutions: As unique as a fingerprint

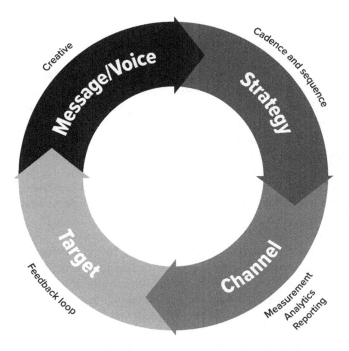

FIGURE 1.2 The solutions to employee communication problems will vary based on the problem at hand. However, those answers typically involve some combination of strategy, channels, target and message/voice.

unique needs, capabilities and influences of any enterprise can combine to further influence an outcome (see Figure 1.2).

Communicating strategically to internal stakeholders demands full use of an ecosystem that combines a full slate of tactics, tools and strategies. The ultimate internal communication strategy selected (upper right) reflects a clear set of choices made to deliver desired outcomes. Those choices include optimal channels (bottom right) for reaching audiences, insights on (often segmented) internal target stakeholders (bottom left) and clear, compelling messaging delivered through a relevant and authentic voice (upper left). Behind these decisions are choices for cadence and sequencing; measurement, analytics and reporting; continuous feedback loops for segmented audiences; and creative applications that engage employees through communication.

Structurally, where an internal communication function reports to within any organization matters, it can have a significant influence on its priorities. Reporting to HR, for example, may drive communication professionals to focus more on people processes, like performance reviews and compensation and benefits, while reporting to a Public Affairs or Corporate Communication function, can lead the employee communication function to align on more comprehensive corporate or externally focused communication goals. Reporting to a Legal or Marketing function also can influence risk taking, creative license and customer orientation.

Regardless of the reporting relationship, all of these influencing functions often do, and should, serve as critical partners to employee communication in driving and executing internal communication. It speaks to the complex, often competing, agendas that live within every enterprise.

Another significant influence on employee communication can be budget allocation. While many organizations successfully drive internal programs on shoe-string budgets, investment in new or emerging digital platforms, money for creative content development and graphic or video production can drive incremental, often significant, budget needs.

In enterprises that have large global populations, translation expenses, along with the need for more creative approaches to "break through" the clutter that employees receive, can drive the need for larger budgets. And underlying all modern-day employee communication is the increasing need for a dynamic and highly functioning IT infrastructure. Everything from email capabilities to intranet and portal development and mobile digital platforms can, and does, drive costs. Ensuring that employee communication has a close strategic partnership with IT will ensure that long-term capital investment decisions are made with at least one eye toward the need of engaging internal stakeholders through technology. But to be clear, it's not just about technology.

Who Are These People?

Today's employee communicators are far more than publication editors or video producers. They are messaging strategists, cultural envoys and technology experts. They are research and analytics practitioners, segmentation gurus and consummate storytellers. The art and science of communication, more than ever, have converged on arguably one of the most complex communication disciplines in the business world.

The skill base required for successful employee communication still remains grounded in exceptional storytelling and message development, but the need to develop deep expertise in more traditional competencies such as writing, measurement and visual production must be complemented with broader and more integrated skills that include an array of social media capabilities, crisis communication, analytics, executive communication and strategy, among others.

And beyond the technological developments that propelled employee communication professionals at the turn of the 21st century is a force far bigger, far more consistent and far longer term in nature: change itself.

Mergers and acquisitions, divestitures and other business portfolio changes demand that communicators help navigate the needs of people and processes that are coming from, and going to, any enterprise. Culture change requires thoughtful communication solutions that engage and inspire. And the introduction of new processes and technologies for everything from customer relations to collaborative, open product design and new finance systems has put most companies on a constant, long-term digital change journey. Effectively managing the introduction, usage and future enhancements of those technologies, in turn, requires highly strategic employee communication solutions.

Not surprisingly, employee communicators increasingly are being asked to develop new skills to ensure success with change management. In an article in *Corporate Communications*, Philip J. Kitchen and Finbarr Daly define *change management* as "not a distinct discipline with rigid clearly defined boundaries," but one that draws on several social science disciplines and "acknowledges the reality that organizations operate in changing environments." It is a management process that ensures the "people side of change" is considered each step along the way in the change process from planning to implementing to reinforcing change. Essential to the change effort is a communication plan that reaches the heads, hearts and hands of those affected by the change and helps get their buy-in. Communication professionals are learning change management methodologies to develop and execute corresponding communication solutions to drive change strategies.

As mergers become more frequent and larger, there's a great opportunity to apply this discipline. An example of change management in practice can be seen in the 2017 Dow–DuPont merger. The DuPont company, inventor of everything from Kevlar bullet-proof vests to Nomex fire-retardant material and Teflon, completed the largest industrial merger in history in 2017 with the Dow Company. The $130 billion transaction was done for a single purpose: to re-allocate the merged-companies' businesses into three new, separate companies. Over a 20-month period of considerable employee uncertainty between the announcement of the merger and regulatory approvals that cleared antitrust hurdles and closed the deal, employee communicators deployed a significant change management communication strategy. They developed a strategic corporate narrative, "A Journey to Three," and launched timely, relevant content through innovative channels to help both employees and managers understand the change journey and to increase belief in the future state of three industry-leading businesses. Communicators measured the impact of their change communication, showing impact on everything from understanding and belief in the future states to reduced voluntary attrition and greater organizational health results.

A Brief History of Employee Communication

Those who cannot remember the past are condemned to repeat it.

Spanish philosopher, essayist, poet and novelist George Santayana in his work *The Life of Reason* gave us this important warning, and when it comes to the history of employee communication, that history is all quite recent in the grand scheme.

That's because relatively little has been chronicled about the origins of this discipline. What has been recorded largely says that, until the late 19th century, organizations used tactical methods, namely publishing newsletters and magazines, to tell employees what leaders wanted them to know. While we can surmise that even those "employers" working before the time of the ancient Egyptians provided laborers with clear communications on what needed to be done, it really wasn't until the Industrial Revolution, when people started being employed by formal industries, like the textile mills of England, that organizations had to start thinking about how to engage workers in the tasks of the day beyond simply being paid.

From its early stages as a distributor of leaflets and other simple communications to its role today as a critical enabler of business and organizational performance, employee communication has covered a lot of ground. Think about modern issues that put employees squarely in the middle of significant business issues: employee activism over sexual harassment at Google; diversity and racial equality at Starbucks; "Momazonians" at Amazon demanding child day care to improve career prospects for women in leadership. These are real issues that employers are facing and require far more than "top down" broadcasting or publishing.

The early history is a tale staged on two continents in two countries, one written in Great Britain and the other in the United States. That's not to say that other countries on other continents didn't practice employee communication until more recently, but rather these were the places that drove industrial growth during those early periods, meaning they had more of an organized need for the type of communications we're talking about. Each contributed something unique and important to the early days of employee engagement and created the first touchpoints that led us to where we stand today.

The Beginnings of "Modern" Employee Communication

Employee communication wasn't always labeled as such. Back in the dawn of employee communication of the mid-1800s, the approach used by management was *paternalistic propaganda*. This idea of paternalistic propaganda is described by Burton St. John in an article in *Public Relations Review* as "propaganda attempted to direct the unsophisticated crowd for the benefit of a client through the spreading of selected information." Essentially, when talking of employee communication, this is the idea of management telling employees what they needed to know. This evolved slowly to more strategic forms of communication intended to persuade and engage. Concurrently, the role of the communicator shifted from that of editor to one of a strategic counselor.

These initial efforts of employee communication were meant to inform employees through communications, such as internal newsletters and magazines, also known as *house organs*. According to research from British public relations professionals Kevin Ruck and Heather Yaxley that traced the history of employee communication, the first formal employee publications date back to 1840 and were written *by* employees *for* employees. Journalists of the time were hired as "industrial editors." These industrial editors' quests for journalistic freedom came at a significant expense: as they gained management support for doing their work, they essentially surrendered any intent to involve employees in their own communications.

For many decades, these house organs were the dominant, if not sole, way to tell employees what the company wanted them to know. Although a simplistic approach compared to what's involved with employee communication today, it is representative of most organizations' efforts to inform through top–down methods.

Another concept, *industrial propaganda*, came to be during World War I. Although the term took on a negative connotation during the war due to the way in which misleading or patently false information was spread through mass media, that idea changed over the next two decades.

In the period between the World Wars, a key figure in the history of employee communication arose in Sir Basil Clarke, known as the Father of Public Relations in Britain. In the 1920s, Clarke brought forward the idea that worker pride could be amplified through an understanding of how a company's product was superior to that of its competitors.

If instilling pride didn't work, Clarke believed fear of competition could also be used as an alternative motivating factor. He used the example of a Midlands, United Kingdom, firm that had a competitor's advertising placed around its own site. While he thought industrial propaganda represented a huge opportunity, he acknowledged the challenges that came with it. In his book about Clarke, Richard Evans quotes him as saying that industrial propaganda "involves the most difficult and delicate type of propaganda work that can be imagined."

Meanwhile, in the United States

About 100 years after employee communication began in the United Kingdom, the field received its first official notice in the United States. A book by *Alexander Heron*, published in 1942, mentions a small but important first-ever meeting that took place in 1940 in Burlington, Vermont, where fewer than 150 self-described "industry relations specialists" met to talk about employee communication.

Heron's book, *Sharing Information with Employees*, became the first book of its kind on employee communication. This groundbreaking text by the Stanford University associate professor took into account both societal and cultural influences on employees and companies.

Promoting community and company pride already was the practice for some organizations, but Heron's methods were the first to acknowledge the relationship between manager and employee as something human, and just as important, emotional. As Stanford University's Paul Eliel wrote in the foreword of Heron's book, "The problem, as Mr. Heron so graphically points out, is not how to convey information but how to share it. Conveying is mechanical; sharing is personal."

From transparency in messaging to the need for cadence, consistency and strategy in employee communication, Heron identified a number of practices in 1942 that are commonly used today. Consider a few of these assertions from Heron's book:

- *The first element in sharing information . . . is the understanding by employees that facts about the enterprise are not being concealed from them. The knowledge that they can get the information they want is more important than any actual information that can be given to them.*
- *The program of communication should be a continuous one, a method of conduct rather than a campaign . . . it must not become an institution apart from the actual work or operation of the enterprise.*
- *The American idea has no place for a class predestined to be wage earners incapable of understanding a world beyond the workbench, no place for a class which is denied the opportunity to reason its conclusions on facts which it helps to create, no place for a class which is happier because ignorant of anything beyond the daily task. And those whose sense of superiority leads them to believe in either the necessity or the desirability of such classes are themselves enemies of the American idea or ignorant of its genius.*

One thing that is clear from these early histories in the United Kingdom and the United States is that communication with employees was, in vision and in practice, one dimensional. It was all about what the organization wanted to say or sell.

The Fast Forward Button for Employee Communication: 1980 to Present Day

To say that nothing changed with employee communication between the 1940s and the turn of the century would be misleading, if not altogether false. The advent of audio and video technologies, for example, certainly gave employee

had never produced a late-night talk show before, but once I had committed to the approach, I attacked it with zeal. Finally, make sure communications—notably those that cost time and money—deliver on the promise of a strategic communication activity (that is, it is two-way and designed to move a needle).

Case Study

HILTON EMPLOYEE COMMUNICATORS BOOST PARTICIPATION AND REVENUES

Situation

Global hospitality company Hilton in 2016 had an underused Team Member Travel Program and wanted to increase occupancy and revenue, while increasing Hilton's competitive advantage in recruitment and retention and positioning the company as an employer of choice. The benefits team developed and launched an enhanced travel program, Go Hilton, that consisted of three programs: Team Member HHonors, a Team Member Travel Program and a Family and Friends Travel Program. Each offered unique perks to Hilton's 325,000 Team Members and their families and friends across 104 countries.

Based on the results of a global employee survey, the team found that the existing Team Member Travel Program was being underused as a lever to increase occupancy and revenue, sometimes leaving up to 30% of inventory unused. They discovered that a paper-based authentication system made processes inefficient and inconsistent across hotels/brands/regions. They also learned that the program lagged in comparison to what key competitors were offering. Hilton communicators used survey results to leverage the channels that Team Members rely on most to ensure successful delivery and receipt of campaign messaging.

Campaign

The Communication team developed an internal communication campaign for all Hilton Team Members designed to drive Team Member awareness and excitement for Go Hilton, leveraging proven channels and tactics and to inspire action and participation in Go Hilton. The campaign included contests to show best practices from individual hotel locations that were promoting the new program, photo and story contents for employees to share how they were using the program and headquarter location displays that created excitement about the programs. Ultimately, the team sought to improve Team Member sentiment about travel perks and increase the overall workplace satisfaction in the process.

Based on these goals, the team set specific objectives to track the program campaign's success. Those included increasing hotel-level awareness by driving 46,000+ leader toolkit downloads (about 10 per property); generating 20,000+ contest submissions (employees sharing photos and stories of their use of the program) to keep Go Hilton top of mind; motivating 162,500 Team Members (50%) to register for Team Member HHonors (TMHH); and inviting at least 162,500 family and friends (one per registered Team Member) by the end of 2016.

They went beyond outputs to business-based outcomes with their goals and targeted one million nights booked online by the end of 2016 that would result in at least US $50M in revenue. They also sought to increase Team Member sentiment by at least 10%, as reflected in 2016 global team member survey results, and targeted recognition as a Great Place to Work in the United States and other countries.

The team created a strategic rollout plan with five phases to introduce and sustain interested in the three programs.

Those phases included the following:

- Phase 1: Go Hilton stakeholder prep/communication prep (Duration: 4 weeks)
- Phase 2: Go Hilton announcement and launch TMHH Card Contest
- Phase 3: Announce TMHH Card Contest winners, launch TMHH enrollment and continued Go Hilton teasers
- Phase 4: Go Hilton travel programs launch
- Phase 5: Steady drumbeat and reinforcement

Results

The Go Hilton campaign impacted the company's bottom line with the addition of over US $120M in room revenue, as it met or exceeded each of the campaign's objectives. Those included 134,841 downloads of Go Hilton Toolkit content (more than 29 times per property), practically three times the goal.

Six employee contests generated more than 25,000 submissions and almost 200 winners, as the program enrolled more than 235,000 Team Members. Expanding to include family and friends, more than 318,000 new Hilton HHonors Members joined, practically doubling the goal and more than 2.2 million room nights were booked by Team Members, their family and friends by the end of 2016.

Finally, Hilton was recognized as a Great Place to Work in 14 countries, including debuting on the U.S. list at No. 56 and ranking No. 1 in both China and Turkey that year.

Source: PRSA Silver Anvil Awards (2017)

Bibliography

Burns, S. (2015, December 18). A brief history of internal communications. *Tribeinc.com*. Retrieved from http://blog.tribeinc.com/2015/12/18/a-brief-history-of-internal-communications/.

Collins, R. F. (2015). Myth as propaganda in World War I. *Journalism & Mass Communication Quarterly, 92*(3), 642–661. https://doi.org/10.1177/1077699015573006.

Evans, R. (2013). *From the Frontline: The Extraordinary Life of Sir Basil Clarke.* Cheltenham, United Kingdom: The History Press.

Fisher-Buttinger, C., & Vallaster, C. (2008). Brand ambassadors: Strategic diplomats or tactical promoters? In Kitchen, P. J. (ed.) *Marketing Metaphors and Metamorphosis.* London: Palgrave Macmillan. https://doi.org/10.1057/9780230227538_9.

Grunig, J. E. (1992). *Excellence in Public Relations and Communication Management* (Routledge Communication Series, 1st ed.). Oxfordshire, England: Routledge.

Heron, A. R. (2021). *Sharing Information with Employees* (H. Milford, Ed.). Oxford: Oxford University Press.

Howard, C. M. (1998). How your employee communications programs can boost productivity and pride. *Public Relations Quarterly, 43*(3), 15–23. Retrieved from http://search.ebscohost.com.proxy.mul.missouri.edu/login.aspx?direct=true&db=buh&AN=1317828&site=bsi-live&scope=site.

John, B. S. (2006). The case for ethical propaganda within a democracy: Ivy Lees successful 1913–1914 railroad rate campaign. *Public Relations Review, 32*(3), 221–228. https://doi.org/10.1016/j.pubrev.2006.05.023.

Kitchen, P. J., & Daly, F. (2002). Internal communication during change management. *Corporate Communications, 7*(1), 46–53. https://doi.org/10.1108/13563280210416035.

Lewis, R. M. (2004). *The Planning, Design and Reception of British Home Front Propaganda Posters of the Second World War.* Doctoral thesis (PhD), University College Winchester.

Santayana, G., & Gouinlock, J. (2011). *The Life of Reason or The Phases of Human Progress: Introduction and Reason in Common Sense, Volume VII, Book One* (M. Wokeck & M. Coleman, Eds.). Cambridge, MA & London: The MIT Press. https://doi.org/10.2307/j.ctt5hhk7j.

Wilcox, D. L., Cameron, G. T., & Reber, B. H. (2014). *Public Relations: Strategies and Tactics* (11th ed.). London: Pearson.

Yaxley, H., & Ruck, K. (2017). Tracking the rise and rise of internal communication. In *Exploring Internal Communication* (pp. 25–36). Oxfordshire, England: Routledge.

2
WHAT MAKES EMPLOYEE COMMUNICATION STRATEGIC?

What makes employee communication strategic? Fundamentally, it's communicating with employees to achieve a predetermined outcome. It's about moving past the idea of informing internal stakeholders, to influencing how they think about a particular topic, and—ultimately—how they behave.

Additionally, to drive belief and behavior change, it takes more personal kinds of communication delivery to affect a change with employees (see Figure 2.1). That's because it affords the opportunity for direct, instantaneous feedback and—if done well—prompts dialogue that helps employees trust management and truly engage in both the strategy and tasks they're being asked to deliver.

Communicating with employees can serve many purposes, but what most organizations value are communications that engage internal stakeholders in ways the prompt action or behavior change. This model shows how broader-scale communication with employees can deliver awareness and understanding about a topic or organizational need. Getting internal stakeholders to believe that the information they're given is relevant, trustworthy and of value to them more often demands more face-to-face communications and opportunities to question, comment and share concerns. The same is true for efforts to prompt action or behavior change. Communications from direct managers, and among peers, for example, will be more effective in driving that kind of change, versus newsletters and broadly distributed videos.

These foundational concepts of employee communication are shared with other, similar fields such as public relations, advertising and marketing and can be seen in the definitions of each. For example, according to a 2016 article in the *Journal of Advertising*, *advertising* is defined as "brand-initiated communication intent on impacting people." *Marketing*, however, was defined in 2017 by the American Marketing Association as "the activity, set of institutions and processes

DOI: 10.4324/9781003024118-2

What employee communication can influence

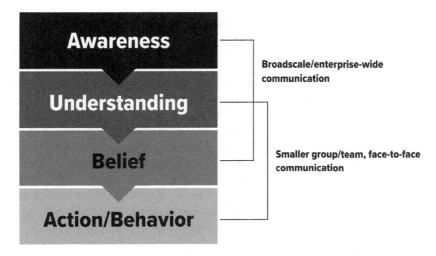

FIGURE 2.1 When communicating with employees, there are several possible goals to the messaging. Typically, you're working with your messaging to influence awareness, understanding, belief or action/behavior.

for creating, communicating, delivering, and exchanging offerings that have value for customers, clients, partners and society at large." Then there's public relations, which, as discussed in Chapter 1, was defined by Wilcox, Cameron and Reber as "strategic management of competition and conflict for the benefit of one's own organization—and when possible—also for the benefit of the organization and its various stakeholders or publics."

While each of these fields has sub-fields that also deal with issues related to the business world, what makes employee communication stand out is that it can, and does, go deeper into these issues and opportunities.

Additionally, the way that employee communication goes about influencing awareness, understanding, belief and action/behavior is similar to what's done in strategic communication as a whole. One way to describe it is that finding strategic employee communication solutions to business problems is a lot like chemistry. The best answers come from choices we make on everything from what we put into the solution to the timing, cadence and sequencing selections we make. In this case, our chemicals are messaging, channels, target audiences and timing to push and pull levers that deliver the results we seek. This idea fits well within the definition of *strategic communication* provided by Kirk Hallahan in the *International Journal of Strategic Communication* as "the purposeful use of communication by an organization to fulfill its mission." However, while employee communication aligns with the strategic communication definition, it goes beyond that in terms of its focus on employees and related elements.

Strategic Employee Communication

So where does this leave employee communication? Essentially, strategic employee communication is foundational to the employee communication ecosystem model (refer back to Chapter 1 to review the model). To expand on our definition based on the model used at the start of this chapter, we need to delve more into the elements contained within employee communication. In his book, *The Dynamics of Persuasion*, Richard Perloff explains how managers spend about 80% of their time communicating with others, typically dealing with persuading others to do, or accomplish, specific tasks or goals. Whether it's changing employee behavior on a manufacturing floor to reduce or eliminate accidents or driving a belief in a vision of a business and driving recruiting and retention numbers, employee communication is uniquely positioned—and expected—to influence how employees think and act on behalf of the enterprise that employs them.

Additionally, thinking about what employee communication can influence strategically, it can certainly deliver awareness about an existing or emerging priority to the workforce, and understanding around why it's important and how employees' work ties to the big strategic picture. This idea can often be done today through larger-scale communication efforts that can be delivered efficiently through digital communication.

To complete the influence of strategic employee communication, we can be guided by the article "Employee communication for engaging workplaces" in the *Journal of Business Strategy* that states that we need to find ways of delivering employee belief that our topic or cause is worth believing in, and that it requires a new or different action on the part of our workforce. Achieving these objectives through employee communication more often demands a higher-touch experience, delivered in compelling, creative ways from leaders and other influencers in smaller groups, or with face-to-face, live interactions. This can take the form of equipping managers with toolkits that include key messaging, questions and answers, discussion guides and/or short, simple presentations. The core idea is that communication takes place in a forum that allows employees to express comments, ask questions, seek clarity and better understand "What's in it for me?"

Having great tools and compelling content is a good start for employee communication, but using those resources strategically demands unique, relevant insights from internal stakeholders, clarity on success measures, creative ideas and clear messaging that sticks. In this chapter, we share how all of those elements must be woven together to deliver clear and compelling results. And, as internal communication strategies are created and executed, the importance of using flexibility and creativity invariably drives the ability to execute a strategy and still deliver intended results.

There once was a time that simply telling employees what was going on, or what they needed to do, was enough. "Work faster," "make more product" or "sell more to customers" were pretty straightforward commands.

The problem now, however, is that employees are smarter than they've ever been about how businesses operate and care a lot more about context than ever. Commands like those are far more likely to be met with new questions in response. How do we work harder? Why do we need to work faster? How do we sell more when there are disruptive technologies, products and services that may be better than what we offer?

The answers to those kinds of questions—combined with the need to understand how employees best process information, what they care about, what change is required and what factors are influencing an enterprise and its market(s)—begin to illustrate why employee communication must be increasingly strategic.

This brings us to the use of persuasion in communication. Dr. Robert Cialdini came up with the concept of the *six principles of persuasion* consisting of reciprocation, consistency, social validation, liking, authority and scarcity. Through the use of these principles in employee communication, one could be more effective in motivating employees and moving beyond just telling employees what's happening and explaining why.

To do this effectively, organizational communicators must have insights about their employee base, develop effective methods of connecting with them, measure the impact of their communication efforts and report progress to executive management. In other words, they must move from *outputs* to *outcomes*.

Employee communicators historically have taken refuge in reporting on the volume of activity they've achieved. We'll cover concepts about this type of measurement in Chapter 4, but when thinking about outputs, it's more often along the lines of reporting how many articles have been written, how many emails were opened, when, and/or who they reached. Those all add up to outputs—actions that may show how busy they've been but have less to do with producing an outcome that the enterprise cares about.

To be clear, executive management cares about outcomes. And they're increasingly holding employee communicators accountable for delivering them with the resources they've been allocated. That's not altogether a bad thing. Employee communicators who produce solid, continuous outcomes more often get additional resources with which to work versus those who don't.

The building blocks of strategic internal communication include a clear set of objectives, supported with strategies and tactics that deliver on those objectives. The building blocks of the strategy and their related tactics include internal stakeholder segmentation (often referenced as "personas"), audience insights, content and creative development, channel effectiveness, feedback loops, measurement/

Six principles of persuasion

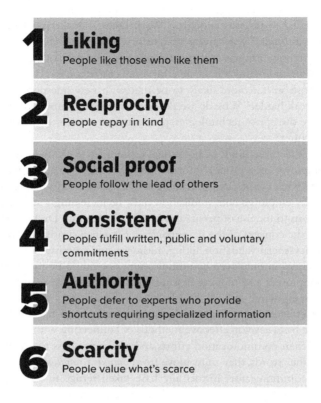

1 Liking
People like those who like them

2 Reciprocity
People repay in kind

3 Social proof
People follow the lead of others

4 Consistency
People fulfill written, public and voluntary commitments

5 Authority
People defer to experts who provide shortcuts requiring specialized information

6 Scarcity
People value what's scarce

FIGURE 2.2 Developed by Dr. Robert Cialdini, the six principles of persuasion—reciprocation, consistency, social validation, liking, authority and scarcity—can be used in employee communication to motivate a workforce and help explain what's happening and why.

analytics and reporting. We'll explore each of those building blocks in the rest of this chapter.

Segmentation

No two employees are exactly alike, just as no two people are exact duplicates. While we may never be able to communicate uniquely to every employee, we certainly can begin to understand that, as organizations become bigger and more complex, we can't think of mass communicating the same message in exactly the same way if we're going to influence thinking and behavior. What's needed is the ability to segment audiences.

According to Michael Slater, *audience segmentation* is defined as the process of taking a homogenous group of people and dividing them into smaller groups based on their attributes, such as beliefs and demographics. Through this segmenting process, communication professionals are best able to create messaging that is audience-centered and relevant, instead of using a single broad message that may only have passing relevance to a larger audience as a whole.

Global message creation and distribution certainly have its place in creating awareness of information that employees may need to know, but it's got to be supplemented with increasingly targeted, specific content that connects to more unique "personas" that better define who employees are and what they believe.

Personas are, quite simply, the identity (typically public) of an individual that has been "accrued and curated." In terms of employee communication, it deals with attributes allocated to employees by role, location, work group, history with the enterprise or other experience relevant to achieving the communication goal.

Rolling out a global IT platform, for example, can require unique segmentation based on what platforms employees are coming from. So, if an organization is rolling out Microsoft Office 365 after a merger, it's possible one part of the new combined company could be coming from a different Microsoft platform, while the other could be coming from Google's G Suite. In this example, communicators would need to segment audiences with insights from stakeholders representing both existing environments to create a viable set of communication strategies and related content.

Organizations going through significant cultural change, as another example, likely would need to segment employees by role; managers and leaders may need more unique insights and assessment tools than a broad employee population, which may need more inspiring stories or modifications for performance incentives. Creating strategies for senior executives, or employees who are driving the change agenda (e.g., HR professionals), could require segmented insights to create unique content and deliver sequencing of communications that help them drive that plan. Communicators also may need to assess how individual locations or countries are impacted by the change agenda and segment internal stakeholders by geography or business unit, accordingly.

From gender to generational diversity, effective employee communication strategies for difficult or complex issues demand that communicators know more about who they're communicating to, what they know and don't know and how they best receive and absorb communications. In going through this process of segmentation, one could ask the following questions:

- What do our segmented audiences know about the topic we're communicating?
- What are their attitudes toward it?
- Where are they getting information about the topic now?
- What resistance should we anticipate?
- How do they communicate what they like and don't like?

- Who needs to understand what we're doing first?
- How do they best learn? Are they visual learners? Do they prefer face-to-face communication from their managers?

Internal Research and Insights

In addition to better defining who internal segmented audiences are, communicators also must better understand what they know about a particular topic, what attitudes they have toward it and the voice behind the communication and what resistance they've registered or could put toward the efforts to inform and motivate them.

Through the research process, including existing (and hopefully recent) results from organizational health and/or smaller-scale employee pulse surveys, communicators can gain a greater understanding of the segments of the audience. This leads to *insights* about the audience to assist the process of developing a communication plan to attempt to change behavior, attitudes or beliefs.

Organizational health surveys are tools used by companies to get a sense for employee feelings and opinions on topics such as company culture and operations. These typically are executed on a routine basis through HR functions, or more specifically organizational development teams within the HR function. *Pulse surveys* are shorter versions of organizational health surveys, done with greater frequency to assess smaller numbers of employees, particularly when organizations are going through significant change periods.

Both of these kinds of survey results may not be specific to the topic communicators are tackling, but they often can paint a picture of existing attitudes toward management, current change initiatives and the general landscape of employee sentiment toward, and about, the organization.

Of course, communicators also can create and deploy surveys of their own to assess what their segmented audiences are thinking about a particular topic. If the survey design is done well, it can paint multiple pictures by segmented employee populations and serve as a strong baseline measurement—to which future measurement efforts can be compared.

Perhaps the most under-used insight-gathering technique is simply identifying internal thought leaders who might influence peers in their respective groups and talking with them.

Communicators can do something more formal, like structured focus groups, or less formal, like calling a cross section of leaders, representatives from segmented employee target groups, and HR business partners who often have their fingers on the pulse of the employee groups they support.

Time and resources often dictate how much, and how deep, communicators can go to develop insights that will fuel their resulting strategies, but like anything else, the more effort we put in to better understand our targets, the better formulated our strategies and the more on-target our communication will be.

Content and Creative Development

Strategic communication is part science and part art. While science is covered with insights, measurement and analytics, the art of communications also is strategic—particularly when it's woven into the broader strategy and connected to the building blocks we're covering.

Great copywriters often fall into the trap of creating content solely to entertain and engage when it comes to employee communication. It's not to say that writing in entertaining and engaging ways isn't good; it's just not enough.

In fact, if we can't engage our employee targets with great stories that inspire employees to believe in compelling visions, we risk losing the battle for heads, hearts and hands. To be clear, great content is able to touch employees' heads intellectually, their hearts emotionally and their hands practically. If done well we deliver content that does all three with the intent of influencing their thinking about our topic, and the desired behavior(s) that our communications should affect.

This may sound like it's a bit on the "soft side" of employee communication and it is. The reality is if we communicate only facts and figures, our audiences—no matter how we segment them—will simply tune out. Research done by Deborah Small, George Lowenstein and Paul Slovic at Carnegie Mellon University bears out this idea. Through an experiment done by the researchers, they found that stories dealing solely with a personal narrative would elicit greater compassion than stories that were primarily focused on data. Not that data can't, or shouldn't, be used—as they can help build trust and confirm information. But the personal story must be the primary element.

Each and every piece of content we create, ideally, should have a clear goal—one that drives employees a bit further down the path to the ultimate destination, or communication goal, we've set. Rarely, if ever, can a single communication or single piece of content accomplish a change in attitude or behavior. But a well-thought-out, sustained strategic deployment of inspiring content can work wonders. We'll cover more about what that content looks like, with particular emphasis on storytelling, in Chapter 11.

Creativity isn't only about writing. It also applies to how great content can be uniquely deployed. When PepsiCo in the early 2000s began shifting its portfolio to lower salt, less sugar and more "good for you" and "better for you" snacks and beverages, it started the education process first with its employee population base of over 100,000 workers.

Employee communicators at PepsiCo developed simple, entertaining product cards that explained how healthier ingredients were going into their products, while ingredients such as salt and sugar were being reduced. They distributed the cards globally to employees, put key questions related to the cards in their global employee newsletter as part of an engaging game with prizes, and distributed "PepsiCo pride" wearable pins to anyone who wanted to be questioned at random on the content of the cards. "Pride" button "spotters" would look for employees wearing the buttons, ask them a question about the changes in products. If the button-wearing employee answered the question correctly, that employee received a T-shirt, sports bottle, cap or other branded prize, literally, on the spot.

The program created significant buzz across the organization, but more importantly, delivered a measurable improvement on employee knowledge of the changes in the portfolio, and their self-reported confidence in talking with family, friends, neighbors and customers, about the evolution of their products.

Channel Effectiveness

The best strategies and most engaging content in the world won't work if communicators don't have access to a reliable set of channels to deliver them. In terms of communications, *channels* refer to the outlets we use to get our messages out to our target audiences, such as email or newsletters. Not surprisingly, then, investing in, monitoring and measuring the channels we use to reach our segmented employee populations are a highly important, yet often overlooked, building blocks of strategic employee communication.

Picking the best channel(s) to deliver communication strategies is fundamental. That means communicators must understand the reach, efficacy and reliability of communication channels that reside in their organizations. Done well, the efficacy of employee communication channels can build trust and transparency with employees. Ignored or poorly managed, the unreliability of employee communication channels can erode trust and build disengagement.

To offer a specific example, it means understanding how quickly an email with critical, time-bound news can reach locations across the enterprise, both locally and globally.

One organizational communicator from a U.S.-based, multinational technology company was shocked to learn that his company's IT system could take up to 15 minutes—after hitting the send button—to "pick up" his global email to all employees. And that it could take up to four hours for that same email to reach parts of his workforce in Asia. And this particular email was delivering significant news that impacted the future of his global organization. Google Alerts, however, delivered the same news from the media to employees in minutes. Frustrated and angry, he said, "I could have put on rollerblades and skated around my headquarters' campus faster to hand deliver the news faster than our email system could do it."

Beyond email, the increasingly central role of digital communication demands communicators know more about how those channels work and why. It includes knowing how quickly video and other digital assets can be uploaded and available. It demands understanding how mobile employees can gain real time access to content. And it means having access to back-end digital metrics that assess open rates, click-throughs and time spent with content.

Getting answers and solutions to digital channel issues demands a close working relationship with IT functions. It requires governance across all parts of an organization that have access to larger-scale employee communication channels. For example, if other parts of your organization are executing a larger-scale employee email at the same you're delivering your time-bound news global email, it's possible you could experience a range of technical issues that interrupt the ability to deliver news to employees, including log jams in computer servers required to distribute the communication. This necessitates communication and planning among the communicators to make sure all messages can reach their intended audiences effectively.

Not all communication channels are digital and not all digital channels reach all employees. In fact, the more impactful communications for driving behavior change often are face-to-face, and many manufacturing environments limit digital channel availability in the workplace, believing it to be a distraction to other internal communication that are more specific to shift work.

So, when communicators are thinking strategically about channels to reach employees, they also have to assess how well their enterprises can deliver face-to-face communication. Leaders not only need strong, relevant content that can be easily digested and delivered to their teams, but many also may need further support in the form of interpersonal and small-group communication skills development. Therefore, when we think of efficacy, reach and reliability, communicators must evaluate and continuously deliver care and feeding to all channels required to reach their targets.

Feedback Loops

Every strategic employee communication plan has one or more feedback loops. *Feedback loops* allow segmented internal audiences to share their response to communication content and delivery methods or more general attitudes toward the communications they're receiving.

The challenge is to implement those feedback loops in ways that do not tax the organization, but do provide insights that lead to actionable decision-making and prompt communicators to show how they're using the feedback. They can include the performance of channels, the content placed in them and alignment across multiple geographies or business units.

It sounds easy enough to the average reader, but challenges quickly arise when employees are overburdened with too many surveys to complete in a given period; see no reason to complete a communication survey if no action is ever taken; or another function attempts to block the creation and use of a feedback loop for a variety of reasons, including administrators or managers not wanting to know how employees feel or "protecting" employees from survey overload.

Continuous Feedback Loops
It's not just one loop; it's the sum of three loops working together

FIGURE 2.3 This feedback summary from the DuPont company illustrates how employee communicators used a series of feedback loops to measure and assess effectiveness during its merger of equals with the Dow company in 2017 and 2018.

Whatever the challenges may be, there are ways to eliminate or reduce their impact. Simple coordination, for example, with HR or other functions that survey employees, can dictate timing and tools communicators can use.

Sharing feedback loop results and corresponding actions with employees delivers a clear and compelling message that "the organization" is not only digesting employee feedback but also taking action to improve what needs improvement, eliminate what isn't working or bolstering what does work.

Of course, the use of one or more feedback loops demands that communicators look holistically at each and every feedback tool, identify the unique type of feedback each delivers and integrate when and how those feedback loops are administered. In other words, all feedback loops must work as a single ecosystem inside the enterprise to paint the full picture of progress toward a communication goal, or destination.

Measurement/Analytics

Having feedback loops is fundamental to demonstrating how employee communication is working. This process also can be strategic, but it is what communicators do with the data that make it relevant.

We will cover more about measurement and analytics in Chapter 4, but for the purposes of showing its importance as a building block of strategic employee communication, the critical takeaways are that the data needs to be pulled from sources in timely ways; different data must contribute to the big picture; and the analytics need to tell a story, presumably one of progress against benchmark or beginning data, against the objectives of the communication strategy, and/or progress against previous reporting period(s).

While many digital tools today come equipped with data dashboards and a degree of analytics, communicators who possess data analytics skills quickly demonstrate significant strategic value to their respective organizations and functions.

Today's communicator needs to supplement digital analytics with other measurement tools that explain how communications are enabling metrics such as employee understanding of a business issue, their belief in the future vision or transparency from leadership in guiding an organization through change.

Delivering solid analytics and reporting on feedback loops builds credibility with executive management and trust with other functions that may doubt what feedback loops can deliver and convince them that they need to know what those loops deliver.

The human ability to see patterns and connect the dots—often developed through basic statistics classes—is what helps communicators see the impact of their work and equips them to share their results with senior leaders and other stakeholders.

Reporting

A great story untold isn't a story at all. Equipped with data and analytics, the onus on communicators is to turn the numbers into a compelling story and to share it with leaders who have vested interests in the outcomes of their communication efforts.

Communicators often get so absorbed in the execution of their strategies that they neglect to take stock of the accomplishments the data reflect and judiciously share it with leaders who need to know.

Successful employee communicators also will identify who needs to see, read or hear their measurement stories, with what frequency, and through mechanisms that work best for their sponsors. Sending an email with a summary attachment may work for some decision makers, while face-to-face reviews of the measurement story may be far more effective for others.

When employee communicators at DuPont wanted to share the impact of their efforts to executive leaders during their merger with the Dow Company from 2015 to 2018, they told a story with numbers that linked employee attitudes to belief in the future state of the business to voluntary attrition (employees leaving the organization voluntarily) during a period of intense change. As results driven by communication (increased understanding and belief in the future state and belief in management communication transparency), employee engagement (as measured through a pulse survey) and voluntary attrition rates improved.

However, reporting isn't just about the numbers. As we'll explore more in Chapter 4, it's about sharing what those numbers mean, what decisions they prompt and what actions they generate. Whether it's reporting results for a specific communication event or a longer-term communication goal, reporting is the lynchpin of every strategic employee communication initiative. It's not necessarily the end of a cycle but an ongoing discipline of demonstrating strategic value to the enterprise.

Profile: Neil Griffiths

Senior Manager Global Communication Environmental Resources Management London (UK)

Career Bio

I got my start in nonprofit, working in different member relations and project roles. I made the shift to communications when I graduated from the McGill University PR Management program, heading up the communications function in a college, before moving into corporate communication at a global engineering firm. I have only been focused solely on employee communication since 2014, having worked across brand, strategy, external and media relations and volunteer management.

Making Employee Communication Strategic

There have been numerous occasions where I've been called in to a meeting and told that the person I am talking to needs me to create something tactical. It is very often clear to me very quickly that the tactic has not been thought through and, especially, that the people on the potential receiving end of that tactic have not been sufficiently researched. One example was with the training and development team. They called me to tell me they need my help to create a video. After talking them through the strategic communication planning process, we determined that a multi-channel and audience-specific campaign would achieve the outcomes they were looking for (which was to change perceptions of the function as a strategic partner in the business).

Asking questions is really important. If you know the right questions to ask, such as "What does success look like and how will you know when you're there? What do you know about your audiences and what do they know about your project? What do you need them to know-think-do?" and "How will communication facilitate the achievement of the outcomes you're looking for?" then it's easier to work with your colleagues on putting a strategy in place. If you start by telling people that you disagree and they need to do something a different way, it can lead to conflict. By asking questions and building your own understanding, it's easier to get people on-side for communicating strategically.

Often people associate the value of communication with the things they can see (or read, or experience, etc.). That's understandable because not everyone fully appreciates what goes into creating a communication tactic. It's no good being defensive about this—you have to put in the work to help people understand why jumping straight into communicating doesn't work, without first understanding what the desired outcome is and who the audiences are who can help to get to that point. Most people I have worked with are very open to working strategically once they can see why the process matters and how it improves the outcomes.

I would say that the most fulfilling projects have been those where I have not only had a positive impact on the outcome of a project but also managed to show people the value of effective communication. Taking someone on the journey from starting with a tactic to stepping back, planning properly and executing with a real plan is hugely rewarding. Working this way has helped to change attitudes/perceptions, build culture, increase understanding and encourage action across a multitude of projects.

It's OK to ask questions, it's acceptable to challenge the temptation to dive straight into communication and you can still run a strategic planning process without anyone knowing. There have been times when my colleague had no interest at all in planning properly. In those projects, I just did the plan in secret and they were none the wiser!

Case Study

WHERE THERE'S A WILL, THERE'S A WAY: NEW SOUTH WALES TRUSTEE AND GUARDIAN CONNECTS CUSTOMER SERVICE PRINCIPLES TO EMPLOYEE BEHAVIORS THROUGH COMMUNICATIONS

Situation

New South Wales Trustee and Guardian is an Australian state government agency that provides will-making and deceased estate administration services. In 2018, slumping customer satisfaction metrics highlighted a need for employees to reposition the organization as customer-centered. The Communications & Engagement team developed and implemented a communication strategy that included an interactive experience to support the launch of the company's new principles and bring them to life. The results of the program demonstrate how experiential learning through team activities is a key contributor to changing staff behavior and improving customer satisfaction.

Customer satisfaction indices (CSI) across key service streams were either low or declining, complaints were rising and staff morale was declining, following an organizational restructuring in 2016. The Communications & Engagement team worked to develop Customer Excellence Principles as a tool to turn these trends around and embed a culture of customer service excellence. They identified six principles—reflecting the key attributes of service their customers wanted.

Campaign

To bring the principles to life in a way that would impact customer experience, the team focused on translating principles into behaviors. The Communications & Engagement team members also segmented internal targets into three primary, and one secondary target, and created learning and development solutions for each.

Team leaders comprised the first target audience. While employees viewed team leaders as their most trusted source of information, team meetings were irregular and there was an opportunity to strengthen this powerful communications channel. Feedback indicated team leaders didn't always know how to talk to staff about poor or inconsistent customer service. Further, there was a strong belief by team leaders and supervisors that their roles did not include leading training.

The second target, frontline staff in branches, had daily face-to-face interactions with will-making customers. This gave those workers a high awareness of each customer's personal situation and experience. However, qualitative customer satisfaction research indicated that service did not always reflect the Customer Excellence Principles. Comments such as *"Left to wait over one hour with no explanation"* and *"Australian language. No need for legal jargon"* represented what customers were feeling.

Specialist teams, the third primary audience, included professionals from Legal, Finance, Tax and Audit functions. Feedback indicated that specialist teams had the perception that they did not have "customers" because they didn't interact with people outside of organization. Consequently, they valued their technical skills and felt they were of greater importance than those of customer service employees.

A secondary audience of senior management and executive leadership was targeted as a strategy to endorse the business need to improve awareness and understanding of the principles. These audiences had a high level of engagement with communication channels including the intranet, management forums and email.

The team's goal was to achieve a significant improvement in customer service outcomes by changing behavior and creating a shared language and framework for customer service within the company. Its measurable objectives included achieving a 40% increase in awareness of the principles, measured by pre- and post-campaign surveys; a 40% increase in understanding of the principles, measured by pre- and post-campaign surveys; a 5% increase in customer service survey scores for all customer streams over 12 months; and a benchmark of 80% of teams complete all five team activities the team created, tracked through completion rates.

The communication team designed a series of five team activities that used an experiential learning approach. Each activity focused on a principle, including the following:

- Activity 1: Personalized—External and internal customer personas were created to build awareness that all teams had customers with different needs.
- Activity 2: Empathy—A video of company senior leaders describing the organization in three words was used as a basis for group discussion about empathy.
- Activity 3: Insightful—A company service was documented to test it was being delivered consistently.
- Activity 4: Convenient and Timely—A service was interrogated to see if it could be delivered in a more convenient and timely way.
- Activity 5: Value—Working together, teams created their own customer value statement.

Results

Pre- and post-campaign surveys provided data for awareness, knowledge and attitude, and the team tracked progress through the completion of all five activities. Reflection sheets provided honest sentiment from staff and were helpful to gauge the effectiveness of improvements in processes, such as the Accounts team revising its payment system. This process of iterative feedback demonstrated the link between the activities and the results achieved.

With 60 teams (80%) completing all five planned activities, "increasing 'high awareness' of Customer Excellence Principles" was achieved at 42%, 2% above the target. A 40% increase in staff "high understanding of Customer Service Principles" was recorded, right on target.

Beyond communication metrics, the efforts increased Customer Satisfaction survey results by 7%, surpassing the 5% goal across all customer work streams.

Source: IABC Gold Quill Awards (2020)

Bibliography

American Marketing Association. (2017). *Definitions of Marketing.* Retrieved March 9, 2021, from www.ama.org/the-definition-of-marketing-what-is-marketing/.

Cialdini, R. (2001). The science of persuasion. *Scientific American, 284*(2), 76–81. Retrieved January 9, 2021, from www.jstor.org/stable/26059056.

Dahlen, M., & Rosengren, S. (2016). If advertising won't die, what will it be? Toward a working definition of advertising. *Journal of Advertising, 45*(3), 334–345. https://doi.org/10.1080/00913367.2016.1172387.

Hallahan, K., Holtzhausen, D., van Ruler, B., Verčič, D., & Sriramesh, K. (2007). Defining strategic communication. *International Journal of Strategic Communication, 1*(1), 3–35. https://doi.org/10.1080/15531180701285244.

Marshall, D. P., Moore, C., & Barbour, K. (2019). *Persona Studies: An Introduction* (1st ed.). Hoboken, NJ: Wiley-Blackwell.

Mazzei, A., Butera, A., & Quaratino, L. (2019). Employee communication for engaging workplaces. *Journal of Business Strategy, 40*(6), 23–32. https://doi.org/10.1108/jbs-03-2019-0053.

Perloff, R. M. (2017). *The Dynamics of Persuasion: Communication and Attitudes in the Twenty-First Century* (Routledge Communication Series) (6th ed.). Oxfordshire, England: Routledge.

Slater, M. (1995). Choosing audience segmentation strategies and methods for health communication. In Maibach, E. W., & Parrott, R. (eds.) *Designing Health Messages: Approaches from Communication Theory and Public Health Practice.* Los Angeles: Sage Publications, pp. 186–198.

Small, D. A., Loewenstein, G., & Slovic, P. (2007). Sympathy and callousness: The impact of deliberative thought on donations to identifiable and statistical victims. *Organizational Behavior and Human Decision Processes, 102*(2), 143–153. https://doi.org/10.1016/j.obhdp.2006.01.005.

3

COMPETENCIES FOR EMPLOYEE COMMUNICATION

In the first two chapters, we explored the definition and history of employee communication as well as some of the factors that differentiate employee communication from other fields, such as advertising and marketing. With that foundation established, it's time to look inside the profession at one of the biggest factors in what makes for a successful employee communicator: competencies.

Success in any career fundamentally reflects acquiring and demonstrating skills—those skills are what gets a candidate the job and improving and building on those skills is what leads to career growth. However, beyond what's listed in a job posting, it can be difficult to know what communication skills, or competencies, are needed to move up the corporate ladder.

This is about more than just doing a regular performance review and showing how an employee can grow. This is becoming a critical issue with millennial and Gen Z employees as they expect true mentors in the office. Research from Deloitte showed that 73% of millennials said they were more likely to stay with a company after five years if their employers were strong educators and trainers. The last thing any organization wants is employees getting frustrated because they don't know what skills are needed and aren't getting proper advice for how to advance, causing them to leave the organization for other jobs.

In this chapter, we'll provide a macro view around how employee communication competencies fit within the broader world of the professional communicator and review the ecosystem model of business actions, strategies and initiatives; then we will delve into the micro view, providing context around how they connect to what is needed for leadership positions. Although the specifics will be different by organization and industry, this will serve as a starting point for how to grow a career in the world of internal communication.

DOI: 10.4324/9781003024118-3

So, let's start with a basic definition of a *competency*. A U.S. Department of Labor report defines a competency as "the ability of applying or using knowledge, skills, abilities, behaviors, and personal characteristics to successfully perform personal work tasks, specific functions, or operate in a given role or position."

Technical competencies are competencies that are specific to a job or function within an organization (even though some may have little or nothing to do with technology). Developing and demonstrating technical competencies are important in meeting the responsibilities of an employee's current role and in preparing them for future potential roles. One example of a technical competency that is specific to a communication professional would be storytelling. Think of technical competencies as a "means to an end"—in that, they help employees perform their roles effectively and give them a runway for future growth and development.

Organizations also may have what are called *leadership competencies*. These are skill sets that are used to assess and develop current and future leaders. As employees continuously gain proficiency with the technical competencies required for their roles, executive management concurrently is looking at future leaders through the lens of leadership competencies. Developing talent in others, such as their team members, could be an example of a leadership competency.

Competencies can fall into both technical and leadership categories, but the way they are framed will be different. Leadership competencies are often broad and more general in nature, whereas technical competencies would be more specific. Communication is a great example of a competency that fits both. A leadership competency for communication might define it to include listening, interpersonal communication and/or small-group communication. Communication as a technical competency for a communications professional would go deeper to include skills such as editorial excellence, positioning and reputation management.

So, if we look at how these technical and leadership competencies fit together within employee communication, it looks like this (see Figure 3.1 on next page).

Competency Variables

Is there a set of universal competencies that apply to internal communication? The short answer is yes and no. Yes, there are skill sets defined by trade organizations such as the International Association of Business Communicators (IABC) and the Public Relations Society of America (PRSA), and other recognized national communication trade organizations in countries across the globe. Some of those skill sets include strategic planning, professional development participation, negotiating and coaching senior management, benchmarking best practices, leveraging technology, developing policy, management (with projects, change, crisis, etc.), communication audits, creative conceptualization and presentation, measuring return on investment and general business literacy.

However, there is not a universally accepted set of internal communication competencies that every organization has adopted. And there are good reasons to

Types of competencies

Leadership competencies
Broad skill sets applied to develop and assess current and future leaders across an organization

Technical competencies
Specific skill sets identified for employees to deliver their work and grow in their fields, like communications

EXAMPLES: Media relations, crisis communication, writing, employee communication

Subsets of technical competencies
More detailed technical competencies that deliver deep expertise, like with employee communication

EXAMPLES: Change management communication, internal stakeholder engagement, employee social media management

FIGURE 3.1 There are three main types of competencies: leadership, technical and subsets of technical.

explain why. Mainly, these competencies can vary depending on the maturity, size, industry and where the communication function reports within an organization.

First, the *maturity* of any communications organization will influence which competencies it values more than others. A "new" or start-up employee communication function or job may value putting more basic levels of competencies in place across multiple skill bases, while a more mature communications group may want to go deep into several skill areas.

Additionally, the way an organization handles its stakeholders can alter its approach to competencies. Organizations that practice an integrated approach to general stakeholder engagement may fold employee communication into a broader competency definition for stakeholder engagement. Enterprises that want more focused attention specifically on internal stakeholders likely will carve out competencies specifically for employee or internal stakeholder communication.

The *size* of an employee communication team also will impact how it defines the competencies it values. A team of one, versus a team of 20 or more, will have different approaches to competency definition. Larger teams likely will identify a greater range of skills within a competency they want their members to have, simply as a result of having a larger pool of talent with the ability to go deeper into those skill sets.

The *industry* in which the organization lives also can be a substantial influence on the employee communication skill sets it defines. An organization in the technology sector, for example, likely will define internal social media skills in ways that are more advanced—heightened analytics skills or coding—than other industries that do not have, or rely on, digital communication channels or tools.

Finally, where an employee communication function reports within an organization also influences which competencies it values, and how it defines them. For example, an internal communication function that reports through HR may have more emphasis on understanding compensation and benefits issues versus a function that reports through Marketing, Legal or Corporate Communication.

Progressing With Core Competencies

So, with all these variables, how can a practitioner of employee communication gain an understanding of the core competencies they should develop? Despite the aforementioned lack of uniformity in how skills for employee communication professionals are defined, there is less disagreement on a number of what competencies are "must haves" for development.

North Star Communications Consulting, LLC, a U.S.-based agency that focuses on communications talent development, has worked with local, regional and global companies on defining skill sets for professional communicators. As a result of working with companies such as Toyota, Visa and Xerox, North Star identified nine core communication competencies needed for employees. From there,

Understanding a safety problem doesn't necessarily mean employees can, or want to, do anything about it. Communicators have to find the right voice, tone and compelling case study (or studies) that will help employees come to believe that there's something in it for them to change, and that the new safety rule or process will work. That would require providing opportunities for employees to have conversations, and potentially input, into the solution.

And finally, third in this scenario, communicators could assess whether employees are actually following the new safety protocol(s), and how communications about the solution either helped or hindered their ability to adopt the new procedure. That, in turn, can connect communication measurement efforts more directly to a financial result, or return on investment.

Each of these challenges offers unique opportunities for communicators to measure the effectiveness of their work. More importantly, if measurement is done correctly, the insights will enable the communicator to course correct what isn't working, or introduce new communication solutions for any part of a communication campaign that needs help.

As with everything in communication measurement, metrics will line up in one of two camps: out*puts* and out*comes*. Both categories are critical enablers of communication success, but employee communicators need to understand the differences and how different measurement approaches combine to assess efficacy. To be clear, communication *outputs* reflect more passive measurement metrics around communication reach, tone and engagement levels, such as data found through social and digital analytics. *Outcomes* reflect sentiment, behaviors and—ultimately—business or financial results like return on investment. This can also include relational outcomes, such as those examined by Tom Kelleher in his 2009 *Journal of Communication* article, including trust, satisfaction, control mutuality and commitment.

Measuring for Awareness

For more than 150 years, starting with the AIDA model (awareness, interest, desire, action) in the late 1800s, awareness has been a foundational element in communication efforts. John Rossiter and Larry Percy discussed the role of awareness in advertising in their book *Advertising and Promotion Management* saying that "without brand awareness occurring, no other communication effects can occur."

Within employee communication, our primary question is, based on the content we create and distribute, are employees getting the basic message that something is happening that we need them to know about?

In order for us to break through the clutter of digital, broadcast, print and live/verbal messaging that employees receive both from internal and external sources, our content absolutely must be delivered in a way that is relevant and timely for our internal stakeholders.

When they are aware of the information we're sending, we essentially have an output that can be measured by way of recall and interest levels through a survey or focus group.

If we've got great content, but it's not reaching our intended internal audiences, we've got a big problem, too. That's why measuring the effectiveness of our channels is a critical output that can be measured as well. Assessing email open rates, click-throughs, intranet site visits and preferred channels through surveys or focus groups can paint a vivid picture of our ability to reach our internal stakeholders. Auditing, covered later in this chapter, also can help us assess what's working, and what's not—and why.

Measuring for Understanding

When employees are aware of a business issue or initiative that's important to their enterprise, the foundation is laid to deliver a better understanding of why it's important and what the organization wants its internal stakeholders to know or do about it. Then that understanding has to be measured.

For example, knowing that an organization is experiencing higher rates than normal of attrition—employees voluntarily leaving their company—is important for employees and people managers to know. But it's far more important to ensure that they understand what's driving the higher rate of attrition, and what can be done to address the problem. Are there new policies or procedures being introduced or training that's being offered? Do they understand what behaviors are contributing to more employees leaving than usual? And do they have any understanding of what it means for them?

So, using this example, communicators could ask employees and people managers a number of content-based questions to assess not only if they're aware of a business problem, but also if they understand the importance of it to the organization, and to them. A survey, for example, could ask a series of questions such as:

Please Indicate Your Agreement or Disagreement with the Following Statements.

The company is experiencing higher-than-usual attrition rates with employees (employees leaving voluntarily).
Strongly Disagree   Disagree   Unsure   Agree   Strongly agree

I understand why more employees are leaving voluntarily than usual.
Strongly Disagree   Disagree   Unsure   Agree   Strongly agree

I understand how higher attrition rates impact me personally.
Strongly Disagree   Disagree   Unsure   Agree   Strongly agree

I understand how higher attrition rates impact my team.
Strongly Disagree   Disagree   Unsure   Agree   Strongly agree

I know what the company is doing to address higher attrition rates.

Strongly Disagree   Disagree   Unsure   Agree   Strongly agree

I know what I can do to help the organization address higher attrition rates.

Strongly Disagree   Disagree   Unsure   Agree   Strongly agree

Collecting these kinds of insights can tell communicators definitively if their content is reaching their intended internal stakeholders, and if it's effective in delivering an understanding of the issue and remedies being offered to address it. That, in turn, can influence additional content and strategies planned for remaining communications.

Of course, communicators would need to apply logic to sequences of questions. For example, if a survey responder disagrees with the first statement in this series about being aware of higher-than-usual attrition rates, that individual would be routed out of the remaining survey questions that dive deeper into understanding the issue.

Measuring for Belief

Awareness and understanding metrics for communication most often are a reflection of broader-scale communication strategies. In terms of more efficient ways of delivering broad-scale awareness of a business issue, enterprise-wide portal posts, company-wide emails or digital signage posts can certainly provide the reach and speed that are highly desirable.

But there also are drawbacks, depending solely on wide-scale communication tactics. An email about an important topic can easily be overlooked by large portions of internal stakeholders in many organizations. And the time an email or intranet reader may invest in a digital communication can be minimal. Broad-scale employee communication channels, by design, often are created for short, focused content versus more in-depth content required to help employees fully understand a business problem and its related solutions.

All this is a precursor to measuring for *belief* through communications. Based on the book *Belief, Attitude, Intention, and Behavior: An Introduction to Theory and Research* by Martin Fishbein and Icek Ajzen, beliefs "represent the information [a person] has about an object. Specifically, a belief links an object to some attribute."

While internal stakeholders may be aware of, and understand, a business issue or opportunity, they may be less likely to believe in its importance, or the efficacy of the enterprise's solution, unless they're given more direct, in-depth interpersonal communication.

That means someone needs to talk with them. Belief in a solution most often demands employees must engage in a dialogue about the issue and trust how the organization's approach to solving it can work for them.

Measurement for belief spans both outputs and outcomes. For outputs, we can measure things like the frequency of opportunities for employees to express their voice in a proposed solution and in the content analysis of blog posts (how many comments our content is generating, of the numbers of "likes" or "shares").

Looking to outcomes, as we get closer to what leadership cares about, we can measure *sentiment*. Using tools such as focus groups, surveys and digital analytics and content analysis of social posts, we can use a *sentiment analysis* to assess how employees are feeling (favorably or unfavorably) about an issue or proposed change, and their intent to act on what the organization is asking them to do. Through a sentiment analysis, organizations can assist efforts related to competitive and marketing analyses as well as risk management.

According to researchers Tetsuya Nasukawa and Jeonghee Yi, sentiment analysis "involves the identification of sentiment expressions, polarity and strength of the expressions, and their relationship to the subject." The researchers argue that the examination of the relationships between the sentiments expressed and the subject matter is crucial.

So essentially, we're moving beyond what internal stakeholders know about an issue or opportunity and assessing how our communications are influencing how they feel about it—a strong gateway to their intent to act on it.

One example that we'll use through the rest of this chapter to show aspects of measurement relates to the DuPont merger with Dow in 2017. In this case related to sentiment, DuPont assessed employee sentiment about the future of its businesses after the merger was complete. Using a word cloud (see the bottom left corner in Figure 4.1), the communicators were able to illustrate how employees felt about their future, which largely reflected their awareness, understanding and belief in the future state of the organization.

Measuring for Change/Behavior

When we measure for change, we're moving to the treasure chest of employee communication efficacy. When we can correlate how communication influences awareness, understanding, belief and behavior change, we're demonstrating the ultimate value of strategic internal stakeholder communication. In Figure 4.1, it shows how various measurements can be used, in this case related to the Dow/DuPont merger mentioned previously, to show change in various areas of the employee experience.

Going back to our example of employees following a new safety procedure, there are clear ways of showing how communications led to fewer recordable incidents/accidents and the financial benefit attached to reduced numbers. The only way for employees to follow new safety procedures, one could easily argue, is for them to understand those procedures and to be motivated to use them. Effectively communicating the problem, giving employees the opportunity to engage in conversation around it, and providing compelling reasons to follow the procedures, each demand successful communication strategies and tactics.

However, it's not only compliance with safety procedures that can impact with business results. Communications can be aligned with an endless number of

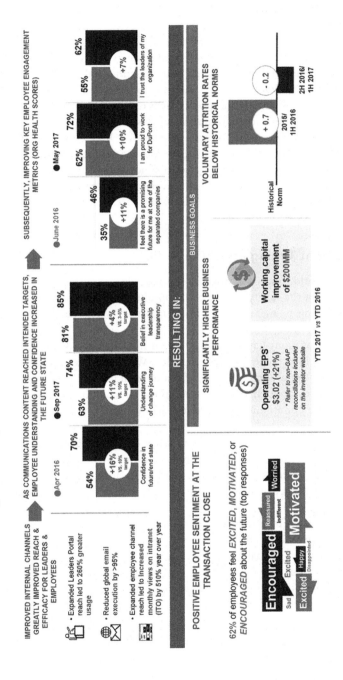

FIGURE 4.1 This summary from DuPont employee communicators, which connects communication metrics with other business metrics taken outside of the communication function, shows outcomes that reflect attitude and behavior, not outputs.

business priorities. Behaviors connected to the use of new IT systems, to retaining employees in the organization, to employees behaving as brand ambassadors—all can be measured.

What's critical is to have a clearly defined business metric up front, and agreement about communication strategies that can influence the desired outcome. That means talking with business leaders—up front—about results they care about, before the first communication tactic is executed.

Whenever possible, and not surprisingly, establishing a *baseline metric* with internal stakeholders is critical to being able to show how communication strategies and tactics affected a result. A baseline is typically a quantitative measure to determine where an organization or process stands at a specific point in time, typically before a change is about to occur (e.g., a new messaging effort or campaign). Said another way, if we don't know where we're starting from, how will we know how far we've come?

Measurement Timing and Other Influences

In a perfect world, communicators would have free reign to measure anything, at any time. But the reality professional communicators face is that they are not alone in wanting to measure what their internal stakeholders are thinking or feeling.

Many organizations have existing internal measurement disciplines that may or may not include communication metrics. Whether it's organizational health and engagement measurement or specific additional internal measurement efforts by various functions (such as legal functions on topics such as ethics and compliance), employee communicators have to learn not just what to measure but also how and when.

To be sure, it can be a complex task in larger organizations to navigate around, and through, existing large-scale internal measurement programs. The key? Alignment. It's critical to have a strong working relationship with HR and Legal departments, in particular, to understand what those functions are measuring, how and when.

In some cases, there may be opportunities to collaborate with other functions that measure internal stakeholders and their beliefs, understanding and behaviors. For example, organizational health surveys, typically administered by HR departments, could include a few questions that are specific to communication. Answers to questions like where employees are getting their information and insights about their organization; where they'd prefer to get their information; their belief in management transparency with communication; and their belief in the strategic direction of the company, for example, are questions that could provide meaningful insights for employee communicators.

But there typically are longer-lead times required to work with larger-scale internal measurement efforts, so communicators need to understand the mechanics of how these programs are administered in order to influence how to be a part of them.

Also, *survey fatigue* can play a factor in when, and how, we can measure. Survey fatigue (also used in conjunction with the larger concept of *respondent burden*, which deals with more than just surveys) was defined by the federal Office of Management and Budget in 1976 as dealing with the amount of time it takes to complete a survey or questionnaire. That definition has evolved to include not only time but also frequency of surveys.

Related to employee communication, this deals with the impact of asking internal stakeholders to respond to multiple or concurrent or closely sequenced measurement efforts. That's why coordination with any, and all, measurement efforts with internal stakeholders is critical.

These kinds of issues to navigate—to be clear—do not mean communicators cannot measure the impact of their work. Sustained employee communication campaigns should include a range of event-based measurement efforts (e.g., the impact of an employee town hall live meeting); focus groups seeking clarification or insights around broader trends; and more involved surveys that look at more attitudinal metrics.

Rarely with employee communication is a single communication metric able to tell the full story. The key is to know what each discrete measurement effort is designed to uncover and to identify specific points in time to aggregate data from multiple measurement tools.

That's where analytics and reporting come in. Far too often, communicators look to a single event for reporting purposes to executive management, or, for that matter, to their employee population. However, internal and external assessment must occur. Communicators should learn how employees are responding to communications and what impact their feedback is having.

Using the Dow/DuPont merger as an example, during the merger planning period, town hall meetings began with a summary of survey results from the previous CEO town hall meeting, and what changes were enacted as a result of the feedback. Whether it was the length of the meeting, the quality of the Q&A session or even the quality of the video streaming signal, communicators reviewed feedback inputs, enacted change and shared the results with both executive leadership and the global employee population. That kind of continuous feedback and reporting activity ensured response rates for surveys and other measurement efforts remained consistently high.

The key in this example is that data from multiple internal communication efforts were aggregated, analyzed and then fully assessed. Communicators were looking for, and made, actionable decisions that were transparently visible to a full range of people who had vested interests. Executives received a "flash report" within 24 hours of town halls, indicating early trends on employee understanding of their messages and their belief in transparency in senior management communication. They received a more detailed analysis of write-in comments within a week. Employees received updates on what their feedback included and what was done about it. Communicators received insights to make better decisions on content, sequencing, cadence and delivery of their communication services.

All in all, the cycle proved to be a win for everyone, as the strong reporting and analytics helped paint a clear picture of where efforts were succeeding and where they were falling short. That—in turn—secured greater confidence and resources from management to invest in employee communication.

What does good reporting look like? Best practices show that an easy-to-read dashboard or scorecard with key metrics is most helpful in telling a story about how employee communication is moving the dial. They should show baseline data and the change attributable to employee communication efforts. So, for example, quarterly reporting with bar graphs can illustrate trends that management finds helpful in assessing what's working. Metrics around engagement—how employees are digesting and interacting with communication content (in digital terms, "likes," "shares" or "ratings")—often are included. And attitudinal responses to belief in management strategy and transparency in communications are likely included as well.

The frequency of sharing these scorecards, and to whom, and how, is something that communication leadership and business leadership should align on.

Auditing and Benchmarking for Effectiveness

Two additional overlooked practices in employee communication measurement are benchmarking and auditing. While there are always "never-been-done-before" organizational strategies, the vast majority of business initiatives have been done in one way or another.

Benchmarking was defined by Robert C. Camp in the *Journal of Business Strategy* as "the search for the best industry practices which will lead to exceptional performance through the implementation of these best practices." Related to employee communication, strategies that have been executed, and their results, can often help communicators set reasonable expectations and correlated goals, as they create their customized approaches.

When Toyota North America consolidated multiple U.S. headquarter locations into one—located in Plano, Texas—there were almost 5,000 employees and their families that needed significant communications in order for them to make the decision about whether to move or not.

Communication and HR leaders at Toyota benchmarked other companies that had moved their headquarters locations significant distances and came up with targets that they wanted to exceed.

Communications ran over a several-year period from the time of the announcement in 2014 until the new headquarters opened in 2017. When all was said and done, the number of employees relocating to Texas surpassed other companies that were benchmarked and Toyota's own internal goals.

Auditing is another critical practice that can make or break employee communication effectiveness and it's all about measurement. According to the Institute of Internal Auditors, internal auditing is:

> an independent and objective assurance and consulting activity that is guided by a philosophy of adding value to improve the operations of the organization. It assists an organization in accomplishing its objectives by bringing a systematic and disciplined approach to evaluate and improve the effectiveness of the organization's risk management, control, and governance processes.

As with any measurement effort, clearly defining the scope of what you want to audit, and why, is fundamental to getting the insights you want. That can include the types of employees you want to ask, differences in businesses or functions to which they are deployed, geographies where they work, or job levels, among other demographics.

Once that scope has been articulated, communicators can use primary research such as one-on-one interviews, facilitated group discussions, formal surveys and less formal feedback tools attached to current outreach efforts (e.g., a single question on a manager guide like "Was this guide helpful to you in preparing to talk with your team about this topic?"—with a comment box) to get the data they need.

Employee preferences are always changing. The advent of mobile technology, changes in workplace meeting practices and the evolving nature (and corresponding talent) of managers and their ability to communicate impact how employees are receiving their information. Just as importantly, when we audit those channels, we often can learn not just where employees get their information, but also where they want to get it.

Auditing can reinforce the good communication practices we're using and expose those that don't work or are outdated. Print publications like employee magazines, once believed to be irrelevant in the day of instant digital communication, have resurfaced in some organizations as tools that can reinforce organizational culture, values and behaviors and reputational issues. The practice of auditing is what helps employee communicators identify where and how content should be delivered.

Full-scale internal communication audits don't necessarily have to be done every year, but every two to three years between them can be an effective practice.

Measurement Is a Discipline

While there are many approaches to measuring internal communication, the discipline of building in a measurement component to every significant employee communication strategy is the key takeaway.

Doing our homework to understand what our internal stakeholders know about the topic or issue we're addressing is job No. 1. Next, looking at driving awareness and understanding through broader-scale communication, and using interpersonal or small-group communication strategies to drive belief and behavior or action, should be part of any strategic solution.

Finally, ensuring that data gleaned from our measurement efforts is analyzed, reported and actionable is what makes the numbers tell a story or show progress—and ideally that story ties to business metrics that are pre-aligned before the first communication begins.

Profile: John Gregory Clemons

Founder, President and Senior Communication Consultant Clemons Communications Huntersville, NC, USA

Career Bio

I began my career as a newspaper reporter and later a national magazine editor. For more than 25 years, I have worked as a communication professional primarily focused on employee communication at several Fortune 500 companies and organizations (AT&T, Marriott International, Raytheon and Walmart).

Measuring Employee Communication

While working at a major retail company, it was important to establish a connection between associates and the leadership of a newly formed business division. It required development, implementation and measurement of a strong and strategic employee program designed to recognize the value of associates' input, and look for opportunities to curate their ideas for consideration by leadership, then share with associates any feedback or actions that resulted from their input.

With the establishment of this new division, formed by combining several organizations representing different disciplines, I quickly realized that to gather the best ideas, associates must first understand their organization and fellow teams—and have a voice in its development. As a result, I created and launched a new program called *Listening Circles*.

The program was designed to provide a structured process for information flow between division associates and division leadership. *Listening Circle* sessions were held quarterly and generally lasted around 90 minutes each. Additional stakeholders included the company's HR leadership and key members of the company's global associate communication team. The program also spawned a new group of company "ambassadors"—supporters of the company, both internally and externally.

We wanted to create a venue for gathering real-world, unfiltered associate insights on several "hot topics," establish an associate sounding board for proposed company messaging, workplace programs, tools and develop a new pool of company "ambassadors."

When creating the *Listening Circles* program, it was important for participants to understand that this was neither intended to be a series of gripe sessions, nor was it designed to get associates to "rubber stamp" decisions that had already been finalized. This had to be different than the typical roundtable-type discussions; associates had to be convinced that their ideas and input would be considered for action at the highest level of the organization. In addition, we needed to find a way to open a dialogue within the division leadership and continue to enhance its culture through associate insights.

In launching this initiative, I learned that I have a key role in listening to, respecting and trusting employees on what works best to help a company successfully implement its vision, strategy, values and goals. Employees are valued assets who can help shape the reputation, visibility and success of a business or organization. Their voices counted and led to several meaningful actions, including creating a monthly division newsletter (to supplement the parent company's existing channels); reviewing and improving the company's associate career development program; reviewing and supporting key HR programs prior to rollout; and responding to participants' feedback and comments, which were well received from division leadership. As a result, several changes were made in programs and communications throughout the division.

Most importantly, a survey of *Listening Circle* participants revealed that the program was viewed as "a sounding board on key internal issues, a program where employee-related programs can be reviewed and changed, as necessary, before rollout, and a worthwhile employee program" within the company.

Regardless of the company or organization, seize the opportunity to provide a "safe space" for employees to share their thoughts, concerns and issues. Employees' input is beneficial to the culture, two-way trust and operational integrity of an organization. Take the time to listen.

Case Study

DUPONT'S JOURNEY TO THREE LARGEST INDUSTRIAL MERGER IN HISTORY SHOWCASES VALUE AND IMPACT OF EMPLOYEE COMMUNICATION

Situation

In December 2015, global science and technology company DuPont began an unprecedented change journey that would alter the 215-year-old company forever. The company announced its intent to merge with competitor, Dow, in a $130 billion deal, initially projected to close within a year's time, and subsequently spin three new industry-leading companies in 12–18 months.

The deal, which closed on August 31, 2017, was the largest industrial merger in history. In the 20 months it took to close the deal, many internal and external influences created a sea of uncertainty for leaders and employees. This business environment demanded a comprehensive employee and leader communications engagement plan that also addressed significant business issues, including a large-scale (about US $1B), cost restructuring plan that would eliminate approximately 10% of the global workforce as the journey began; a new chairman and CEO (the first CEO hired from outside the company in DuPont's history) just weeks before the merger announcement; critical planning and adjusting for extended regulatory reviews, resulting in portfolio divestitures and acquisitions; and multiple activist investors seeking a realignment of the proposed portfolio.

Campaign

With a heightened need to retain top talent and improve business performance, internal communication took center stage. To keep employees and leaders engaged and confident in the change journey—and focused on immediate business performance goals—DuPont developed a consistent employee narrative, created continuous feedback loops, rebuilt its internal communication infrastructure for employees and leaders and implemented a robust measurement, analytics and reporting discipline.

DuPont Communications conducted primary research via surveys, web metrics and organizational health data shortly after the merger announcement was made. It gauged baseline employee attitudes; reviewed messaging; assessed channel effectiveness; reviewed demographic information; and partnered with HR to conduct ongoing surveys during the 20 months between the announcement and the transaction close.

To support business goals and communication objectives leading up to transaction close, DuPont communicators developed and implemented innovative communication strategies that fostered engagement and built excitement around the changes taking place, while also giving meaning to the intended companies' new value propositions. These efforts, in turn, helped drive retention and stabilize organization unrest.

Specific employee communication strategies included driving employee engagement through delivery of a powerful narrative, centered on compelling content and future opportunities for employees—called the *Journey to Three*; empowering leaders to deliver transparent communications through relevant content, training and tools; extending content reach and penetration and increased speed of delivery by significantly modernizing internal communication channels and introducing targeted new channels; implementing a continuous feedback loop, while enabling analytics and reporting to drive actionable communication strategy decisions for rapid deployment; and maintaining business continuity by aligning all business, functional and regional communication leaders on all merger-related needs, announcements and plans.

Communicators redesigned the flagship global employee communication channel with simpler navigation, greater interactivity and new video and graphic media storytelling capabilities, while building a global site architecture to support future, anticipated merger and spin activities. They also supported the delivery of the narrative through more than 200 town halls as senior leaders visited local sites and plants across four continents and measured impact of content with employees and tracked message performance regionally and globally. They also introduced a short-format video series called "Take 5"—in which executives answered five "burning questions" on employees' minds (taken from feedback loops), centered on integration planning. And they introduced a new executive blog series called "Compass," through which senior leaders shared their perspectives on various topics of employee interest—integration planning, merger milestones and course-of-business updates. Each of these new executive channels extended opportunities for two-way dialogue and continuous feedback.

After aligning communication plans with the CEO and his leadership team, employee communicators at DuPont instituted a global Communication Program Management Office (CPMO). The CPMO became an effective risk management tool to ensure alignment, secure timely approvals, minimize overlap, identify gaps and harmonize local and global messaging—internally and externally. To do this, the team introduced a "Global Control Tower" site as a central repository to connect the business unit/functional/regional plans to drive change at the local level and connect back to the enterprise strategy. Further, they implemented weekly CPMO meetings with internal and external global representation, and various subject matter experts to minimize risk in an environment with increased scrutiny on restructuring, merger and integration communications. They also began bi-monthly alignment meetings with all business unit/functional/regional communication leaders to align on updates and identify immediate action, interdependencies or support needed.

Results

The impact of 20+ months of uncertainty on leaders and employees could have been catastrophic to talent retention and business performance. Ongoing measurement tools (i.e., feedback options on channels) and surveys revealed that by the close of the transaction, goals and targets were not only met but also exceeded.

Globally, employee/leader understanding of, and confidence in, the change journey increased 11% and 16%, respectively, as already-high belief in executive leadership transparency (81%) grew an additional 4%. Those communication results clearly correlate to Organizational Health scores, which showed 11% improvement in employee confidence in the future and a 7% increase in leader trust. Concurrently, full-year business performance dramatically improved (earnings per share +21%) as voluntary attrition dipped below historical norms (−0.2).

Source: IABC Gold Quill Awards (2018) and PRSA Silver Anvil Awards (2018)

Bibliography

Bruner, G. C. (2017). *Marketing Scales Handbook: Multi-item Measures for Consumer Insight Research* (Library version.). Fort Worth, Texas: GCBII Productions, LLC.

Bruning, S. D., & Ledingham, J. A. (2000). Perceptions of relationships and evaluations of satisfaction: An exploration of interaction. *Public Relations Review, 26*(1), 85–95. https://doi.org/10.1016/s0363-8111(00)00032-1.

Camp, R. C. (1992). Learning from the best leads to superior performance. *Journal of Business Strategy, 13*(3), 3–6. https://doi.org/10.1108/eb039486.

Fishbein, M., & Ajzen, I. (1975). *Belief, Attitude, Intention, and Behavior: An Introduction to Theory and Research.* Reading, MA: Addison-Wesley.

Greenwald, A. G., & Leavitt, C. (1984). Audience involvement in advertising: Four levels. *Journal of Consumer Research, 11*, 581–592.

Hon, L. C., & Grunig, J. (1999). *Guidelines for Measuring Relationships in Public Relations.* Gainesville, FL: The Institute for Public Relations. Retrieved January 26, 2006, from www.instituteforpr.com/pdf/1999_guide_measure_relationships.pdf.

Institute of Internal Auditors (IIA). (2000). *About the Profession*. Retrieved from https://na.theiia.org/about-us/about-ia/Pages/About-the-Profession.aspx.

Kelleher, T. (2009). Conversational voice, communicated commitment, and public relations outcomes in interactive online communication. *Journal of Communication, 59*(1), 172–188. https://doi.org/10.1111/j.1460-2466.2008.01410.x.

Krugman, H. E. (1965). The impact of television advertising: Learning without involvement. *Public Opinion Quarterly, 29*(3), 349–356.

Macdonald, E., & Sharp, B. (1996). Management perceptions of the importance of brand awareness as an indication of advertising effectiveness. *Marketing Research On-Line, 1*, 1–15.

Nasukawa, T., & Yi, J. (2003, October). Sentiment analysis: Capturing favorability using natural language processing. In *Proceedings of the 2nd International Conference on Knowledge Capture*. New York, NY: Association for Computing Machinery, pp. 70–77.

Rodgers, S., & Thorson, E. (2019). *Advertising Theory* (Routledge Communication Series, 2nd ed.). Oxfordshire, England: Routledge.

Rossiter, J. R., & Percy, L. (1987). *Advertising and Promotion Management*. Singapore: McGraw-Hill.

Sharp, L. M., & Frankel, J. (1983). Respondent burden: A test of some common assumptions. *Public Opinion Quarterly, 47*(1), 36. https://doi.org/10.1086/268765.

Wimmer, R. D., & Dominick, J. R. (2014). *Mass Media Research: An Introduction* (10th ed.). Wadsworth: Cengage.

5
INFLUENCES ON EMPLOYEE COMMUNICATION

We've all heard the story about one set of seeds put in fertile ground and another set put in the sand. Those in the soil, watered and drenched with sun, thrive and grow. Those put into the sand wither and die. It's the environment and the care and feeding of the seeds that makes the difference.

And that's pretty much how it goes for employee communication. The environment in which the function operates, how it is structured, where it reports and how it is resourced in any organization can determine its potential for growth, likelihood for success and clear definition of its priorities.

In this chapter, we'll explore the resources—along with the organizational and cultural influences related to employee communication—where it lives, what it focuses on and what limitations and opportunities come with it. No single structure, placement, cultural attribute or budget influences how employee communication is run in any organization. Think of all these influences as an ecosystem surrounding the practice of communicating with employees.

Integrated or Not. That Is the Question

Perhaps the first and most important influence on employee communication is the question of whether or not internal and external communication are "housed" together in the same function, and whether or not they are integrated in day-to-day operations and in strategic planning.

More evolved communication functions tend to look at a 360-degree set of stakeholders, recognizing that the lines between internal and external communicating often are blurred or even non-existent. They look concurrently at all issues and opportunities for communication through the lens of both internal and external stakeholders. Even in the best of organizations, the odds of consistent

DOI: 10.4324/9781003024118-5

effectiveness when internal and external communication teams are separated are much less likely, and efforts tend to be short-term and project-based versus long-term and strategic.

Given that, you may wonder if employee and external communication professionals still work effectively if they report through different functional leaders, such as HR, Marketing or Legal?

The answer is yes, but they would need to be closely "wired" through regular meetings and established protocols for advising each other about what's happening and for reviewing communications planned for both sides of the house.

In these cases, when internal and external communication functions are housed in different parts of an organization, chances are good that they are in different physical locations as well, which typically doesn't foster sharing or collaboration on either day-to-day or longer-term communication priorities. And those priorities themselves can be very different.

There are other significant implications related to keeping communicators together or separating them. Career development, for example, can be fragmented when technical competencies for employee communicators are different because of where they sit within an organization. For example, when HR houses employee communication, compensation and benefits communication expertise may be emphasized more heavily, whereas marketing and branding expertise would be the focus if the employee communication function is placed in Marketing. When internal and external are separated, career paths may seem, or become, less robust for all communicators. Integrated functions often provide greater latitude for communicators to learn "both sides of the house" and, more importantly, apply strategic solutions more often and more effectively.

Where *Should* Employee Communication Report?

There can be arguments made for employee communication reporting to any function or any business leader within an organization. The correct answer tends to reflect the perceived value that the function brings for senior executives.

Let's start with the biggest decision maker of all: the chief executive officer or president. This individual begins to set the agenda for where employee communication reports by deciding where the broader communication function (both internal and external) sits.

A senior executive who values communication and uses it often likely will want a communication leader reporting directly to her or him. This can reflect the executive's experience with communicators who have provided strong, valuable counsel and service. As executive communication is a function often located within the communication department—and often paired with employee communication—many senior executives have a strong preference for direct and immediate access to their communication teams versus having them report through other staff functions such as HR, Legal or Marketing. In many organizations where the communications have a proverbial "seat at the executive table," the function may be a part of what's called Corporate Affairs, Public Affairs or Corporate Communication. Regardless of what it's called, the closer the function reports to the top decision maker, the greater its potential for influence is, along with its ability to secure resources.

On the flip side, executives who don't value communication, or have not had a strong, positive experience with an influential communication professional, may choose to have the communication function report to another senior business executive, like a COO, or to another staff function leader. Said, one 35-year corporate communication veteran, "I can't statistically prove it, but experience has taught me that if a rising senior executive hasn't had a strong communication partnership and experience by the time they are a director, chances are good that when that person becomes a member of the C-suite, the job of a communication leader—and everyone in the communication function—becomes far more challenging." In these cases, communication, and as a result, employee communication, often is placed as a sub-department in other staff functions. So, let's take a look at the influences that those other staff functions have.

When employee communication is placed in a *marketing* function, the influence, as you can guess, most often is placed on aligning internal stakeholders with consumer or customer communication strategies. That could include a greater emphasis both on market-facing activities and on efforts to influence reputation of the company and its brand(s) (in some cases, that can be the same thing). We have a case study on a brand ambassador program in this chapter, but empowering employees to represent the brand, the corporation, or a combination of both, can yield powerful results for brand image and reputation. For larger companies with big marketing budgets, aligning employee communication with the marketing function can provide communicators with more flexibility to ideate and execute their strategies with more resources—even to become part of the PR budget mix. The trade-off, however, could be that other organizational priorities beyond marketing can get downplayed or ignored altogether. For example, internal communication around financial performance, cultural values, employee benefits, ethics and compliance could get less attention under a marketing leader who doesn't value those areas for communication as much as marketing-related activities.

Sometimes, employee communication can be placed in the *legal* function, where the guiding force often is reflected in protectionist philosophy. Delivering communication strategies and content could reflect keeping the organization out of trouble more than fully delivering awareness, understanding, belief and behavior change that's connected to other business strategies.

While there are always exceptions to the rule, many employee communication functions reporting through a Legal department can experience struggles in driving transparency and clarity in communication. In companies that compete in heavily regulated environments, such as energy, financial services and health care, there can be strong cases for aligning internal communication with Legal to ensure any, and all, compliance issues are considered before hitting the "send" button. So, focus areas for employees while placed in a Legal department can move toward ethics and compliance strategies for employees. The challenge is to balance the need to protect with the need to clearly communicate.

Few staff functions inside any organization understand how an enterprise runs and performs better than the chief financial officer (CFO) and the *finance* organization. So, while it may sound like an unusual place to call home for employee communicators, it's not completely out-of-the-ordinary to find it placed there. While the focus of employee communication can gravitate toward financial performance, cost-cutting initiatives and other productivity programs, communicators can receive a valuable education about the business, and, importantly, how to communicate about it. Sub-functions in the finance organization, like Investor Relations also can provide important insights into communicating about the business.

Perhaps the most likely home for employee communication, if not in a centralized Corporate Communication department, is with *Human Resources*. There's a certain logic of placing the communication function with another, bigger function, focused internally on the organization's people. However, when the focus is predominantly on HR-related transactions—compensation and benefits, annual health benefit enrollment and culture, for example—the influence of external issues and related communication can be diminished or ignored altogether.

The bottom line with any of these placements is that when separated from external communication, employee communication professionals can easily fall into siloed ways of working, which can, and does, create gaps in communication strategy and results. Even if by unintentional omission, a lack of transparent communication between internal and external teams is fostered when they report through different parts of an enterprise.

Industry Type and Culture

The type of industry an employee communicator works in can have a significant influence on how internal communication is done. Regulated industries, such as energy, financial services and health care, have particularly stringent guide rails to work within.

Think about internal digital and social platforms that communicators increasingly use to reach dispersed and growing mobile workforces. Companies in those regulated industries have been the targets of well-publicized data breaches, where customer data were compromised. With the advent of more mobile technologies, the temptation for employees to use texting platforms, for example, increases. The particular challenge with texting is that data are not encrypted, something that the Health Insurance Portability and Accountability Act (HIPAA) in the United States requires for personal medical information.

In the financial sector, where massive amounts of customer data are stored digitally, the threat of cyberattacks and hacking is equally as daunting. That, in turn, places greater demands on how employee communication is executed, particularly with an increasingly mobile workforce. The Gramm–Leach–Bliley Act "requires financial institutions . . . to explain their information sharing practices to their customers and to safeguard sensitive data." There has even been discussion gaining traction in the last few years to enact a national data security standard for all entities handling sensitive financial information.

Regulatory governance clearly isn't the only force that can guide culture and the resulting attitudes toward employee communication, but it also certainly can shape it. An organization's approach to what, how and when it communicates with employees is a reflection of other cultural attributes as well.

Private companies, for example, may not see a need to communicate as openly or transparently, as publicly held companies that are required to follow rules for disclosure from the countries in which they do business.

The attitude of the CEO, or most senior leader, and his or her senior team toward employee communication also can color everything from tone and frequency to detail and transparency of communication to employees. Each and every influence on culture, from industry to stated company values, influences strategies created to inform, inspire and engage workers. Does a culture that doesn't foster transparency with employee communication mean employee communication efforts are doomed? Not necessarily. Savvy communication professionals increasingly are diving into traditional organizational cultural norms—"the way we've always done things"—and challenging them with data that tie the impact of that culture and communication on business metrics such as talent recruiting, retention, corporate image and reputation. Those metrics can drive business performance.

Big-Picture Influences: Enterprise Structure

Where those who work in employee communication report is one part of the influence of structure, but that's simply a reflection of plugging in the function where the organization thinks it's an optimal fit. The total structure of the enterprise also is a significant influence on the employee communication function. In smaller, or more simply *structured enterprises*, employee communication would report to a single leader in an enterprise-wide communication function.

But in larger organizations, employee communication professionals often are placed in *matrixed structures*, with communicators reporting both to lines of business (where profit and loss responsibilities reside for distinct product or service lines) and to a global communication function leader. Naturally, this placement has both positives and negatives on how the employee communication group prioritizes activities and resources to accomplish goals for both the business and the global function.

For example, an employee communicator placed to support a specific country or region of the world may find themselves reporting to the president of the business in that specific country; at the same time, the communicator also may report to a regional or global head of communication. Similarly, an employee communicator may report to both the global internal communication leader and a second leader in HR, IT, Legal or Finance. In both examples, the communicator would set goals and report progress to both the global communication function and the business, or additional global function to which they are deployed.

The positives of working in these matrixed environments include greater alignment between functional and business goals, greater communication between those internal organizations, efficiency in implementing global strategies and clear accountabilities for driving both functional performance (employee communication) and business performance.

Those positives come to fruition only when there is a clear partnership and communication between the business or geography leader and the global functional leader for employee communication. When that partnership isn't present, we can see the down side of a matrixed enterprise structure. Competing agendas for the function and business, political complexities of pleasing multiple bosses or leaders and misalignment of priorities all emerge as barriers to getting work done and, inevitably, job performance and satisfaction on the part of the employee communicator.

The key for any communicator working in a matrixed environment is to drive for clarity with goals and priorities and resources—up front and early—with both bosses. Then it's about regular reporting on progress to both managers, and deploying a process for quick resolution of issues that inevitably emerge with competing agendas. In other words, success demands clear goals, clear communication, regular reporting and efficient problem-solving. It's easier said than done, but applying these principles will save the employee communicators from significant stress and surprises in the course of their careers.

Where Are Your People and What Are They Doing?

While structure certainly has an influence on where employee communicators focus their efforts, an equally significant influence comes directly from employees themselves. Specifically, the type of work they do, where they work and the tools they use—or have access to—can influence a great deal of what we'll call internal communication infrastructure.

When we talk about infrastructure, we're talking about channels, systems, processes and protocols in place that allow employee communicators to do their day-to-day jobs.

For example, mobility is a critical issue that communicators must address. As employees move away from their desks (and desktop computers) to work in different locations closer to their customers, employee communicators need to think about what channels can reach them in efficient and effective ways. Cell phones, or other proprietary hand-held mobile devices, can be a part of the solution, but often there can be restrictions on how communicators can use them—through company policy, management practice or even organized labor contracts.

While digital communication can serve some organizations well in addressing mobility, they don't always solve every communication need. In many manufacturing environments, for example, both management and organized labor rules can influence what communication tools and channels employees can have, when they're allowed to use them, who is allowed access for placing content and what that content can and cannot include.

To illustrate this idea, imagine a situation where the corporate communication team wants to send an update on sustainability to the manufacturing floor employees who are working under a union contract. Those employees are paid hourly for manufacturing work. If the company then wants them to read that sustainability update on company time, it would need to be decided who pays for that time and under what conditions. Is it taking an hour away from the production time, or is it asking the employees to read it after their regular shift, which may require overtime pay?

Another example would be a company that wants to send an email newsletter to union employees. In this case, there would need to be a discussion about whether or not the company is allowed to have direct access to personal emails and phone numbers (since some production workers won't have company email addresses). Unions often want to see and/or control what company information reaches employees, particularly on topics related to pay, benefits and policies.

In every instance, employee communicators must partner with professionals in functions, such as labor relations, Legal and HR, to ensure they understand the behaviors of their employees, the processes to which they must adhere and the policies that guide how the enterprise communicates with them.

For example, using the manufacturing environment again, before workers begin their shifts, they often will attend short "stand up" meetings with local managers to review topics like safety or productivity. While employee communicators would like to tap into these kinds of regular face-to-face meetings, they need to navigate around issues such as time constraints (these meetings often are relatively short), and local management control on content, which is prioritized on production, versus other more "corporate" messaging on topics such as sustainability, community engagement or even diversity, equity and inclusion.

Similarly, on proprietary hand-held devices, local management more often than not holds tight control on what employee communication "corporate content" can be put through tools designed predominantly for customer service or sales. It's a challenge every employee communicator faces and the solutions only come through partnership and clear, compelling strategies.

All of these issues can influence how a strategic employee communicator builds and operates an infrastructure that enables efficient and effective communication.

An employee intranet or portal, email distribution lists, town halls at local or global levels, measurement and reporting strategies—among other channels and processes—all must reflect the unique attributes of the enterprise.

Policies and protocols also can influence internal communication channel effectiveness. A global organization in the chemicals industry, in an effort to empower people leaders, operated a "leader's portal" with special communication tools for people leaders.

While this sounds like an effective strategic effort, there was a problem. As one employee communicator said, this portal had a flawed process for giving access to the channel and unclear protocols for deciding what constituted a people leader. "We basically had the process in place that said—if your manager sent an email requesting access to the leader's portal on anyone's behalf, they got access," he said.

> So, while we were creating great content to empower leaders through communication, we were not reaching thousands of bona fide people leaders who didn't even know we had a leader's portal for them. Needless to say, we fixed it using HR-generated data that clearly identified leaders who managed other employees, versus individual contributors.

The big learning here is not to assume that existing communication channels for leaders or employees simply run themselves. The policies, protocols, systems and technologies in place when they were developed, launched or last updated can quickly become outdated and inaccurate. These tools need care and feeding, and the strategic communicator knows the importance of reviewing how they're working on a regular basis.

Geographic Reach

When organizations have employees that all live and work within the borders of a single country, employee communication certainly will be challenging enough. But when they have employees in multiple countries, the employee communicator's job is made even more challenging.

For starters, there's the issue of language. Communicators must understand and/or decide how many languages are either required by law or necessary to be effective in their communication efforts.

In Quebec, Canada, for example, the Official Language Act of 1974 requires employee communication to be delivered both in English and French. But beyond what is required by law, employee communicators must decide which communications need to be translated and the variables of time and money clearly factor into the decision mix.

For run-of-the-mill communications, it may not be necessary to translate content into 15 different languages. For communications connected to crises, or ethics and compliance priorities, the pressure to translate communications into every language used where the company does business may be non-negotiable.

Other kinds of global communication present communicators with different choices for translation. With plenty of advance notification, communicators can plan for, and execute, translation services—factoring in the time required, and any money, that may be necessary to do those translations. While some organizations use an internal network of bilingual employees to translate global content in local language, others use online or contracted translation services to do initial translations, followed by review of the translations by in-market, bilingual employees.

Again, how much time any communicator has to work with, and the nature of the content, will drive how many languages need to be included, how the work will be executed and what it will cost.

Beyond translations, government notifications and organized labor contracts also will dictate how and when employee communication in some markets must be executed.

In Europe, for example, the European Works Council requires notification from multinational companies that do business in the region to communicate with them about significant changes (such as restructuring or potential facility changes) within specific time frames. This demands close coordination between internal and external communication professionals, labor relations and government affairs representatives of the company.

In the United States, the *Worker Adjustment and Retraining Notification Act* (WARN) requires employers to provide 60 days advance notice of plant closings and mass layoffs to their employees. It may sound simple enough, but there are complexities involved here, too.

There are both federal and state requirements that trigger notification and disclosure requirements. In larger organizations, which can have multiple operations operated through different lines of business, tracking timing and scope is crucial to understanding when the law requires notification not only to employees but also—by nature of notifying federal or state authorities—to a variety of external stakeholders, too. So, consider the example of one business in a company that may not have the impact to trigger notification. But when we combine that business with a second or third business in the same company that is considering layoffs or plant closures, it may well require notification. The communication group will need a clear partnership and tracking accountability with other professionals in the company, likely in HR.

When translation and notification compliance don't come into play for multinational organizations, chances are good that other forces will. Consider the issue of multiple time zones. Communicating to North American employees on a significant issue in the afternoon most certainly will miss employees in Europe, the Middle East and Asia. If the message, or content, is of great significance, the unintended consequences of timing can create distrust and less engagement for parts of the organization that feel slighted.

Of course, no list of multinational influences on employee communication would be complete without including culture. How global messages are delivered in some parts of the world is every bit as important as what is said. The importance of a leader facing employees, live and in person, to deliver significant news and insights or context around that news, can make a big difference in how the news is accepted. Rather than sending an email, and expecting employees will "get it," savvy employee communicators will reach out and learn—in local markets—to understand employee communication practices and preferences and to localize a global message to make it relevant to workers in any given market.

To illustrate how the complexities of the global marketplace can influence employees (and external communication), consider the case of one multinational consumer goods company which faced a communication challenge around global sustainability goals.

While there was a global goal to reduce CO_2 emissions over a multi-year period, the company was introducing packaging in one market that was oxo-degradable and would increase CO_2 emissions temporarily in that single market. Why? That particular market had a significantly bigger issue with disposable packaging—no landfills. The company needed to clearly articulate what the packaging solution was globally, and in that market, to employees and other stakeholders. It went to great lengths to ensure employees understood the packaging solution was temporary until an alternative solution was developed, yet highly relevant to environmental priorities in that market; at the same time, it ensured all stakeholders understood that the global CO_2 reduction goals remained in place.

Budget, Staffing and Technology

We'd love to believe that driving employee engagement through communication can always be done on a shoestring budget and with limited staffing. Actually, many of our CEOs and CFOs not only would like to believe but, in fact, are also totally committed to that way of thinking. Those also are organizations that are likely to have disengaged employees who are unaware of what the company's priorities are and how their work and behaviors connect to their mission, vision and/or values.

Budget, staff size and investments in technology all go hand in hand in the bucket we'll call resources. While there is no hard-and-fast rule that dictates the number of professionals that are optimal for an employee communication department or function, some previous benchmarks suggested that one employee communication professional for every 1,000 employees made sense.

Certainly, there are organizations that are above and below that 1:1000 ratio, reflecting the unique natures of each enterprise and management's interest and commitment to engaging employees through communication.

Similarly, most employee communication functions must compete for funding annually, to get what they believe they need and to keep what they're given when cost cutting inevitably occurs. As we said in Chapter 4 on measurement, there is no better ammunition to make the case for budget and headcount than achieving and sharing communication results that are clearly connected to business goals and priorities.

The higher the budget and headcount to work with, the more options will be available to create strategies, develop content, execute initiatives and measure the impact of our efforts. It's not that we can't be creative and effective when we have shoestring budgets, and we are limited to no dedicated headcounts, but sustained results and high employee communication performance are not likely to be reported in most organizations that are underfunded and understaffed.

A 2018 global employee communication report from UK-based internal communication agency Gatehouse included insights from 650 global employee communication practitioners. Communication budgets reported by respondents to the Gatehouse's survey reported budget ranges in line with the size of their respective employee populations, ranging from 6,700 to 30,000 Euros (US $8,100–$36,000) for companies with fewer than 250 employees, to a range of 323,000–529,000 Euros (US $390,000–$640,000) for companies with more than 50,000 workers.

Employee Communication Budget Size

With increasing use of digital communication for, and with, employees, organizations across the globe are sifting through technology options. They range from highly customized mobile solutions to off-the-shelf collaboration platforms that come with internal communication suites from companies such as Microsoft and Google, which include email, video streaming and conferencing and cloud-based file transfer and sharing for collaboration purposes.

Any and all of those offerings can fall under the purview of employee communication as channels to promote, use or even regulate. But fundamentally, employee communication professionals must have a clear connection to IT professionals and, ideally, a line of sight and influence on longer-term investments in communication technology.

Without a seat at the IT table, employee communication professionals will find themselves in the position of the proverbial "tail wagging the dog"—meaning they'll spend more significant time, energy and money retrofitting a digital communication platform to the needs of the enterprise if they're brought in after the purchase decision has been made for that platform.

As enterprises increasingly look to digital collaboration platforms to drive innovation and productivity, a greater strategic partnership between employee communication and IT has become more critical than ever.

While the number of organizations adopting social channels is rising the numbers of employees actually using them is a different story. The same 2018 Gatehouse global employee communication survey (see Figure 5.1) showed that launching new social

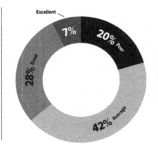

What social channel(s) have you implemented in your organization?

SharePoint	56%
Yammer	49%
Twitter	25%
Internally branded/purpose-built social platform	22%
Chatter (Salesforce)	11%
Slack	9%
Jive	8%
Google+	7%
Workplace by Facebook	7%

Excellent 7%
20% Poor
28% Good
42% Average

How successful was the adoption of social channels in your organization?

FIGURE 5.1 This table and chart represent 2018 Gatehouse global employee communication survey data related to social channel usage and adoption.

platforms for internal adoption clearly is not an "If we build it, they will come," kind of story. In fact, the report showed 62% reported average or poor adoption. These findings suggest that social digital communication channels require thoughtful, strategic change management communication to internal stakeholders—something we will cover in Chapter 10.

The types of influences on what the employee communication function does, and how it does its work, are widespread. From reporting structure and enterprise organization type to technology enablement and staff size, any one of them could easily alter the focus and success of an internal communication team. Together, they represent an ecosystem of influences that must be understood, navigated and managed. When all that is done effectively, employee communication professionals will have the resources, clear priorities and enabling environment that allows them to deliver business results that matter.

Profile: Craig Smith

Client Communication Expert
McKinsey & Company, USA/Chicago

Career Bio

I started my career as an intern in the U.S. Congress and the British Parliament before joining the oil company BP. I worked in the employee communication team, creating publications and videos and writing articles, speeches and content for employee meetings. Employee communication was then mainly about information dissemination—we were measured on how quickly and effectively we got information out. But great copy can only go so far in aligning attitudes and behaviors around business strategy, and I started to get intrigued by the untapped potential of communications to inspire and motivate people. This has kept me hooked now for more than three decades.

Today, I help our client teams, and our clients, communicate more effectively. There is no typical day at work. I might be working with a client to design and build out a transformation communication strategy, or helping a CEO prepare for an employee meeting, or coaching a CFO on communication skills. Or I could be delivering training to our consultants or to clients. We tailor communication solutions to the specific needs of clients, so my job is one of endless variety and intriguing challenges.

Understanding Employees Influences the Best Strategies for Engagement

I worked at a large U.S. company emerging from a near-death experience after the 2008/2009 financial crisis. The share price had plummeted, people were laid off and there was real doubt about whether the company would survive. A new CEO embarked on a program of radical change that included the sale of a large business. Not surprisingly, employee engagement was low.

I was convinced that, despite all the upheaval, employees had a strong attachment to the company and wanted it to succeed. But with all the crises and changes, they were unclear on what success looked like. I shared this with the CEO and suggested that we needed a new vision statement that would inspire and motivate people—it is much easier to embark on a hard journey if you have a clear sense of the destination. But, words alone, no matter how well crafted, cannot inspire and motivate people. I pulled together a small team and for the next two months we visited company sites across the United States, conducting focus groups and interviews with the goal of capturing employees' thoughts on what made the company special. We filmed all the sessions and used the transcripts to uncover common themes. This approach helped us create a vision statement that resonated with employees and by involving them in the process—and sharing the footage of the focus groups at the launch event—we engaged them as well.

This experience really drove home for me the importance in communication of starting with the audience and thinking deeply, and with empathy, about their feelings and concerns. Leaders can only lead if people choose to follow them, and companies can only be successful if people are willing to give their whole selves to the job. You can't make that happen with facts, statistics and market analysis, you also need to appeal to people's hearts. You need to communicate in a way that taps into the source of meaning that is important to them, and you can only do that if you really understand the audience you are trying to reach.

We certainly saw an increase in engagement scores. But more than that, because of the way we created it, people had embraced the new vision. I visited a company call center a couple of weeks after the vision had launched and saw that a wall in the break room had been decorated with the new vision—employees had, on their own initiative, come in on the weekend to create it from cut-out letters.

If you are only focusing on the sender's needs—that is, what leaders want to tell their people—the best you can achieve is effective information delivery. To actually communicate, and do so well, you need a detailed and intimate understanding of the audience—what motivates them, what irritates them, how they like to be communicated with, what their sources of meaning are. If you do that, employees will feel a sense of connection with leadership and with the organization's goals and be much more engaged.

Case Study

PEPSICO AMBASSADOR PROGRAM

Employee communications pilot boosts knowledge and confidence as brand ambassadors

Situation

PepsiCo's global internal communication team in 2011 recognized a desire among employees to talk about the company's commitment to operating responsibly—something the company called "Performance with Purpose." However, employees did not feel they had sufficient authority, information or tools to do so. The company had been immersed in a major external brand reputation campaign, and the internal communication team saw its opportunity to amplify and assist in that effort by marshaling engaged and mobilized employee advocates. The team developed a six-month pilot to test a variety of techniques for empowering employees to serve as ambassadors, with the goal of applying key learnings to a broader rollout.

The pilot's objectives were to educate, equip and engage employees as PepsiCo ambassadors focused on three pillars:

1. Increase pilot participants' understanding of PepsiCo—and their willingness to share stories about the company and comfort level in doing so—as measured by surveys conducted at the program's beginning and end.

2. Encourage participants to share stories with at least three people or social media platforms per month, as measured by social media monitoring and a monthly self-reporting activity survey.
3. Engage with all participants at least once per month through meetings, information, training and online networking.

Once the team secured senior leadership support for the pilot, the team partnered with internal stakeholders to promote the pilot, attract pilot participants and identify ambassador captains. Individuals targeted were salaried employees with good communication skills who were willing to contribute up to six hours of discretionary effort a month.

Once identified, the 120 participants completed an online survey gauging their understanding of PepsiCo, its brands and "Performance with Purpose" vision, as well as how comfortable they felt describing the concept to others. Eighty-five percent described PepsiCo's reputation as good or excellent, and 100% said "Performance with Purpose" was the right direction for PepsiCo. However, 14% were not sure they would be comfortable describing the company's "Performance with Purpose" vision to others.

Campaign

With the baseline established, the team moved to help employees become ambassadors through three broad strategies:

Educate: Give ambassadors the knowledge to talk credibly about PepsiCo.

- An orientation outlined PepsiCo's product portfolio and "Performance with Purpose" initiatives and a separate message training session helped employees speak credibly on the subject.
- Monthly virtual/in-person meetings focused on one of the company's major brands along with responses to common questions ambassadors may be asked. Ambassadors were provided samples of new products to better acquaint them with the portfolio and help them explain their attributes to others.
- Social media training outlined PepsiCo's social media policy and empowered and encouraged ambassadors to talk about the company on their social media.

Equip: Make ambassadorship easy with convenient tools, resources and inspiration.

- An ambassador information hub on the company's intranet included talking points on sensitive, "hot" subjects, step-by-step guides to writing blog posts and filming videos, and sample presentations.

- A bi-weekly inspirational *Advice for Ambassadors* email outlined creative ideas for spreading the word about PepsiCo.
- Conversation starters included handouts to trigger discussions, such as coupons and product samples. Ambassadors were provided with two versions of printed leave-behind cards for restaurants—one thanking them for serving PepsiCo products and another encouraging them to include PepsiCo products in their restaurant offerings.
- A "25 Quick and Easy Ambassador Tips" sheet focused on specific actions employees could take to share the PepsiCo story.
- A new tool allowed employees to easily share PepsiCo intranet stories with their external social networks.

Engage: Build a sense of community and mutual learning.

- An Ambassador Facebook group allowed participants to network and share real-time examples of how they use social media to be ambassadors.
- Pilot participants were encouraged to learn from each other by highlighting their successful efforts in the bi-weekly newsletter. Round-table discussions at monthly meetings highlighted successful ambassador interactions.
- Ambassadors were recognized through social media-based contests spotlighting posts that generated the most comments and conversations.

Results

At conclusion of the pilot, measurement showed clear progress against stated objectives:

- 97% of ambassadors felt comfortable talking about PepsiCo and its "Performance with Purpose" vision, an 11% increase since the pilot's inception.
- After the pilot, there was significant behavior change—with 95% of ambassadors acknowledging they talked about the company vision outside work, reflecting a 26% increase.
- Asked to describe the pilot in one word, the most common response was "informative" followed by "empowering."
- Ambassadors engaged an average of 22 people each month about PepsiCo, its portfolio and "Performance with Purpose" vision, and an exponentially larger amount with social media posts.
- Per month, ambassadors collectively developed an average of three external blog posts, two intranet stories and two self-produced videos highlighting the company's products and vision.

- 75% completed social media workshop training and referred the voluntary module to hundreds of other employees.
- A third of the ambassadors volunteered to help facilitate a broader program rollout.

The ambassador pilot program won a "Best of the Best" International Association of Business Communicators (IABC) Gold Quill award. Furthermore, the pilot's success and its learnings provided the basis for an expanded program that continued to evolve in the succeeding years. Voluntary PepsiCo ambassador programs were rolled out to all interested employees at the company's three U.S. division sites, and smaller programs were launched in Brazil, the United Kingdom, Mexico, Australia/New Zealand and the United Arab Emirates. The program continued to evolve through participant feedback and in the convening years more than 6,000 U.S. employees and hundreds of international employees volunteered to become PepsiCo ambassadors.

Source: Sharon Phillips and Sharon McIntosh (2021)

Bibliography

Gatehouse. (2018). *State of the Sector, Volume 10.* Retrieved from www.iabc.com/wp-content/uploads/2018/11/SoS-report-2018.pdf.

Mobilearth. (2017). *Are Your Employee Communications Regulatory Compliant?* Retrieved from www.mobilearth.com/mobile-banking-news/are-employee-communications-regulatory-compliant.

6
ETHICS AND EMPLOYEE COMMUNICATION

If you were to ask people about the ethics in the field of communication, some might cynically say there aren't any. For many on the outside, communication can be seen as a profession that fosters pop-culture depictions of spin control, gerrymandering of information and bold-face lies. While that may be an attractive trope in the entertainment industry, the truth in the majority of cases is far from what viewers see on television shows like House of Cards. It does, however, call into question the practice of ethics in communicating—both externally and internally.

For example, how do employee communicators—when asked to communicate good news about bonuses to employees one week, yet knowing about upcoming layoffs—ethically communicate the positives while ignoring pending, confidential negatives? It's a scenario faced by many internal communication specialists and it puts the issue of ethics squarely in the bullseye.

Let's start with a definition of *ethics*. According to Patrick Plaisance in his book *Media Ethics: Key principles for responsible practice*, ethics is the "inquiry concerned with the process of finding rational justifications for our actions when the values that we hold come into conflict." The definition is slightly altered when placed in the context of *public relations*. Patricia Parsons in *Ethics in Public Relations* defines ethics as "the application of knowledge, understanding and reason, to questions of right or wrong behavior in the professional practice of public relations."

This latter definition fits the world of employee communication if we modify the setting (the corporate world) and the audience (employees). However, these concepts were first formed long ago. In fact, codes of ethics were established almost from the beginnings of modern public relations around the turn of the 20th century. In many cases, ethics in communicating is more broadly defined

DOI: 10.4324/9781003024118-6

under the umbrella of public relations, but the reality is that internal communicators are bound by the same constructs.

The foundation of the ethical codes was created by *Ivy Ledbetter Lee* around 1905 during a time when he was representing coal mine owners who were dealing with an employee strike. Lee was a pioneer of a new tool, the press release, which he decided to use in this case to provide the newspapers covering the strike with daily informational updates in a printed form. These updates were seen as corporate publicity or advertisements by the reporters of the day, and Lee's efforts were met with hostility. In order to fight these accusations, Lee issued what he called a *"Declaration of Principles"* explaining his work and intent stating:

> This is not a secret press bureau. All our work is done in the open. We aim to supply news. This is not an advertising agency; if you think any of our matters ought properly to go to your business office, do not use it. Our matter is accurate. Further details on any subject treated will be supplied promptly, and any editor will be assisted most carefully in verifying directly any statement of fact. Upon inquiry, full information will be given to any editor concerning those on whose behalf an article is sent out. In brief, our plan is frankly, and openly, on behalf of business concerns and public institutions, to supply the press and public of the United States prompt and accurate information concerning subjects which it is of value and interest to the public to know about. Corporations and public institutions give out much information in which the news point is lost to view. Nevertheless, it is quite as important to the public to have this news as it is to the establishments themselves to give it currency. I send out only matter every detail of which I am willing to assist any editor in verifying for himself. I am always at your service for the public of enabling you to obtain more complete information concerning any of the subjects brought forward in my copy.

This declaration by Lee, essentially stating that public relations practitioners have a responsibility to present the general public with accurate information, is a cornerstone of the ethical mores communicators follow today. For communication professionals, there are specific guidelines in place provided by local, regional or global trade organizations supporting communicators as led by groups such as the International Association of Business Communicators (IABC), the Global Alliance for Public Relations and Communications Management and the Public Relations Society of America (PRSA). Specifically related to IABC, when members are facing difficult issues, IABC's Ethics Committee serves as a global resource. The Ethics Committee offers advice and assistance to communicators regarding specific ethical situations and assists with professional development activities dealing with ethics. Each member agrees to adhere to strict conflict of interest and confidentiality guidelines.

Along with the concept of presenting accurate, honest information to the public and internal stakeholders, there are other commonalities related to the ethics of the profession between these organizations, including protecting confidential information, not representing conflicting or competing interests and supporting the ideals of free expression.

While these ethical guidelines provide a solid framework for the profession of employee communication, ethics are not that simple. Along with these professional organizations, companies may have their own ethical policies, and each individual has unwritten ethical rules that are determined by their families, peers and experiences they go through in life. In general, ethical guidelines should conform with accepted societal norms and cultural values.

Foundations of Ethical Decisions in Employee Communication

When it comes to taking ethics from theory into practice in the workplace, research shows that there is no real commonality in approach. The way people go about making ethical decisions tends to vary based on the environment in which they work—agency vs. corporate vs. nonprofit—as well as the age and years of experience the person has been in the field. Katie R. Place, in her article "More Than Just a Gut Check: Evaluating Ethical Decision Making in Public Relations," explains that this idea of age and experience being a factor in ethical decision-making can be guided by *Kohlberg's Theory of Moral Development* in which "individual moral development occurs over time, in six stages that build upon each other." This theory espouses the concept that at an advanced stage "individuals' moral actions are guided by their own self-chosen principles or values, such as justice, equality, human rights or dignity."

In her research, Place found that there were five themes that arose in how public relations professionals assessed their decisions in ethical situations including informal "gut checks," posing specific questions, considering the impact on and accurate reflection of society, reflecting on the values of their organizations and considering the needs and feedback of key publics.

Another study done by Marlene S. Neill included a Delphi survey and personal interviews with communication practitioners to determine the most common ethical issues facing professionals as well as what skills are needed and which skills were lacking. Neill's findings yielded a model of the ethical counselor/conscience and spin doctor, two opposing concepts of how ethical decisions are handled within the profession. According to Neill, the counselor/conscience "advocates for right action through the exercise of practical reason and wisdom," while the spin doctor "advocates for causes based upon one's own or client's self-interests without consideration of the actions' impact on others." As seen in this model (see Figure 6.1), the "virtuous" counselor/conscience is talking to others, seeking counsel and listening to determine a correct path, as opposed to the spin doctor

Model of the ethical counselor/conscience and spin doctor

Ethical counselor/conscience	Spin doctor
Advocates for right action through the exercise of practical reason and practical wisdom	Advocates for causes based upon one's own or client's self-interests without consideration of the actions' impact on others
Virtues • Humility • Truth/honesty • Integrity • Moral courage • Caring • Empathy • Candor	Vices • Arrogance/hubris • Deception • Moral relativism • Fear • Uncaring • Unsympathetic • Secrecy
Impact on practice • Sincerely seeks and listens to the concerns of stakeholders, internally and externally • Serves as a boundary spanner and voices of the concerns of stakeholders to help organizations make ethical decisions • Engages in moral reflection before making decisions	Impact on practice • Feedback falls on deaf ears; communication is one-way • Is silent/complicit about the concerns of stakeholders and moral consequences of decisions • Acts without moral reflection; obeys orders from superiors

Source: Neill, 2020

FIGURE 6.1 Model of the ethical counselor/conscience and spin doctor, as developed by Marlene S. Neill.

who is not seeking or ignoring feedback and is solely focused on making sure the end result desired by the client or boss is met.

This is only one model related to ethical decision-making, however. One of the most famous of these in the communication world is the *TARES test*, created by Sherry Baker and David L. Martinson. This test (see Figure 6.2) asks communicators to go through five principles for ethical persuasion as they make their decisions.

Each of these studies provides a foundational understanding of how employee communicators can go about the decision process related to ethical situations. It's critical for professionals to embrace these concepts, as appealing to—and recruiting the next generation of—employees depends on it.

For example, in order to appeal to Gen Z, companies need to show, not just tell, that they are following an ethical path. This includes reporting on topics such as corporate social responsibility and efforts related to diversity, equity and inclusion. A national survey done of 18- to 24-year-olds by the MOJO Ad agency at the University of Missouri found that 69% of respondents agreed that they would walk away from a job offer if a company didn't actively support DEI efforts, and 60% worry about finding a workplace that treats them equally and well. This research supported the finding that those in this age demographic would have no

T.A.R.E.S. test

T **Truthfulness**
of a message

A **Authenticity**
of the persuader

R **Respect**
for the persuadee

E **Equity**
of the appeal

S **Social responsibility**
for the common good

FIGURE 6.2 The TARES test helps communicators work through ethical decisions.

problem walking away from a job, essentially ghosting an employer, if they didn't see these types of ethical behavior in play.

Ethics and Corporate Social Responsibility

One of the ways to show ethical practices to employees and consumers alike is through *corporate social responsibility* (CSR). The idea of CSR goes back centuries but began to emerge widely as a formal concept in the middle of the 20th century and has evolved significantly over the years. CSR took a huge step forward in public consciousness in the early 2000s when a series of corporate scandals, such as Enron and Tyco, and stories such as the corporate practices of using child labor, handing out golden parachute bonuses to C-suite executives and committing serious environmental hazards were all exposed by the news media.

In fact, many external reputation issues have significant implications for employees, too. Several consumer goods companies, when called out by People for the Ethical Treatment of Animals (PETA) over Research and Development testing practices, found themselves having to explain to concerned employees exactly what they were doing with animals.

Many retailers, when the global pandemic hit in 2020, were faced with a series of ethical decisions in developing employee guidelines for everything from remote-work provisions to testing protocols and return-to-work standards. Defining "essential personnel," for example, presented employers with significant challenges to define and communicate. Depending on whether an employee was defined as "essential" or not could mean greater risk, greater rewards or greater protection, among other things. These may seem like cut-and-dry decisions, but, in each case, the company had to make ethical calls about the right way to take action and communicate what, how and—importantly—why those decisions were made. Many, if not most of those decisions, were guided by the organizations' articulation of values and executed by employee communicators.

In turn, the decisions and actions of organizations facing ethical dilemmas influence corporate social reputation. A wide array of researchers including Archie B. Carroll from the University of Georgia, Alexander Dahlsrud of the Norwegian University of Science and Technology and Shafiqur Rahman at Kent Institute Australia have published studies that explore how to define CSR and the evolution of the concept. Most of those who study CSR seem to agree that what began as social responsibility in the 1950s with a focus on an obligation to society has emerged today as a construct that deals with a wide array of concepts.

Rahman summarized the iterations of CSR over the years through 10 dimensions, which include an obligation to society, improving the quality of life, ethical business practices, human rights, protection of environment and transparency and accountability. Dahlsrud also worked in terms of the dimensions of CSR and found those included environmental, social, economic, stakeholder and voluntariness dimensions.

Based on these ideas and collections of definitions that comprise them, we can define CSR related to employee communication as an effort by organizations to go beyond what is required by law to manage the impact they have on the environment and society, including how they interact with employees, stakeholders, customers and the public at large.

Salesforce is a company that is walking the walk when it comes to CSR. The company was founded in 2000 with a philanthropic 1–1–1 model, which refers to giving 1% of Salesforce's product, 1% of its equity and 1% of its employees' time to philanthropic causes and the nonprofit sector. The company has created a Philanthropy Cloud with more than 1.4 million causes to which employees can donate, volunteer or advocate for a cause. As of the fiscal year 2020, Salesforce had given away more than $406 million in grants, had employees donate more than 5 million volunteer hours and hosted over 870 interns and apprentices through untapped talent programs.

Along with the philanthropy, Salesforce has been active with its DEI efforts, such as adding $3 million to the pay of its female employees to balance pay disparities by gender and creating programs to increase diversity among coders and other technology sector jobs. These efforts have made Salesforce a place people, especially young people, want to work.

Employee communicators must determine the best way to show CSR efforts that ring as true with both the public and their internal stakeholders. A study done in 2011 from the *Journal of Business Ethics*, explored the idea of *greenwashing*, which is defined as "the tactics that mislead consumers regarding the environmental practices of a company or the environmental benefits of a product or service." For large companies, CSR communications can be a costly endeavor, ranking as the third-largest expense for corporate communication departments back in the early 2000s. Therefore, making sure that communications to employees and the public are seen as authentic is critical.

What this study found was that CSR communications needed to connect with the organization or brand to ring true to employees and consumers alike. So, if a company is known to be altruistic—like a Salesforce—a positive CSR message would be taken to heart. However, if a company has a history of poor ethical and CSR efforts and is sending out information about its dedication to CSR, it will only reflect negatively on the brand and be seen as greenwashing.

A solution born out of the need for transparency and standardization has begun to influence CSR communication. In an increasingly complex landscape, with myriad standards and criteria to judge corporate behavior against, CSR communication had begun to fall out of step with companies' sustainability agendas. Enter environmental, social and governance (ESG) criteria. ESG, the latest evolution of the intentions behind CSR, provides a framework for greater transparency, greater efforts and greater good. These agendas, and the results of strategies that organizations deploy, increasingly must be part of employee communicators' content and programming strategies.

Astroturfing and Avoiding Unethical Communication

It shouldn't be hard to communicate in an ethical manner. As we've explored already, there are professional organizations that provide codes of ethics to make this an easy process. However, in this digital age, where people can hide behind fake names and organizations, nothing is easy.

One of the most prevalent forms of unethical communication involves *astroturfing*. According to a *Journal of Business Ethics* article from Charles H. Cho, et al., astroturfing is defined as "fake grassroots organizations usually created and/or sponsored by large corporations to support any arguments or claims in their favor, or to challenge and deny those against them."

While astroturfing is often associated with political and policy efforts, this practice extends to behaviors like creating false product reviews; creating fake profiles to post on social media and blog sites; false advertisements that redirect consumers to corporate pages; and efforts to attack rivals (be it business or personal, in the case of politics) with false information. Back in 2012, *The New York Times* published an article that quoted Bing Liu, a data-mining expert at the University of Illinois-Chicago, as saying that he estimates that about one-third of all consumer reviews on the internet are fake.

Several corporations have been found engaging in these activities, including Fox News and Walmart (twice—in 2006 and 2010). These practices typically had the companies employing bloggers, many of whom live in countries such as Bangladesh, the Philippines and Eastern Europe, and who were paid very little for each post.

Employee communicators also need to be wary of creating video news releases that aren't clearly labeled, so as not to be confused with actual news stories, and disclosure or sharing of financial information.

One company that's successfully delivered ethical brand communication is Dove—through its Real Beauty campaign. Dove completed research in 2016 in its Global Beauty and Confidence Report, which showed that 77% of women thought all images seen in the media were digitally distorted. On top of that, 69% of respondents said the pressure to reach the standards they saw in those images led to feeling "anxious about their appearance."

This led Dove to create the No Digital Distortion Mark, which is an icon that appears on all of Dove's promotions and advertisements that let viewers know that the women featured in the image have no alterations.

According to Jess Weiner, cultural expert for the Dove Self-Esteem Project, "Viewing unrealistic and unachievable beauty images creates an unattainable goal which leads to feelings of failure," she told us. "This is especially true of young girls who have grown up in a world of filters and airbrushing."

While the campaign was externally focused, communicating those insights with internal stakeholders would be an equally important strategy. From female employees to women and girls in the families of employees at the company, a project of this magnitude would merit significant investment in authentic internal communications. The TARES test, for example, could guide an ethical approach to communicating with employees.

Living With Ethical Communication

When it comes to ethics and employee communication, it's important to communicate with your organization in honest and authentic ways and disseminate information about expected behaviors so there aren't any questions about what is, and isn't, acceptable. That begins with executives in the C-suite, who should serve as models of ethical behavior.

Global science and technology company DuPont makes a regular practice of sharing compliance data—built on compliance with the company's established code of conduct with employees. Its CEO includes, as part of town hall agendas, insights on trends—positive or negative—and shows executive sponsorship of making decisions, and taking actions, in ways that are consistent with the DuPont's Code of Conduct.

Additionally, using internal communication tools, such as an intranet or newsletters, to send reminders and policy updates, and to hold training sessions as ethical standards change, can help keep a workforce informed and feeling like the organization is staying current.

Many, if not most, organizations have an ethical code of conduct in place. The challenge is to bring the contents of the code to life through more engaging and thoughtfully sequenced content. For example, some Compliance functions, typically residing in Legal departments, have online and live annual training that is mandatory for all employees—often as a requirement from the company's board of directors. Employee communicators often are asked to support efforts to create awareness about the required training and/or bring a sense of urgency and importance to it.

Regular efforts about employee satisfaction, such as surveys (as explored in Chapter 4), can help alert communicators and management to new issues that arise, or signal if additional education efforts are needed. Using a quiz or situational exercises, for example, can help gauge employee understanding of policies. Similar internal communication efforts that create awareness of reporting mechanisms for suspected ethical violations, such as anonymous hotlines, also merit employee communication support.

By following ethical guidelines, an organization can build a positive culture and a place where people want to work and stay. Employee communicators play a significant role in bringing focus and prioritization to ethical behavior through thoughtfully created strategies, content and tactics that bring ethics to life.

Profile: Jillane Kleinschmidt Rochin

Senior Director, Client Delivery
Gagen MacDonald
Chicago, IL, USA

Career Bio

I started out doing traditional PR at an agency. It was a great way to start, exposing me to consumer, tech, food and business-to-business clients and their challenges. I had one experience with a client who needed employee communication and culture change . . . and I was hooked. I ended up getting an internal communication role at that company and taking a few other corporate roles before I found my way back to consulting. Using my agency experience served me well in my corporate roles and my corporate experience makes me a more effective consultant, because I've been in my clients' shoes.

My team and I work with clients, who are often in communications or change program roles, to help define strategies for how to engage and equip employees to do their best work, align their behaviors and contribute to the goals or purpose of their company. We start by understanding our audiences and what it is we want them to know, feel and do. Then, we create strategic plans and help to execute on those plans. On any given day, that may include developing core narratives and messages, executive speeches, videos, articles, FAQs, toolkits for leaders, monitoring metrics and feedback and tailoring the approach accordingly.

Driving Ethical Behavior Through Employee Communication

There is a corporate governance concept called "tone at the top," used to describe the climate or culture set by leaders for ethical behaviors and compliance throughout the company. When facing an accounting issue, the Board of Directors questioned whether the company was measuring it and what we were doing to ensure a strong "tone at the top" to help prevent unethical behaviors.

Our communication team added several specific questions to our employee survey related to perceptions of the importance of the code of conduct for leaders and self, and whether it is safe to speak up. We also increased the frequency of the survey to annual, made a bigger push for the annual ethics training, raised awareness of the compliance hotline and surrounded it with guidance and tools for people managers to discuss ethics and integrity with case studies.

Sometimes there are true ethical dilemmas in our workplaces and the answers are not clear. It's important to teach employees that it's OK to question, discuss and explore the best solutions, and that there are resources to turn to for advice and counsel, be it a leader, a hotline or an ethics officer.

Open dialogue and use of the resources increased. Survey scores also went up when employees saw that their direct managers and leaders truly cared about doing business ethically versus getting results at any cost.

You can face resistance to teaching about ethics in the workplace when people view ethics as related to personal morals or rooted in religion. So, it's important to frame communication about ethics in terms of integrity and business standards. For example, when you are representing our company, we must all share one common set of ethics standards, values and behaviors; it is what our customers, shareholders, employees, partners and communities expect and deserve.

Case Study

UTILITY PUTS POWER BEHIND ETHICS COMMUNICATION

Situation

There are few industries that rely on public trust quite like the electric utility business. With power lines that span nearly every residential and commercial corner of our country and rates set by public commissions, electric utility companies must continually earn and retain trust to maintain their license to operate, expand their services and operate profitably.

In the early 2000s, one of the nation's largest electric power providers confronted a crisis in trust. In 2003, several employees were discovered to have falsified data on both customer satisfaction and safety reporting surveys, both of which were instruments used by the state's utilities commission to determine electricity rates. The falsified data's discovery led to an internal and external reckoning, resulting in reputational damage, substantial fines and a mandate to change. An internal investigation into the scandal concluded that one factor ultimately led to the company's missteps: Culture.

When surveyed about their beliefs, employees' attitudes about the company's values were startling to top executives. For instance:

- a majority of employees surveyed believed that management was willing to get results at all costs;
- less than 5% of employees surveyed believed that the value of "integrity" was a priority for management;
- 59% of employees surveyed reported that top performers who violated ethics were promoted or tolerated.

Campaign

To regain public trust and achieve its long-term plans, the imperative was clear: the company would need to transform its culture.

The company embarked on a comprehensive, multi-year initiative to fundamentally alter their employee experience to inspire new beliefs. The logic of the program went as follows: if you change what employees experience each day, you will change what they think and feel about their company's values. By discarding old values (such as "getting results at all costs") and instilling new ones (such as "makes decisions for the greater good"), new beliefs would produce new behaviors. These new behaviors—grounded in ethics—would result in the company operating in a manner worthy of public trust.

This transformation took shape in innumerable ways.

The company went through an exhaustive, bottom–up exercise to define its values. Using surveys, focus groups and mini-workshops, the company solicited the views of all employees to better understand their aspirations for the organization. Synthesizing those inputs, the company's top 27 leaders together went through an immersive deep dive to create a new strategic framework, articulating not only the company's desired values but also corresponding guiding behaviors.

This new strategic framework was then expressed with a unique visual identity and rolled out in a careful and deliberate cascade. First, in a special session for the company's top 200 leaders. Next, in a series of small "roadshow" presentations to different clusters of employees featuring various executive leaders. The message was clear: we're serious about change and leading with new values.

While the new values and strategic framework's introduction were important, maintaining and sustaining momentum proved the eventual key to success. Using a variety of cultural levers, the company continued to disrupt old messaging to tell a new, refreshed story. There are many powerful examples of how the company changed its reality to change its future. For instance, on the communication front, the editorial strategy and guidelines of all enterprise-wide vehicles, such as the company's newsletter and intranet, were overhauled to feature content that profiled employees who demonstrated its new guiding behaviors. Similarly, to drive behavior change, the refreshed values and guiding behaviors were embedded into the company's performance management and goal setting processes, so employees were actually evaluated according to stated ideals.

Recognizing that communities drive change, the company convened local appreciation events, small gatherings to celebrate team-based examples of the new values in action. In addition, leaders were supplied with ongoing communication tools to discuss and advance culture change within the micro-structure of their teams.

Finally, and perhaps most memorably, the company developed and implemented a new Chairman's Award program. Using a peer nomination system, employees at all levels could submit written nominations of their colleagues to be considered for a prestigious annual award based on the nominee's record of exhibiting the company's values and guiding behaviors. Hundreds of nominations were received each year, which were vetted and considered by a committee of executive leaders, including the chairman and CEO. Ultimately, 40 employees each year were recognized as Chairman's Award winners, receiving $10,000 prizes and the opportunity to attend a black tie recognition gala. The award program was transformational. It showed the company's seriousness about adopting new ways of doing things and recognizing top performers.

Results

Five years later, the results spoke for themselves. According to surveys, 86% of employees agreed that "how I act is just as important as what I contribute to the company," and 80% agreed that "living the company values is important to meeting our business goals."

By using communication and other cultural levers to change the company's reality, leaders in corporate communication and HR, along with partners across the business, created a window for transformation. They gave employees the freedom to experiment with new behaviors without fear of punishment. Rewarding these new behaviors created a positive feedback loop. The company's reputation for ethics has been dramatically improved ever since.

Source: Gagen McDonald (2020)

Bibliography

Baker, S. B., & Martinson, D. L. (2001). The TARES test: Five principles for ethical persuasion. *Journal of Mass Media Ethics, 16*(2), 148–175.

Carroll, A. B. (1999). Corporate social responsibility. *Business & Society, 38*(3), 268–295. https://doi.org/10.1177/000765039903800303.

Cho, C. H., Martens, M. L., Kim, H., & Rodrigue, M. (2011). Astroturfing global warming: It isn't always greener on the other side of the fence. *Journal of Business Ethics, 104*(4), 571–587. https://doi.org/10.1007/s10551-011-0950-6.

Dahlsrud, A. (2008). How corporate social responsibility is defined: An analysis of 37 definitions. *Corporate Social Responsibility and Environmental Management, 15*(1), 1–13. https://doi.org/10.1002/csr.132.

Dove.com. (2021). *100% Real Beauty: Introducing the Dove 'No Digital Distortion' Mark.* Retrieved from www.dove.com/us/en/stories/about-dove/no-digital-distortion.html.

Hutton, J., Goodman, M., Alexander, J., & Genest, C. (2001). Reputation management: The new face of corporate public relations? *Public Relations Review, 27*(3), 247–261.

International Association of Business Communicators. (2020). *IABC Code of Ethics for Professional Communicators.* Retrieved from www.iabc.com/about-us/purpose/code-of-ethics/.

Kohlberg, L. (1981). *The Philosophy of Moral Development: Moral Stages and the Idea of Justice* (Essays on Moral Development, Vol. 1). San Francisco, CA: Harper & Row.

Kohlberg, L., & Hersh, R. H. (1977). Moral development: A review of the theory. *Theory Into Practice, 16*(2), 53–59.

MOJO Ad. (2019). *2020 State of the YAYA Report.* University of Missouri School of Journalism.

MOJO Ad. (2021). *2021 State of the YAYA Report.* University of Missouri School of Journalism.

Morse, S. (1906, September). An awakening in Wall Street. *The American Magazine, 62,* pp. 457–463.

Neill, M. S. (2020). Public relations professionals identify ethical issues, essential competencies and deficiencies. *Journal of Media Ethics, 36*(1), 51–67. https://doi.org/10.1080/23 736992.2020.1846539.

Parguel, B., Benoît-Moreau, F., & Larceneux, F. (2011). How sustainability ratings might deter 'greenwashing': A closer look at ethical corporate communication. *Journal of Business Ethics, 102*(1), 15–28. https://doi.org/10.1007/s10551-011-0901-2.

Parsons, P. J. (1994). *Ethics in Public Relations: A Guide to Best Practice (PR in Practice)* (2nd edition by Parsons, Patricia J., Published by Kogan Page (2008) (61089th ed.). London: Kogan Page.

Place, K. R. (2015). More than just a gut check: Evaluating ethical decision making in public relations. *Journal of Media Ethics, 30*(4), 252–267. https://doi.org/10.1080/237 36992.2015.1082913.

Plaisance, P. L. (2008). *Media Ethics: Key Principles for Responsible Practice* (1st ed.). Thousand Oaks, CA: SAGE Publications, Inc.

Public Relations Society of America. (2020). *PRSA Code of Ethics.* Retrieved from www. prsa.org/about/prsa-code-of-ethics.

Rahman, S. (2011). Evaluation of definitions: Ten dimensions of corporate social responsibility. *World Review of Business Research, 1*(1), 166–176.

Russell, K. M., & Bishop, C. O. (2009). Understanding Ivy Lee's declaration of principles: U.S. newspaper and magazine coverage of publicity and press agentry, 1865–1904. *Public Relations Review, 35*(2), 91–101. https://doi.org/10.1016/j.pubrev.2009.01.004.

Salesforce.com. (2021). *Philanthropy.* Retrieved from www.salesforce.com/company/philanthropy/overview/.

Streitfeld, D. (2012). The best book reviews money can buy. *The New York Times,* August 25, 2012.

7
INTERNAL AUDIENCE SEGMENTATION

Imagine, as a communicator, being asked to convey an organizational change about your company's structure. Executive A is leaving the company and her role won't be back filled. Executive B is getting most of Executive A's former team, and Executive C is getting a few smaller teams from Executive A. The task given to you is simply to communicate those changes to those in the organization.

It may sound simple enough to write something up, put it in an email, and hit "send." After all, people understand change happens, they can read emails and it's not that complicated, right?

But what if this were the third significant structural change for these team members in six months? And there's a higher-than-normal attrition rate in one of these teams—say, with new product development? And what if Executive B has no previous history or experience running the kinds of teams coming to him from former Executive A?

Start adding a few of those circumstances, and hitting a single "send" button would be akin to throwing gasoline on a burning fire. Chances are that this one email message sent to all internal stakeholders simultaneously would engender a response from those receiving it of confusion, distrust and even anger. Employees who are most directly impacted rightly feel they should know about a change impacting them before broader audiences are informed. Leaders in the organization likely would feel blindsided and unable (or even unwilling) to speak to the rationale of the decision(s) and the potential positives it could yield. And as a result of how this change was communicated, leader and employee engagement wanes, productivity takes a hit and everything from failure to meet quality standards to increased code of conduct violations can follow.

Treating all internal stakeholders the same fails to recognize and address the unique needs of several different internal stakeholder sets. This is where audience

DOI: 10.4324/9781003024118-7

segmentation comes in. As stated in Chapter 2, *audience segmentation* is defined as the process of taking a homogenous group of people and dividing them into smaller groups based on their attributes, such as beliefs and demographics. Through this segmentation process, you can assess the unique communication needs of employees and sequence messages in ways that optimize how, to whom and when, the change news is delivered.

How internal stakeholders feel about the change, and the way it is communicated, can make a significant difference in how the change is accepted, the time it takes to implement the change and how effectively that new structure will work once it's fully implemented.

Consider how different the outcome would be if you used audience segmentation with the messaging approach. Instead of a mass email, there was a pre-wired message about the expected change with administrators and thought leaders in the organizations touched by the new change in structure. Imagine how differently the news would be accepted if you delivered the news in a meeting, with context, to Executive A's team members before they read it in an announcement sent to the entire organization? Consider how much more easily change would be implemented if leaders in Executive B's and C's organization were pre-briefed, and provided with tools and messaging that enabled them all to work off the "same page," so to speak.

All of this is not to say that there's never a time or place to send one mass communication to all employees. However, with today's communication needs to internal stakeholders it's important to consider what the message is and if a "one size fits all" approach is appropriate for what you want to achieve.

Common Internal Segments

There are many ways to segment internal stakeholders, and combinations of internal segments can seem endless, but a good reference point is to think about segmentation across two dimensions: role and affiliation. A summary of common employee segments is included in Table 7.1.

TABLE 7.1 Common Internal Segments

Common roles for segmentation	Senior executives	Executives	People managers	HR business partners	Impacted employee(s) or teams	All employees
Examples of affiliations for segmentation	Line of business or business unit	Location: Facility Region or Geography	Function	Union or organized labor	Hourly (non-union) or salaried	Employee Resource Group(s) (e.g., Gender, LGBT, Ethnicity)

Different Segments Have Unique Needs

The unique needs of each internal stakeholder segment can be as unique as the organization's culture. When internal communicators start segmenting by level in their organizations, they're solving not only for preferences and needs of those segments but also for behaviors that exist in the culture. For example, fewer organizations today rely on cascading information from top to bottom. The speed of social/digital media makes it—for all intents and purposes—impossible for top–down communications to be effective.

The size of an organization will dictate levels of roles and the numbers of them, so the list of roles that follows may not directly apply in every organization, but directionally they signal the types of content that are best suited for some of the more common levels/roles in larger organizations. While there may not be universal agreement on what those unique needs are, there are a few core consistencies in the kinds of content each likely would prefer.

Senior executives: While the CEO and C-suite executives won't get into the minutia of large-scale communication, they most often want to see the big picture of what the communication plans are, what the core messaging is, what questions and answers they should be anticipating and what their roles are in communicating the topic or issue.

Executives: Often defined leaders with the vice president and director-level roles, these executives will want to understand more detailed communication plans, including sequencing and the unique messaging needs for their organizations. They may, or may not, have significant roles in communicating themselves, but if they are being positioned as key communicators, they will need some level of customized messaging, detailed Q&A and detailed sequencing on any supporting communication planned for their organizations.

People managers: Supervisors and managers are critical enablers of communicating change. They need to be, and feel, empowered, with the messaging and associated tools to confidently share information with their respective direct reports and extended teams. This often will include additional materials to what their bosses need, such as presentation materials and more detailed Q&A tools.

HR business partners: Many internal processes require support from HR professionals who provide counsel to people leaders and directly to employees. Whether it's compensation and benefits insights, or strategy and counsel on restructuring teams, these partners often need advance preparation and specific communication support tools to effectively help drive change or support critical business processes.

All employees: Broad employee communication most often is, and needs to be, clear, concise and written in plain language. Beyond a broad announcement, and depending on the magnitude of change or actions required, all-employee communication plans often can include an abbreviated Q&A series, visuals to clearly support the topic (e.g., infographics or organizational charts) and messaging that encourages employees to engage with their supervisors for more in-depth discussion needs.

Location Is Important, Too

Segmenting by location also matters. We work and live in a global economy, which has advantages and disadvantages. While the flow of digital information across time zones and continents can drive substantial impact for many organizations, it also demands that internal communicators be deliberate in planning where their efforts are prioritized. For example, the timing for announcing significant news should include consideration of when employees who work as much as a full day ahead of where their headquarters is located will learn about it.

This can be seen with global organizations in the United States, which often schedule CEO town halls earlier in the business day to catch employees in Europe and the Middle East before they head home. Or they may host live events in the evening (e.g., U.S. Eastern time) to ensure employees in the Asia/Pacific reason can participate during their early morning/next day. If you've got big news on a Friday, many employees in the Middle East will not be in the office, as it is a day of worship for them.

Does this kind of planning have to be done with every communication event? No, but when the big news is scheduled to be delivered, every internal communicator would be well served to factor in the importance of all (or as many as possible) employees learning about it together. When employees feel like they're overlooked, or treated as second-class citizens, they can become distrustful of leadership and less engaged in the organization's priorities.

Segmenting by line of business, or business units as they're often called, is yet another tool to have in the employee communicator's box. Typically, announcements limited to a single line of business can be executed through channels dedicated to employees in that business. Organizational restructuring, senior leadership changes and similar news can effectively be communicated within a single line of business without having to assess how it affects other lines of business (unless, of course, a leader from one business is moving to another).

However, communicating issues such as cost cutting or layoffs in one business unit, for example, can quickly be interpreted as a harbinger of bad news for other businesses in the same company. In those kinds of circumstances, communicators need to fully assess how the news could be interpreted by other audiences who are not primary targets. Naturally, they would need to coordinate with other business units and corporate—or more centralized/enterprise-wide communicators—to ensure the right employees get the right message at the right time and in the right way. The lesson here is not to assume that any intentionally discreet internal communication to a targeted group of employees will not impact other internal or external stakeholders.

A tangible example of location as a factor in communication can be seen in a multinational company that was preparing to spin off significant pieces of business and needed to re-issue company credit cards to employees in specific markets. Rather than only communicating to impacted employees in those markets, internal communicators segmented employee populations into those who needed new credit cards and those who didn't. Both received information about the credit card program, but the messages were quite different. One group needed to take action, and the second needed to understand that no action was needed.

Why take this approach? Because employees communicate with each other in ways that go far beyond what organizational communicators do. They talk directly, they exchange emails, texts and direct messaging on social digital platforms, and they post observations and questions in social media channels. So, getting in front of this particular issue, and communicating to those who were NOT affected, made a lot of sense and helped avoid confusion.

Tailoring Messaging in Action

In times when there is significant news or change inside an organization, it demands different levels of insights, or details, for different employees. So, the message we communicate about a single initiative often needs to be segmented by stakeholder. This practice is often referred to as message tailoring. According to Matt Kreuter, tailoring is "any combination of information or change strategies intended to reach one specific person, based on the characteristics that are unique to that person, related to the outcome of interest, and have been derived from an individual assessment." Kreuter's definition was focused on his work in health communication. For our purposes in employee communication, the definition of *tailoring* is taking a general message and making it relevant on a personal level to an audience or individual, typically to inform, educate or change behavior.

Consider a global technology company on a mission to transform its entire HR function. From implementing more manager and employee-self-service tools, changing the traditional role of its HR partners and launching new employee call centers for HR support in markets across the globe, communicating those transformation efforts took place over several years.

In this case, not surprisingly, messaging requirements were significantly different for HR business partners, managers, employees and even senior leaders. While all communications tied back to a single shared narrative and key messaging, the content was tailored differently for a wide array of internal stakeholders. HR partners needed to understand the details of how their roles were changing and the specifics of how to transition parts of their former roles to new self-service tools or new HR call centers. Managers needed to understand where to go for some of the services previously offered by HR partners, and employees had to understand how the new call centers worked and how to access them.

It isn't just multi-year transformation projects that demand this level of tailoring. A host of business initiatives, ranging from layoffs to benefits changes and new safety procedures, often require supplying different details about the same issues to segmented internal stakeholders. While broad employee communication may focus on what's changing and why, tailored communication to people managers often includes answers to "What if?" types of questions, exceptions to the rules, or how to address resistance to the initiative. Tailored executive communication may often focus more on reinforcing rationales behind the change or initiative, or big picture insights from the business, marketplace, competitors or customers.

Messaging tailoring also can be particularly useful when considering how compensation or benefit-related details are communicated. Hourly employees versus salaried employees most often have different pay and benefits. The same is true for collective bargaining units, or unions, versus non-union employees. Employee communicators who work with HR compensation and benefits professionals must clearly understand the implications of communicating to those discreet internal sets of stakeholders.

Communicating From the Inside Out

Not all employee communications stay inside the organization. In fact, many roles inside an enterprise have responsibilities for interacting with external stakeholders. Customer-service roles, supplier-facing jobs, government or regulatory agency facing roles and media relations jobs all, for example, require specific communications to segmented internal audiences. Here again, they may all share core messaging from a consistent narrative and/or set of key messages, but more detailed content needs to be shaped by and tailored for the unique needs of stakeholders that each manages.

When food and beverage manufacturers have to recall products for safety reasons, most would think that communication is only externally focused, but nothing is farther from reality. Employee communicators inside those companies must meet internal communication needs for suppliers, regulatory agencies, retail customers, consumers and media. They can only do that by deploying an employee communication strategy that includes internal segmentation of stakeholders who must understand what's happening and be fully equipped to communicate to a wide array of both internal and external stakeholders.

Segmentation and Sequencing: They Go Hand in Hand

A natural strategy that goes hand in hand with segmentation of internal stakeholders is the answer to the question "When?"—and that's all about *sequencing*.

Not everyone inside an enterprise does, or should, receive news or instruction at the same time. If we turn back to the organization change example at the beginning of this chapter, we're reminded that departure of one single executive had significance for three different teams. In that scenario, the sequencing of who is told what, and when, can make the difference between a relatively smooth transition and chaos.

If communicators sent a broad announcement to all three teams simultaneously, a significant opportunity to successfully engage direct reports of all three executives would be lost. Those leaders would not have the opportunity to understand the changes, see how their roles would be impacted, convey the rationale for the solution and keep their respective team members engaged. In other words, by cutting them out of the sequencing, they would not be empowered and equipped to support the change.

If the executive departure in this scenario was at a senior-enough level, there likely would be external communication notification requirements, whether required by law for disclosure or simply for customer relations reasons. The key point here is that internal sequencing, many times, must be balanced with external sequencing needs as well.

As we think about internal segmentation and planning, the most successful of larger-scale employee communication strategies feature three critical stages of sequencing:

Pre-wired communications: These are communications required anywhere from one day to a week in advance of a significant announcement. There are many influences on how far in advance this period can last, reflecting basic confidentiality requirements to laws about disclosure for publicly traded companies. During this period, key communicators are pre-briefed on the content of communication events, fully engaged on their roles as communicators, and advised on the timing and sequencing of all communication (so that they understand how their role fits into the bigger plan or strategy).

"Day-of" communications: As the name implies, these are communication activities that follow a prescribed sequence on the day of a significant news announcement. Depending on what the event is, this sequencing likely would be in concert with planned external communication with media and/or investors.

Post-communications: In the days following a significant internal announcement, strong communication strategies most often will have a number of follow-up activities, ranging from collecting feedback from communicators and employees to assessing messaging and channel effectiveness. The concept of a continuous feedback loop should be central to measurement efforts, which are covered in Chapter 4. Efforts also will include the need to follow up with teams or individuals who need clarification or additional information to support the news. The post-communication plan will capture these activities—in advance of the event—to ensure all communicators understand who will collect feedback, when and how.

Communication planning template

Date/Time	Stakeholder(s) (Who is receiving communication?)	Who is communicating?	Channel	Key content	Who executes the communication?
	If more than one stakeholder set and sending at different times or using different content, use separate lines	Who owns the message?	Email distribution, conference call, etc.	What tools will be shared? Organizational announcement? Any key messaging?	Who hits the "send" button or schedules a call?

Key questions

Pre-wiring (1-2 days prior to announcement)	Day of announcement	Post-announcement/follow-up communications
1. Who needs to know about this change before the communications begin?	1. Who needs to have this schedule to ensure clarity around execution?	1. Are there any immediate follow-up communications needed after this broad organizational change is communicated?
2. How should they be informed and by whom?	2. Are there any competing communication activities that need to be considered?	2. What feedback loops will help assess how employees are responding to this change announcement?
3. Are there any unique sensitivities that need to be addressed?		
4. Who else needs to be aligned with the communication process?		

FIGURE 7.1 Employee communication planning template.

Communicators can ensure their segmentation decisions are fully incorporated into their plans by using basic communication planning templates that address each of these three stages. A full plan summary also would include specifics on dates and times; details on who is communicating (the voice delivering the news); specifics on what channel(s) would be used; key content and/or tools required by each segmented internal stakeholder group; and details on who is scheduled to execute each discreet communication activity. Consider the template above for illustration purposes (see Figure 7.1).

Channel Selection With Segmentation

It stands to reason that as communicators segment internal stakeholders, the channels they use to reach those segmented audiences may likely change as well.

Selecting small-group communications, such as team meetings, where leaders are empowered to deliver content to teams, may be more appropriate for more sensitive or complex communications, while broader-distribution digital channels such as all-employee emails or videos may suffice for simpler and/or time-sensitive information.

The choices most often reflect a thorough assessment of the communication channel, the unique attributes of organizational culture, effectiveness and efficiencies of existing channels and timing available or required to execute an internal communication plan.

Segmentation and Crisis Communication

In a perfect world, communicators would have the luxury of time to plan in advance, make decisions on segmentation and execute their plans accordingly. The most common barrier to this ability to plan and segment is the lack of time that most often comes with crisis communication needs.

While some crises can be anticipated, and segmentation pre-assessed for those events, many events come with unique circumstances that make real-time segmentation more challenging, if not impossible, during the early stages of a crisis. By early stages, we are talking about the first hour or two. That doesn't give employee communicators a "pass" for not having to think about internal segmentation. It means they must learn to quickly assess those unique audiences and factor more customized communication solutions to them soon after the early stages of a crisis pass. They also must continue those segmented communications until the crisis is resolved.

In many consumer-packaged goods companies—foods and beverages in particular—product recalls demand immediate communication responses not only for consumers but also for a range of internal stakeholders. Customers, defined by food and beverage manufacturers as retail outlets, such as grocery and convenience stores, require segmented communications about which products are being recalled and why. Communications within supply chains of the manufacturer and its retail customers must have clear, customized communication about processes for retrieving and destroying recalled products. Sales professionals must understand what's happening and what their roles and guidelines are for replacing recalled products with new products. And customer and consumer service professionals, often reached by web or toll-free numbers, must fully understand what to share with their stakeholders.

All of these internal stakeholders can be pre-assessed for potential crisis events like product recalls, but a crisis communication "playbook" should fully assess the most common or likely types of crises that employee communicators should be ready to address.

Clearly, one size does not fit all in larger and more complex organizations. Whether it is by role, location, line of business, topic or channel, the strategy of segmenting internal stakeholders is not a "nice to do." It's considered a base-line strategy in the work of today's employee communication professional.

Profile: Ricardo Martinez

**Global Corporate Communication Manager
Nemak
Monterrey, Mexico**

Career Bio

My career path has always been tied to employee communication. Right out of college, I worked for three years in communication for my alma mater. Then, I spent some time doing graduate studies abroad in Management and Organizational Communication.

I came back and did consulting work for several large Mexican corporations, and focused on strengthening their employee communication strategies. My next move was to join the Mexican operations of one of the largest food and beverage companies in the world. My tenure was three years as part of the communication team and another three years as part of the strategic planning team.

Finally, I took on the challenge of my current job, overseeing the strategic development and execution of the corporate communication area, including employee and executive communication.

Using Segmentation of Internal Stakeholders as a Strategic Tool

A few years ago, the company embarked in the project of renovating its corporate brand and strategic positioning statement, what I would call its ethos, in order to better connect with current and future trends of the industry. The project was beyond a simple aesthetic/visual renovation. I tapped into changing the way all employees should understand the higher purpose of the organization and how they contribute to it.

Segmentation was fundamental for the success of this project. We had to translate the output of the project to make it relevant to everybody, from the C-suite out to our employees at the production line in 16 countries.

We ventured into a robust analysis of all of our strategic cohorts, especially our employees. We followed the premise that, for each cohort, we should be able to not only inform about the change in a clear, simple and sufficient way, but also answer the question of "What's in it for me?"

We segmented cohorts, first, by level in the organization. But we also were evolving our corporate identity, which some of our longer-tenured employees were struggling to accept. That's why we further segmented internal stakeholders by years of service. So, organizational roles, nationality and tenure were elements of the segmentation combos used to communicate.

I learned many things, but I would highlight two. First, devote enough time for planning and research at the beginning of the project; it will yield greater benefits and significantly ease the execution. Second, listening is key. Make sure you carve out time to listen to different audiences during and after the communication process. Some may want to share the excitement, and listening makes them feel more "part of it." Others may need a forum to vent their concerns, but that's a necessary step to help them transition to embrace change.

We successfully delivered a single statement about the company's purpose, which now acts as a cornerstone for many other employee communication efforts. It also factored heavily into our employee engagement efforts, serving as a new strategic positioning statement for our brand to energize our people.

As for segmentation, devote a considerable amount of time to knowing your audiences. The better you understand their needs, concerns and even sub-cultures, your chances of successfully delivering a communication strategy will be higher. It also will make measuring its effectiveness easier. Have a clear picture of how success looks and find the appropriate way to measure it.

Case Study

SAPPI FORESTS EMPLOYEE SAFETY CAMPAIGN SAVES LIVES AND LOWERS COSTS

Situation

Despite initiatives to improve safety, from 2015 to 2016, the number of fatalities increased from zero to six for Sappi Forests. The South African forester acknowledged that its industrial work is demanding, with extended hours in harsh outdoor conditions and ever-present safety hazards. While its employees number only 860, about 90% of its operations were outsourced to 76 private contractors, who employ almost 10,000 workers.

Both injuries and fatalities occurred mainly in contractor operations. In addition to the loss of life, the impact on its business included loss of reputation (goodwill and trust) and financial loss (hiring cost of replacements, training costs, material damage, loss in production, investigation costs and investment in preventative activities), which resulted in a strained relationship between Sappi and its contractors.

Employee communicators created *Stop and Think Before You Act* (STBA) as a central part of Sappi's risk tolerance mitigation strategy and communication campaign. Their efforts were targeted at achieving Sappi's safety goal:

to be twice as safe by 2020. Its four-year initiative was focused on improving safety and eliminating fatalities.

The communication team conducted research with contractors and engaged employees to further understand the safety and communication issues that were flagged in a 2016 employee engagement survey. Primary research included surveys, focus group discussions, in-depth interviews and group discussions and qualitative data from meetings.

Research also showed safety communications to be poor, and directly connected to safety performance. For safety to improve, communicators learned the company had to replace rules-based management culture with a safety culture. The status quo left little room for creativity and innovation. Diverse demographics, multiple languages and psychographic barriers compounded the problem. Contractors came from diverse ethnic cultures. Illiteracy was high among laborers, and employees who were not proficient in English were expected to read lengthy, complex safety policies and work procedures, which they then had to communicate to others.

The communication chain from the company to its contractor staff was complex; communication between management and frontline floor workers was inadequate. Messages were unclear because management and safety leaders were using confusing language. Communication channels were not suitable for their intended audiences, and the tone of voice was perceived as angry and disrespectful. Also, there was a lack of recognition for positive behaviors.

Campaign

To address those issues, communicators developed a robust communication strategy that united the primary audiences in support of a common goal: improving safety. Their three-pronged approach included engaging targets in developing a new approach to communication that transcended barriers such as illiteracy, language diversity, culture and gender, and empowering them through a risk-mitigation tool to guide them to safe behavior. This tool instructs employees and contractors to "Stop and Think Before you Act," and to ask, "If I do this, what could go wrong? If something goes wrong, how bad could it be? What could I do about it?" The third prong focused on giving them clarity of purpose by assigning roles and responsibilities to each stakeholder group.

Communicators segmented their targets, then trained them on communication and facilitation, developed their knowledge and motivated them to train others.

Group 1 included the company's operational team—whose roles were to be both coach and supporter. They needed to lead by example in the new way of communicating and practicing STBA. They had to be mindful of their role as supporter, and not the owner of safety and/or communication in the contractors' operations, thereby showing trust and restoring relationships. Communicators hosted coaching and alignment workshops for them to help guide them in their new roles. In addition to participating in the contractor consultation sessions, they also joined Train the Trainer workshops designed to hone their skills in communication and facilitation and to learn the STBA process.

Group 2 was comprised of contract owners who needed to "own" STBA and take the lead in establishing new ways of communicating. They had to support their safety leaders in implementing STBA and include recognition and affirmation in their approach. They participated in Train the Trainer workshops with Sappi's operational teams and their safety leaders. They received toolkits with campaign materials (toolbox talks, posters, fact sheets, etc.) in hard copy and in electronic format so that they could incorporate the STBA symbols in their operational safety material.

Group 3 targeted contractors' safety leaders as STBA change agents on the shop floor. Communicators followed a process of reflective learning to train them. They also attended Train the Trainer workshops and received instruction on communication, facilitation and the STBA process. They received a certificate of proficiency upon completing the workshop, and the training was recorded as part of their professional development.

Group 4 was comprised of frontline workers who needed to understand and implement STBA. The safety leaders taught them the meaning of STBA and also the process through rhyming. They were shown how to apply STBA to their various daily tasks; in the event of a near-miss incident, they were involved in a team debriefing to discuss the incident.

Communicators also adopted a storytelling approach as a central strategy. Visuals made the STBA concepts easier to understand and teach, increased engagement and improved uptake and recall. Research also showed that symbolism and similes worked well with audiences. Communicators wrote the STBA process into a story to explain the thinking process, introducing a hero and a villain to juxtapose the STBA process against non-compliance.

Audiences named the hero character "Clever Me" and then named the villain "Stupid Me"—as he did not stop and think, was prone to be injured or killed on the job and his family suffered the consequences. The story engaged audiences on how everyone has the power to choose their destiny. While communicators initially were concerned about using the name "Stupid Me" to describe a character, research showed only about half of one small sub-group team objected to the name. Their materials were adopted to reflect the name they gave the villain ("Irresponsible Me").

They introduced a generic symbol to represent hazards throughout the business. Labor considered many symbols but chose the black mamba, which elicited a dramatic response from audiences. The use of a standard set of symbols throughout all safety communication created a universal, consistent language. We catered to color-blind stakeholders by using symbols on the characters' hard hats. Workers learned the meaning of each symbol and could immediately identify the characters and associate them with correct and incorrect behavior. Highly visible STBA symbols served as triggers for workers to apply STBA throughout their workdays. Research indicated that some also implemented STBA at home.

Results

The results of the campaign clearly showed the effectiveness of employee communication efforts. Fatalities were reduced by 83% just in year one. The Accident Injury Frequency Rate (AIFR) was reduced by 3.67%. Lost Time Injury Frequency Rate (LTIFR) fell by 8% and Lost Time Injury Severity Rate (LTISR) plummeted by 64%. The Injury Index (II) improved by 67.49% by October 2017.

The reach of the campaign also was impressive: 486 contractor employees representing all 76 contractor companies were trained in Train the Trainer sessions on communication and facilitation skills. In turn, they trained almost 10,000 people in STBA (almost 100%).

Source: IABC Gold Quill Awards (2018)

Bibliography

IABC. (2018). Sappi Forests employee safety campaign saves lives, and lower costs. *IABC Gold Quill Awards*. Retrieved from https://gq.iabc.com/case-studies/.

Kreuter, M. W. (2000). Tailoring: What's in a name? *Health Education Research, 15*(1), 1–4. https://doi.org/10.1093/her/15.1.1.

Slater, M. (1995). Choosing audience segmentation strategies and methods for health communication. In Maibach, E. W., & Parrott, R. (eds.) *Designing Health Messages: Approaches from Communication Theory and Public Health Practice*. Los Angeles: Sage Publications, pp. 186–198.

8
CHANNEL AUDITING, ASSESSMENT AND ACTIONS

The employee communication ecosystem, as explained in Chapter 1, starts with organizational purpose, mission and values and relies upon communication to enable business outcomes and action adjustments. In this chapter, we'll delve into elements that feed into channel auditing, influence sequencing and segmentation, and define feedback loops that lead to action.

So, let's put this into perspective. As hard as communicators work to get the message right, the ability to effectively and efficiently deliver that message can prove to be a far more daunting task. Employees might not hear about significant news in an internal e-newsletter because they had too many emails to slog through or they assumed news that important would be delivered by a manager.

In these, and in many other instances, where messaging doesn't reach—or resonate with—its intended audience, it's likely that internal communication channels aren't working. The way to assess why that's the case is through auditing channels and analyzing data and then acting on those findings to remedy what's failing.

When we talk about auditing, this isn't what you'd associate with accounting procedures. It also isn't the marketing definition focused on the way linked organizations work together in the process of creating a product.

Contrary to looking for a specific number that's missing, calculation that doesn't add up, or flaw in the process of manufacturing a product, communication *channel auditing* is defined by the Communications Consortium Media Center as "a systematic assessment, either formal or informal, or an organization's capacity for, or performance of, essential communications practices." This may consist of examining a host of potential issues—ranging from email list management, to governance for who gets access to what kinds of information, to preferred channels employees have for receiving specific kinds of information. This kind of

DOI: 10.4324/9781003024118-8

methodical analysis of the communication channels used, and assessment of what's needed, can dramatically improve—and ensure—that the right content is being delivered, in the right channel, to the targeted internal stakeholders.

Auditing isn't a task that's independent of delivering business and communication objectives; it's an enabler of both. With deepening insights into what content is reaching—and resonating with—internal stakeholders, critical audit findings allow communicators to assess everything from how corporate narratives are faring to whether or not social digital platforms are delivering an ROI (and a lot of other things in between).

Who should conduct an employee communication audit? Many organizations will use an outside agency or contractor to design and execute a comprehensive audit. Key benefits to using an outside entity are:

- receiving an unbiased, objective third-party opinion without a vested interest in any particular channel or process;
- getting expertise in designing and conducting audits; and
- receiving meaningful analytics and recommendations based on industry best practices.

Other organizations may choose to conduct an audit with existing internal resources. A key benefit in that scenario would be reduced costs. In either case, comprehensive internal communication auditing requires a significant time investment over a period of a few weeks to several months.

Conducting an Audit

The basics of auditing include collecting samples of all existing internal communication, conducting surveys and focus groups, along with assessing passive metrics and analytics that can come from digital communications—such as open rates and click-throughs.

The key is to think, and act, holistically in assessing the world of employee communication. This means looking at communications created and delivered not only from corporate—or centralized—sources but also from channels that exist within operating divisions, lines of businesses, geographic areas and even individual locations.

The reason that communicators need to be comprehensive in their auditing efforts is to ensure that they understand where gaps and redundancies exist in content, frequency and cadence, and, more importantly, they need to fully understand the employee experience in receiving different messages from different sources, all coming from inside the same organization. In other words, to understand what's working and what isn't, communicators need the full, big picture from the employee's point of view. Mapping the employee experience is the only way to do that successfully.

In all candor, auditing communications across the enterprise can be perceived as threatening to some professionals who "own" unique channels and content, often within geographies, specific locations or lines of business. The key to executing a successful audit, and avoiding turf wars, is to ensure that the results meet the needs of all communication channel owners. There needs to be an appropriate level of participation and buy-in from those owners in designing and executing the approach and in having access to the results and making decisions on actions coming from them.

Many organizations routinely will audit the effectiveness of their internal channels every few years. Others recognize a need when—either through anecdotal evidence or passive metrics from digital channels—they see that internal stakeholders either aren't receiving what they're sending or that there is a lack of engagement with the content they create. Still others use significant events, such as mergers and acquisitions, to comprehensively audit internal communication channels and their effectiveness.

The Survey: Ground Zero

The fundamental tool used for just about every internal communication audit is the *survey*. While anonymity clearly is a way to encourage direct and candid feedback from survey participants, it doesn't mean surveys should not include demographic insights.

Asking employees about the kinds of roles they hold, the number of years spent with the organization, what languages they use or need in communications and what parts of an organization they affiliate with (as covered in Chapter 7) can help research efforts by zeroing in on where, and with whom, communications are not working well. Of course, labor laws in any given country may restrict just how deep it's possible to go in getting demographic insights, but the more detail that can be collected, the better the resulting strategies will be to address the research findings. This can be particularly helpful with the generational differences of preferred communication channels. From baby boomers to Generations X, Y and now Z, increasing preferences for digital communication—and even different types of digital communication—can play a significant role in connecting with them inside an organization (see Figure 8.1).

Additionally, when we look at just 18- to 24-year-olds, and how they prefer communication within the workplace, the data changes. According to survey data from the MOJO Ad agency at the University of Missouri, these youth and young adult employees prefer in-person discussions (38%) as their top choice, followed by email (29%) and text message (19%), with phone calls (6%), video calls, like Zoom, and business communication platforms, like Slack or Microsoft Teams, both coming in at 4%.

A comprehensive survey that lists all existing employee communication channels is the way many start with an audit. Communicators will ask if employees

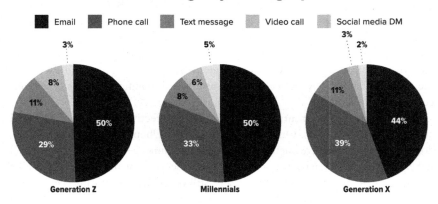

Source: 2019 Yellow Recruiting

FIGURE 8.1 Talent acquisition platform Yello conducted a 2019 survey that illustrated communication preference differences between Generations X and Z and millennials. Understanding these differences can impact choices made about which channels most effectively reach them.

are aware of various internal channels, followed by how often employees engage with each other.

When beginning this process, it's important to think about survey design best practices. These include developing questions that aren't leading and, when measuring change over time, using the same wording and placement within the survey to assure consistency of data. Additionally, minimizing the number of open-ended questions due to the time it takes a respondent to complete them and starting with questions addressing broad topics—such as general questions about communication satisfaction—and then narrowing as the survey moves along, like a funnel, are ideal.

It's common for surveys to ask employees about content provided in each channel and what their preferences are for specific types of content. For example, content about organizational values might be delivered through a weekly e-newsletter, simply because it's a more efficient way to reach employees through a centralized channel. However, auditing could tell a different story about where employees would prefer to get information about cultural values, such as in a printed monthly magazine or through a team meeting facilitated by their managers.

Clearly, what employees have, and what they want, can be the most important gap that auditing can help close. Understanding what information they want, and how they want to get it, can be assessed through a well-designed survey tool. It can also probe to get insights on frequency and tonality of certain kinds of content.

Here's the bottom line: employees want to be heard. In truth, this isn't groundbreaking news, but it commonly is an area overlooked by employee communicators. There's often such a focus on driving communication agendas that, sometimes, communicators forget to ask, "Do you feel we're listening to you?" This is another critical topic on which an audit can yield important insights. If the right questions are asked about whether employees feel empowered to share their thoughts about what the business is doing, it can begin to elevate understanding on how open communication is inside the enterprise. If employees are asked if they feel they have opportunities to share their opinions, and if they believe the company is listening, it aids the creation of a classic tenet of modern-day employee communication—building a continuous feedback loop.

Focus Groups and Interviews: Going Deeper

As insightful as the survey tool can be, quantitative data can only take you so far. Survey data serve as foundational insights that best prepare the organizational communicator to get into more detail through qualitative research, often in the form of *focus groups*. Having direct conversations with individuals and small groups of employees allows communicators to better understand the "why" behind what's working, what isn't, and what their preferences for remedies might be.

Focus groups tend to be smaller in size, providing greater opportunities for individuals to express themselves in a more comfortable forum. They can last anywhere from 30 minutes to well over an hour and are structured in ways that allow communicators to go deeper into specific areas that survey results yield. Questions are designed to test theories and themes that emerge from survey data.

Facilitators guide the group discussion through a series of pre-designated questions with probes to dig deeper into new or emerging insights with follow-up queries. Composition of focus groups should reflect key internal stakeholder groups or "personas" identified as critical targets—for example, by role, level in the organization, affiliation with a line of business, location or other demographic differentiators.

These focus groups can be gathered in a single common place, or increasingly can be conducted through web-based tools that allow participants from multiple locations to engage with the facilitator, and with each other, or to conduct projective exercises to get at thoughts and feelings about a given topic.

Similarly, auditing often will include *one-on-one interviews* with various thought leaders and/or senior leaders in an organization. Collecting insights from a range of internal stakeholders through face-to-face or virtual meetings invariably generates critical insights that should be factored into any strategies and action steps coming from the research.

Another auditing option is conducting *"walk around" tours* in different types of company locations. These activities also can help communicators make decisions about where to place digital monitors, such as in break rooms or common areas with high employee traffic. Federal Express was an early innovator in the use of video monitors in hallways as employees entered their distribution centers from the outside, and headed to their work areas inside. The walk presented communicators with the precious commodity of time to leverage in communicating key company information in a concise digital format.

Beyond the physical insights communicators can gain through walk around tours in specific types of company locations, they also can gain insights around local communication processes, including ownership of channels and content by local management. Shift management, for example, may use pre- and post-shift stand up meetings as a critical internal channel for communicating productivity or quality priorities to their teams. Often, local management may be guarded in accepting additional content that drives or supports a corporate agenda. Collective bargaining agreements and country-specific regulations for issues like language translations also can drive how communications can effectively, and legally, gain access to internal channels.

The value of the auditing process can be seen in an example from a regional electric and gas company. This company conducted a survey and the results showed that employees did not want to receive information about ethics and compliance in a company newsletter. Ethics and compliance were critical topics the company prioritized, given the importance of working in a regulated environment where safety was paramount. The risk of electrocution and gas explosions—whether it was for employees or customers—made ethics and compliance a "must do" for employees.

But communicators wanted to better understand why employees didn't want updates about ethics and compliance in a newsletter. The answer came through loud and clear in focus groups. Employees said they felt the impersonal delivery of such an important topic through a newsletter made it seem less important. As communicators probed more deeply in focus groups, they came to understand that employees felt that focused attention, through the spoken word and delivered by their supervisor, made the company's commitment feel authentic, and much more important. They needed that human touch added to the messaging.

Another example of the importance of qualitative data comes from a consumer-packaged goods company that wanted to emphasize communication around the changes in its portfolio of products. This company recently had shed several non-core businesses and a recent acquisition was performing poorly. Given the changes and poor performance, employees felt unsure about longer-term survival for the company.

Communicators had culled anecdotal feedback that employees were not engaging with digital content delivered through an e-newsletter. Content had been short and concise to fit with the readability requirements of digital content. But to get into the details of the portfolio changes and to deliver them in a format that employees would spend the time with, they dedicated an entire issue of an employee magazine with straight-talk insights about why changes were made to the portfolio and gave them reasons to believe in a sustainable future for the company. Measurement efforts that followed the publishing of that special edition showed dramatic improvements in employee understanding of the portfolio changes, and in their belief that the changes would enable future, longer-term growth. It was clear through the audit that employees chose to engage in the content through printed publication that was delivered to their homes.

Oh, the Things You'll Learn

Auditing internal communication channels will yield far more insights than the basics of who wants what kinds of information and how they want to receive it.

Using the example of the consumer-packaged goods company that used a print magazine to explain portfolio changes, auditing can challenge assumptions that might, on the surface, seem obvious. Contrary to the popular belief at the time, print communications were not dead. In fact, putting longer, more insightful content into a print publication proved to be a highly effective channel in delivering the critical content for that organization. Communicators also were reminded that when print publications are delivered directly to employees' homes, the channel has the added benefit of extending reach into the employee's family. That can be particularly helpful on content around benefits, or continuous employment choices, where family members can influence employee decisions and actions.

The question of print versus digital channels increasingly arises for many organizations. Auditing can help paint a picture where each can work optimally, and both can work together. For example, in locations where manufacturing and distribution employees don't have email accounts, or access to laptops or kiosks, print communications may prove to be the most efficient way of connecting with them.

Working remotely is a critical evolving priority that many organizations are sorting through, and auditing can help articulate what employees have, and what they need, to address the reality of their working environments—namely, that they're outside the office setting more. This is particularly true for employees who have sales roles or provide distribution and delivery services. There often may be existing mobile communication tools in use for the tasks they're required to complete—tools that may include space for communicating other company information deemed critical. The implications for frontline employee access to email, company intranets, portals and other digital channels also are significant. Here again, the audit can highlight how each channel works, and how content and access decisions are made about them.

Not all internal communication channels are mechanical, soulless entities. On the contrary, some of the most important internal channels are living breathing humans: managers and supervisors.

Insights delivered through surveys, focus groups and other methods sometimes can yield what isn't working with managers and supervisors who are relied upon to be effective internal channels. If they don't have the skill base to effectively engage with employees through communications, they clearly need skill building support to develop that capability. If they don't have access to tools and content to equip and empower them to effectively communicate with their teams, auditing can paint a picture of that need, and potentially lead to introductions of new, or modifications of existing, communication channels created for them. It may take the shape of developing a manager toolkit, updating the layout of a leader's portal or creation of a completely new solution, but given the priority placed on people leaders to be effective communicators, this is a critical set of insights to glean from auditing.

Governance, Approvals and Security: Realities Behind the Front Line

If communicators controlled all time and space, reaching employees through the channels we choose would be as simple as hitting the "send" button. But the reality is that communicators must understand and influence a wide range of approval processes, governance structures and tools that are invisible to most others in any organization.

Auditing employee communication successfully demands a deeper dive into these issues to ensure our assumptions about channels and how they perform are accurate; that we understand how digital security standards are observed; and we know how content is developed, reviewed and approved for distribution to internal stakeholders.

Let's start with *governance*. It's a fancy word for ensuring there are clear processes in place for enabling access for the right employees to the right information. As employee communicators work to reach segmented internal populations, it's critical to ensure that digital systems, in particular, have safeguards—whether IT-driven or behaviorally guided, such as social media policies—in place to ensure appropriate access and use for those segmented populations.

Consider the case of a new employee global communication chief (GCC) for a science and technology company. The GCC had assumed that a "management portal" for people leaders in the organization provided access for those leaders through a company database that identified who people leaders were and authenticated them as they logged into the portal. After asking a few questions, the GCC learned that the only requirement for gaining access to the portal was for employees to have their manager send a request to the Corporate Communication department. In other words, there was no governance around who actually was a people leader in the organization. There was no "pull" of company data from an HR platform that would have authenticated who actually was a people leader.

Consider another example of an employee communication leader who initially trusted that an "all employee" email distribution list actually meant ALL employees. After diving into governance processes around distribution list management, it was discovered that the list had not been updated in over four years, and consequently "all employees" actually meant about 60% of global employees.

These may seem like extreme cases, but unless communicators understand how employee data are stored, how it's updated and how it's pulled to create appropriate access to segmented internal targets, they're flying blind. That's what auditing provides. And that is why including IT professionals in the auditing process is critical. A close, working relationship with IT during the auditing process not only will shed light on current practices and capabilities but also can highlight future IT strategic plans that can, and should, impact employee communication.

A rapidly growing communication area that prominently impacts employees is the rise of internal social digital channels—those that promote collaboration, ideation and general sharing of information.

Opening new social channels for internal communication not only can unleash all kinds of innovation, but it also brings significant challenges for professional communicators. Microsoft Teams and Workplace from Facebook are examples of rapidly evolving internal social channels that IT security must evaluate, place behind the organization's firewall and deploy. At the same time, communicators must engage in change management communication to ensure the technologies are adopted quickly and efficiently. In other words, communicators should be working to ensure the company captures its intended return on the investment. Auditing the use of those social channels can effectively highlight action steps that can correct misuse or inefficient use of the technologies and influence content placed in them.

The deeper the communication audit can go, the more it shows how employees are using existing channels and can influence how they are created, reviewed and approved for placement. This isn't only for the content they create in corporate, or centralized, ways. It demystifies how content is developed and deployed for lines of business, geographies and other segmented communication efforts. Why is this important? Because the more communicators know how channels outside of their own "control" work, the more effectively they can work with, or around them. In the case of global issues, like the 2020 Covid-19 pandemic, many organizations had to quickly engage every available channel to communicate global priorities to employees. The pandemic—almost overnight—highlighted significant gaps in organizations' abilities to reach their employee populations instantaneously. Auditing on a regular basis, in those cases, would have exposed those gaps outside of a crisis environment and led to a solution for using all existing channels as an effective web for efficient distribution and feedback.

Whose Voice Is It, Anyway?

While we often think of employee communication channels solely as delivery mechanisms, sometimes auditing will reveal that employees add a different attribute to them: *voice*. A global CEO town hall isn't simply a town hall channel—it is the voice and sentiment of the CEO. A team meeting in which content is delivered isn't "the company"—it's an employee's manager or supervisor. Understanding the connection between voice and an internal communication channel can help communicators develop strategies that best deliver the right content through the right channel and the right voice.

Explaining a significant change in benefits—for example, the elimination of a pension plan or the introduction of new self-service for HR services—could be put into a newsletter. But the odds of resistance or failure to adopt new procedures will be higher with a mass communication. Empowering managers or supervisors to share those changes with team members offers them the opportunity not only to give context but also to respond in real time, to confusion, anger or other types of potential resistance.

Selling or acquiring businesses, as another example, might initially be shared through news channels, but providing a business rationale and reasons to believe in the value of that kind of change would be best served in the voice of a CEO through a live event like a town hall.

The voice of the communicator and the channel used also funnel into another important insight area for employees: trust. Candor and transparency are characteristics that employees can assign to both a communicator and the channel used. So, it also is common for audits to ask employees about their trust in a channel or their belief in its candor and/or transparency.

Turning Insights Into Action

Data delivered from internal communication auditing is only as useful as the actions, and corresponding future results, it drives. The best analytics in the world won't mean much if it doesn't lead to actionable decisions that, in turn, drive the communication performance bar even higher.

There are multiple approaches, or models, that can be used to organize audit insights into more actionable buckets for decision-making. One of the more common approaches includes using the *S.W.O.T. model*, prompting communicators to examine strengths, weaknesses, opportunities and threats.

From an auditing point of view for communications, here's how a communicator might look at each:

Strengths: What are the practices proving to be highly effective in reaching internal targets, and through which communication strategies and messaging are resonating? These are areas not only worth keeping but also reinforcing or building upon.

Weaknesses: What did we discover about our current practices that illustrate a significant gap in our ability to connect with one or more segmented internal communication targets, and/or where is our messaging or strategies not resonating with our internal stakeholders?

Opportunities: Where do we see new practices, channels or content that we can develop to make us more efficient in our delivery of content and strategies?

Threats: What forces exist inside or outside our organization that are, or will, interfere with our ability to reach our segmented targets with meaningful content in efficient ways?

The answers to each of the questions should yield a list of issues that should inform recommendations for action to leverage strengths, close gaps or weaknesses, capture opportunities and reduce or eliminate threats. This step is the most important of any audit, as it reflects the distillation of data into action.

Importantly, there always are metrics coming from internal communication audits. Rather than looking at, and using them, solely as stand-alone data to start a series of potential changes, communicators should look at using that data as baseline metrics for future measurement efforts.

Of course, that means developing an ongoing measurement plan that will assess similar metrics so that there is an apples-to-apples comparison for a fair number of core data points. It doesn't mean that there won't be new areas to measure through ongoing efforts, but it does mean communicators will hold themselves accountable for improving the baseline metrics that the audit delivers.

The resulting plan, in addition to action items and measurement, must also include related budget items for all components. Central to all digital actions, communication auditors will need that ongoing, direct partnership with IT professionals, who will have accountability for leading assessment, deployment and related budgeting actions for internal digital communication initiatives.

Meeting Employees Where They Are

Assessing how best to communicate with employees might seem like a complicated task, particularly in large, complex enterprises. But employees themselves are not particularly complicated. They have preferences on how they want to receive information from their employees and how they want to provide feedback. Under the right conditions, they are usually more than happy to articulate those preferences and tell communicators what's working, what's not and why. The key is simply to ask in the right ways by meeting employees where they are.

Auditing is an avenue that every communicator should follow to acquire a comprehensive look at the effectiveness of internal communication efforts.

The Edelman Trust Barometer, an annual global survey that asks citizens of the world about their trust in particular industries, has routinely discerned that employees inside an organization are a highly valued source of information as they decide to trust or distrust a company or industry. Employees themselves say "someone like me" is among their most trusted sources for information about an enterprise or industry.

With that kind of potential influence, it makes sense to invest in how they view the information they're getting from their employer through the auditing process.

Profile: Shraddha Sankhe

**Program Consultant, Cloud Business Office
Canadian Institute for Health
Information (CIHI)
Toronto, Canada**

Career Bio

I went from being an accounting student to becoming a blogger in India to a path of journalism/strategic communication in North America. I have been in the digital/social media space in organizations very large and small spanning roughly a decade.

Before getting my master's degree in Journalism/Strategic Communication from the University of Missouri, I interned with a nonprofit in Washington D.C., and a renewable energy company in the Silicon Valley. I was also a Smith/Patterson Fellow at Mizzou's Health Communication Research Center. I worked with SciXchange, a collaboration between the University of Missouri and Howard Hughes Medical Institute to promote science journalism. My first job after my master's degree was in higher education in Texas.

My day-to-day activities involve consulting with internal subject matter experts for the promotion of upcoming data releases. I help create digital content and promote it to reach very specific users. This includes product landing pages, social media planning, monitoring and drafting message sets and consulting with graphic designers about the images for social media. I am also involved in publishing content and reporting social media analytics.

Auditing Social/Digital Media Channels

For the past couple of years, I have been striving to create content that's platform-specific. It's hard not to copy and paste, but it's necessary to give each social media platform its own little personality.

A user behaves differently on different social media platforms. Their engagement behavior on social media reflects this as well. Think about Twitter, it's newsy and informative. Facebook is more about family/personal announcements. LinkedIn deals with professional branding. TikTok focuses on self-expression/personal branding, and so on. The same is true of multiple internal channels.

Social media is not a means to an end anymore. It's important to not only reach your target audience but also engage them within the platform.

That includes shares, likes, comments, cross-promotion to other platforms and so on.

Social media platforms reward content that's tailored to their interface. Take Facebook, for example. It has multiple content styles that perform much better than your plain old *text and hyperlink* that takes users out of Facebook (web/app) to a different website. On Facebook, video is the most engaging social media content idea, followed by a question and a photo—all of these keep users on the social media platform.

Most stakeholders in an organization look forward to reviewing social media analytics and comparing them. But ALL stakeholders want to review the data about clicks that the social media content generated. Think about Google Analytics or other web analytics programs and it's important to note that social media analytics are not structured like website analytics.

To make it more interesting, every social network has its own metrics and reporting structure. It's hard not to want to somehow consolidate all the metrics and lump them together. But a reply on Twitter is reported very differently than a comment on Facebook—both of which are essentially serving the same purpose.

Our team has been addressing the need for platform-specific content right from the beginning of a project. But social media managers don't work in isolation. Creating a steady stream of content needs support from the stakeholders as well. Who are the stakeholders? They can be teams that help generate content—the subject matter experts, dedicated graphic designers, editors, project leads, product managers, marketing research or sales teams.

The most valuable lesson I've learned is not to take social media for granted. Being proactive really helped, especially when: defining the scope of the project at the beginning; creating a social media message set that is approved and proofread way before the release date; having a social media calendar and discussing opportunities to plug content on promotional days; incorporating popular hashtags; and engaging collaborators. Also, it's critical not to let deadlines interfere with the creative process. There could be an emoji that works better than just text or a GIF that expresses your idea way better than an image.

As a result of our auditing, social media campaigns started performing better. If we were doing a paid promotion, we got a much higher return on our investment. We started receiving recommendations from the subject matter experts for platform-specific content ideas that were really fun, interesting and doable. That's a huge success. When a subject matter expert points out valuable bits and pieces that could potentially be turned into very sharable content—you jump at it.

Case Study

MICHELIN AUDITS INTERNAL CHANNELS TO DRIVE GREATER ENGAGEMENT

Situation

French multinational tire manufacturing company Michelin had a challenge reaching its 400 North American sales employees. Employee communicators recognized that sales employees, closely linked to customers, know the pulse of the market and are the face of the brand. However, because of their nomadic work, they're also the most removed from the day-to-day inner workings of a company—often resulting in lower levels of awareness, understanding and ultimately engagement. Seeing symptoms of disengagement, the Michelin Internal Communication team set out to transform the employee experience for this critical group.

The communication team identified a negative trend with sales employees across multiple surveys. Those employees said that accessing internal channels was getting more difficult and the types of channels did not encourage dialogue between employees. Overall, they were less satisfied than employees located at the company's headquarters.

By way of background, in 2015, the Internal Communication team launched a substantial communication effort around company growth. As the audience most tied to the customer, closest to the final product and responsible for driving the growth result, communicators anticipated sales employees would be more highly aware of the company's growth goal and certainly understand how they contributed to its success. However, research showed sales employee awareness rates were lower than their counterparts who worked at facilities throughout North America.

Additionally, in early 2016, communicators saw a troubling sign of disengagement—retention rates were highly unstable. That's what prompted employee communicators to improve their channels, content, visibility and reach of communications to this important sales audience.

Primary research, and the auditing process, included field visits to "ride along" with sales employees, one-on-one interviews, focus groups, meeting with new employees and in-person meetings, to cover as much ground as possible. The first key learning was that existing internal channels were not designed for their needs. Internal TV systems, bulletin boards and events were built for employees who work at one location. Conference calls and intranet sites worked for employees who sit at a desk most of the day but not for a sales employee who travels and is in and out of a car 20 times a day and checks email on the phone only sporadically while on-the-go. Secondly, communicators learned that messages were not getting to sales employees. There were cascading issues indicating communications were stalled or stopped—creating a different level of awareness based on the business unit. Additionally, sales employees were hungry for content they weren't receiving—tire industry news and trends—essentially content that was readily available within the organization.

Communicators' benchmarking shed light on the most critical channel problem—that channels weren't adapted for the sales audience. Mobile apps and podcasts were the predominant tools for remote sales employees, and communicators knew they had to meet those employees where they were—on their phones. Also, social distance among field groups led to little exposure or interaction with their colleagues. Their geographic disparity made them feel removed from the company, further weakening their connection to the company's goals and programs. This social distance could also lead to retention issues that the team discovered.

Campaign

With these insights, the employee communication team focused on the goals of improving growth campaign message awareness with sales employees by 5% and improving key engagement indicators by 5% as measured by benefit program participation.

They launched new channels and improved existing channels to fit the sales audience's needs, as they repaired communication cascades, and directly relayed information when appropriate, and better aligned content to sales employee needs.

For example, salesforce online chats were expanded to additional business units, and the team started executing direct distribution of communications from corporate internal communication to sales employees to improve message consistency, expedite timing and deliver relevant content. To better cascade messages within the organization, the weekly headquarters email was moved up one day, enabling more timely relaying in the business units' weekly Friday communications.

An additional segmented audience was leadership, and the internal communication team simplified and clarified manager communications through a pre-packaged email for sales managers to share with teams in the field.

After hearing clearly that employees wanted to be alerted when video updates from senior leaders became available, the team began pushing some communications rather than asking employees to pull from the intranet. Additionally, the team adjusted its daily news summary, which highlights media coverage of the company and industry, and they implemented regular industry news updates for all employees.

Also, a clear gap in how the company shared information with new sales employees prompted the communication team to launch a new process—one that included meetings with all new field sales employees to expose them to key messages and channels.

Finally, one of the biggest successes was the creation and execution of a new, innovative tool that answered the salesforce's needs: podcasts. The tool is a private channel—accessible only to Michelin employees. It had been piloted in one of the business units and had engaged more than 250 subscribers. The channel allowed for easy access to timely content, including recordings of corporate town halls, corporate messages from leadership, monthly business updates, priority call recordings and industry updates. The tool was readily adopted, supported and implemented in a few weeks.

Results

Upon launching new tools and improving the visibility of existing tools, the number of employee users rose instantly. Against the team's targeted goals, its salesforce registered the largest gains in terms of awareness of the company's growth objective (+19 percentage points) and knowledge of their contributions (nearly +10 percentage points). Further, the percentage of salesforce employees who completed Michelin's health review process increased 10% over prior year, and the retention issue stabilized.

Source: PRSA Silver Anvil Awards (2017)

Bibliography

Communications Consortium Media Center. (2004). *Strategic Communication Audits.* Washington, DC: Coffman, J.

Goodwin, J. N., Davis, A., & Telg, R. W. (2014). Communication audits: Adding value and social impact to agricultural communications. *Journal of Applied Communications, 98*(1). https://doi.org/10.4148/1051-0834.107.

Helms, M. M., & Nixon, J. (2010). Exploring SWOT analysis—where are we now? A review of academic research from the last decade. *Journal of Strategy and Management, 3*(3), 215–251. https://doi.org/10.1108/17554251011064837.

MOJO Ad. (2021). *2021 State of the YAYA Report.* University of Missouri School of Journalism.

PRworks. (2020, April 14). *Conducting a Successful Communication Audit.* Retrieved November 26, 2020, from www.prworksinc.com/conducting-a-successful-communication-audit/.

Singh, A., Taneja, A., & Mangalaraj, G. (2009, June). Creating online surveys: Some wisdom from the trenches tutorial. *IEEE Transactions on Professional Communication, 52*(2), 197–212. https://doi.org/10.1109/TPC.2009.2017986.

Tybout, A. M., Calder, B. J., & Kotler, P. (2010). *Kellogg on Marketing* (2nd ed.). Hoboken, NJ: Wiley. Chapter 11, Anne T. Coughlan, pp. 232–357.

Yello. (2019). Meet generation Z: The new high-tech and high-touch generation of talent. *The 2019 Yello Recruiting Study*. Retrieved February 21, 2021, from https://yello.staging.wpengine.com/resource/white-paper/generation-z-recruiting-study/.

9
EXECUTIVE COMMUNICATION

To some, it may seem odd to have a chapter on executive communication in a book about employee communication. However, understanding how to help executives communicate is central to any, and every, successful employee communication effort.

Let's start with a definition. According to a 2020 article in *Public Relations Review*, *executive communication* deals with communication across three main areas: the vision of the organization, passion for the organization and the work and care and support for the organization and employees. That said, executive communication can mean different things to different organizations. For just about any organization, the practical definition will include supporting the CEO or the most senior leader in every organization with communication to a wide range of stakeholders. Many more definitions will include helping C-suite executives in ways that could include providing communication support for the chief financial officer, chief human resources officer and chief digital officer, among others.

Still other communication functions may define executive communication to include providing communication counsel, tools and strategy to support all of those roles—plus managers or people leaders—essentially reaching every leader who has one or more direct reports. Clearly, the broader the definition for who is included in executive communication, the greater the resources required to support them and the greater the differences in levels of support provided.

Regardless of who is included in any definition of executive communication, one thing is certain. Whatever an executive in an organization communicates to a set of stakeholders, inside or outside the enterprise, the line between internal and external communication becomes invisible. A CEO communicating to shareholders and financial analysts that their company is restructuring, or merging with another company, knows that every employee with a Google Alert will know

DOI: 10.4324/9781003024118-9

what's being communicated at almost the same time. Conversely, a CFO communicating cost cutting measures internally knows that the details of that initiative will reach financial analysts almost concurrently.

That's the efficiency and speed of digital communication in action and it highlights why every executive communication function must work in lock step with employee communication and external communication. In fact, in many organizations, executive and employee communication are combined and managed by a single communication leader. In others, it may be separated.

The reason executive and employee communication teams are structured either together or apart can reflect competencies of communication professionals in those roles and the unique requirements that senior executives need. Often, the biggest skill set that can influence whether they are combined in a single organization, or not, is speech writing. It's a competency that demands very deep and specialized skills that include storytelling, writing, executive counseling and audience analysis, among others.

The skill of a gifted speech writer to identify and capture the authentic "voice" of the CEO or senior leader is highly valued. That same communication professional may not have the skill sets or bandwidth to lead broader employee communication strategies. Similarly, those who lead employee communication may not have the aptitude or bandwidth to deliver C-suite communication needs for both internal and external audiences. An executive with a more significant external speaking agenda, for example, may have need for communication support from a professional who is more engaged with external stakeholders. A chief communication officer may choose to have a dedicated executive communication professional, or professionals, to ensure the CEO or most senior leader is fully supported. It can be a puzzle for the CCO to find the right blend of talent and time on their team, and sometimes it can be a combination of the CCO and a speech writer or executive communication leader.

CEO Communication

It sounds simple on the surface, but supporting the CEO communication agenda is demanding, complex, and rewarding for those who do it well.

The unique needs of each chief executive define the level of communication support needed. From the "Bring me my speech writer. I have something to say" tactical needs to the strategic advisor and counselor who sets the CEO's communication agenda, the range is broad.

A strategic executive communication function not only delivers day-to-day communication for the chief executive, but it also sets the agenda. That requires an executive communication leader to understand where, when and how the CEO will deliver maximum impact when communicating. CEOs universally have calendars packed with obligations, demanding that communication activities be efficient and highly impactful. Setting the agenda that delivers on those expectations requires partnership with subject matter experts to understand customer needs, the regulatory environment, media relationships (in concert with external communication professionals), non-government organizations (NGOs), investors and a host of different internal stakeholders.

Externally, CEOs often are drawn to global stages where their voices can be heard in significant ways. For example, the World Economic Forum, held annually in Davos, Switzerland, is one such stage. The nonprofit organization's mission is to pull political, business, cultural and other leaders to shape global, regional and industry agendas. In other words, it's a pretty big stage for a CEO to get his or her message out.

Similarly, the widely popular TED Talks, a collection of influential speeches—recorded on videos—come from expert speakers on education, business, science tech and creativity. It is another popular communication destination for chief executives. In both cases, however, there is a need for considerable research, preparation, rehearsal and logistics from executive communication professionals.

While a broader-scale speaking platform may be the primary driver for any executive to get to Davos, or deliver a TED Talk, the opportunity for media and other influencer communication in, and around, those events is critical for maximizing the investment of time and effort to reach those destinations. Rarely are these kinds of events "one and done." That's where we see the role of executive communication taking on greater complexity and the need for attention to detail rise considerably.

For example, a CEO's executive communication agenda at the World Economic Forum likely would feature an agenda that includes delivering a keynote address, meeting with several media outlets, connecting with heads of state and participating in a panel discussion—all in one morning or day and at different venues. That event, in particular, has stringent requirements that limit the number of visitors to Forum venues and all must complete an involved credentialing process. The logistics of getting the CEO from one venue to another, working through security check-in processes and ensuring introductions and meetings take place as planned all combine to paint a picture of what executive communication often demands.

To be clear, that kind of agenda is rarely executed without significant alignment and coordination with external communication professionals, government affairs leaders and a host of other subject matter experts. The ability to partner with other communicators and subject matter experts is paramount.

This leads us to zeroing in on one of the most critical competencies—speech writing (see Table 9.1). Executive communication professionals with this competency can come from many different backgrounds. Journalists and political campaign speech writers often have strong skills that can more easily transfer to corporate types of environments.

These professionals learn how to optimize their time spent with the chief executives—to understand their thoughts and opinions about critical topics to

TABLE 9.1 Global Beverage and Food Company PepsiCo Illustrates Competency Progression Through Speech Writing, One of Several Core Competencies for Executive Communications Proficiency

Speech writing competencies

Proficiency level	Behavioral indicator	Description
Minimal exposure	Some basic level of understanding and knowledge in this area; uses the right terminology	Understands basic logistics of speech writing and sources research materials in support of developing a speech
Foundational	Working knowledge in this area; ability to apply this knowledge with some reliance on others	Supports the development of professionally written speeches for senior executives
Capable	Solid understanding and knowledge of this area; ability to apply this knowledge	Demonstrates ability to manage public speaking and communication activities for senior executives
Advanced	Extensive knowledge and thorough understanding of this area; ability to apply in-depth understanding to resolve complex issues and to transfer know-how to others	Offers specialized and strategic views on an ever-widening spectrum of economic, regulatory and competitive issues
Mastery	An expert level of knowledge and deep understanding of this area; recognized expertise sought out to provide leadership, set direction and develop new processes and tools in this area	Coaches executives to deliver speeches that motivate diverse audiences

their businesses, to capture anecdotal stories that can engage an audience and help clearly articulate a strategy or response. They not only learn what matters to the CEO in creating communications of the day but also understand the legacy the chief executive wants to leave behind and what personal passions they have that can be integrated into broader communication agendas. Fundamentally, they can connect any and all of these elements to deliver compelling content that engages listeners, viewers and readers.

From writing a short toast to honor or say thanks, to speaking at local business roundtables to doing "listening tours" with employees, the CEO's needs for communication support span a wide range of events and populations. The executive communication professional must be responsive enough to turn on a dime and planful enough to see well beyond the needs of the day—connecting stories, messaging platforms and business strategies with dramatically different audiences.

A key connection point for the executive communicator, beyond the CEO, is a strong working relationship with the CEO's administrative assistant or chief of staff. As requests for meetings or speaking engagements are added to the CEO's calendar, the need to engage executive communication leadership in careful planning and preparation is critical.

Looking at internal communication needs, executive communication professionals have an equally, if not ever greater, set of demands on them. Chief executives have significant demands placed upon them and their chief human resources officers to ensure employees are engaged in the organization's business priorities, and the CEO's communication agenda is a critical enabler.

From leadership development programs to employee recognition, diversity, equity and inclusion agendas to connecting in meaningful ways with Employee Resource Groups (ERGs), chief executives need communication support inside the enterprise to connect and inspire the troops.

And Then There's the Town Hall

Perhaps one of the more common venues for CEOs to use inside their organizations is the *town hall*. Whether they're local/single location events, or "on location" meetings broadcast to locations across the globe, the opportunity for employees to hear "live and in person" from their most senior executive is among the most important for chief executives to get right. From hundreds to tens of thousands of employees can "tune in" to hear what the CEO has to say, and, perhaps more importantly, how questions are answered from internal stakeholders.

Some CEOs depend on PowerPoint slide decks to guide them through what they want to say, while others avoid prepared decks at all costs. Regardless of the preferences, CEOs still need to be fully prepared to communicate to the troops. Executive communication professionals are tapped to develop content, work with employee communication leaders to get a pulse on what employees want to hear about and ensure that the chief executive delivers the right message and with the right tone. This takes something that CEOs often have in short supply and may need convincing to invest in: time to rehearse.

Supporting CEOs with live events is more than writing the speech or bullet points for them to use. It requires executive communication leaders to research what the intended audience knows and how they're feeling about the business. It demands an understanding of the advantages and drawbacks of the space that will be used. If the event is to be recorded, if there are videos on the agenda, or plans to do remote links with executives or employees in other locations, it's the executive communication professional's job to ensure they work as planned and that the CEO understands exactly that those additional elements will be worked in. Whether the CEO wants to advance his or her own slides or wants someone else to do so, wants a podium or a chair, or wants to be introduced or not, all are detailed elements of town halls that must be anticipated, locked down and fully understood by the CEO. If there are other presenters on the agenda, all speakers must understand—in advance—how the event will be run and what information will be delivered by each speaker.

Most employees will tell town hall organizers that they want less prepared remarks and more time for Q&A. It's their way of helping set the agenda, seeing greater transparency in what the CEO says and how it's said. And perhaps the most feared moment in any town hall environment for organizers is when the CEO announces it's time for questions and it's followed by silence. It's rarely a reflection of the fact that the CEO has answered every possible question in their prepared remarks. We've all been there; it just takes someone to break the ice with that first question.

Experienced executive communication professionals have a couple of strategies to address the deafening silence or a shy audience during Q&A time. First, if they've done their preparation homework, they've pre-canvassed the audience for what questions are on their minds. This can be done a week to two in advance of the event, as invitations are sent with "hold the date" messaging. A moderator for the Q&A session can ask a question or two—based on common thematic questions that come from pre-canvassing—to fill the time as others need a little time to gather the courage to ask their own questions.

A second strategy is lining up a question asker or two, in advance, who won't waste time getting to a microphone and asking a question. Of course, key in any advance planning for CEO town halls is to share common-themed questions in advance and include draft answers provided by subject matter experts.

Not all CEO communications are targeted to all employees. An executive communication leader for a global food and beverage company said his team routinely prepared briefing binders for the CEO on every participant in employee *"lunch and learn"* meetings. The hour-long lunchtime events were designed to be less structured, informal opportunities for the CEO not only to share a few thoughts about the business but also to understand what employees were thinking and feeling about where the business was going. He said:

> We made sure that participants were not executive leaders, but rather 'skip-level' participants closer to customers and other external stakeholders. Our job was to make sure the chief executive knew a little something about those at the table and about what that part of the business or location was doing. That was just to get the CEO in the door. Our second responsibility was to capture key ideas generated at the meeting for follow up.

Leadership in the Digital Space

In a world dramatically influenced by social media, the executive communicator also will have responsibility for supporting the CEO's digital agenda, both inside the organization and outside. Chief executives increasingly have a voice on platforms such as LinkedIn, where their voice can have a significant following and influence.

The key is for the executive to understand that social media communication isn't a "broadcast and leave" kind of channel; it's a conversation. They must be prepared to post, follow the responses and respond if they want to be seen as credible, authentic participants on the platform.

With crammed agendas, CEOs can easily lose track of the need to monitor their social media posts and that's where executive communication professionals can help. Whether it's aggregating responses to executive posts, highlighting particularly thoughtful responses or offering suggestions on content for follow-up postings, communicators should play a significant role in helping the chief executive not only prepare any original post but also monitor and follow up in meaningful ways.

As with any social media strategy, a CEO's social media activities should include a content calendar that can align their voice with the right opportunities. For example, a CEO who has an affinity for advancing women in the workplace will want to have a meaningful post for LinkedIn on International Women's Day. Another CEO who has a passion for veterans would have something to say on Veteran's Day each year.

Gina Drosos

**Chief Executive Officer, Signet Jewelers
Posted March 7, 2020**

FIGURE 9.1 Signet Jewelers LinkedIn Example

As International Women's Day approaches on March 8, we are getting ready to celebrate this year's theme of #EachforEqual across all of our banners: Kay, Zales, Jared, H. Samuel, Ernest Jones, Peoples, Piercing Pagoda stores, JamesAllen.com and at our headquarter campuses. The #EachforEqual theme is drawn from the concept of "Collective Individualism"—meaning we are all connected to something bigger than ourselves. This concept really resonates with me and my colleagues and has helped guide me as a leader throughout my career. We are all responsible for our own thoughts and actions. Individually and collectively, we can change the world.

At Signet, our "People First" value is critical to the success of our business as it is grounded in decision-making that reflects a range of different perspectives, inclusive of diversity of gender, background, age, sexual orientation and thoughts. To maintain relevance and a competitive edge in an age of continuous disruption and transformation, our employees and our experiences reflect the people who choose our brands; our People First core value also informs our "Customer First" strategic priority.

This mindset is beautifully complemented by our "Own It" core value. In order to deliver on our commitments, each of our team members needs to feel empowered when she or he comes to work and encouraged to unleash their full potential. To that end, leadership development, particularly for women, is a central component to Signet's long-term strategy, and we have lived up to this commitment for more than a decade. We're also empowering our businesses around the world to give back, through corporate giving and our Signet CSR efforts worldwide.

Today, I am proud that Signet is setting the standard for the retail industry—and public companies in general—with regard to gender equality. We have a workforce that is made up of 75% women, with women comprising 70% of our store leadership. Five of the eight members of our executive leadership team, including our CFO, are women. And 5 of our 11 Board members are women. Earlier this year, Signet was again recognized in the Bloomberg Gender-Equality Index in acknowledgment of our continued commitment to fostering an inclusive workplace. Out of the 325 retailers included in the index, Signet is the only specialty jewelry retailer.

We have always believed that diversity is not just a nice-have, it is a must-have. We developed a Culture Action Plan to further strengthen the training, development and advancement opportunities of all team members. Our recent accomplishments include completing required diversity and inclusion training for over 4,000 store managers and the creation of new Business Resource Groups (BRGs) for women, members of the LGBTQ community, multicultural team members, veterans and young professional team members. Since 2018, our Women's BRG has grown to more than 500 team members across our Dallas and Akron Store Support Centers—with the plans to expand across the field organization this year. The group also engages male allies. We also offer training programs, advancement opportunities and best-in-class policies to recruit, retain and develop female leaders in our community, and we encourage the men in our organizations to do the same. We emphasize diversity throughout our supply chain, not only with our employees but also with our vendors, suppliers and partners—including supporting women-owned businesses.

Of course, while it is vital to reinforce our commitment to equality every day, we want to take this opportunity to celebrate and call even more attention to the importance of these efforts on International Women's Day. Our Women's BRG is hosting several employee training sessions and conversations to support #EachforEqual. Team leaders across the organization will facilitate workshops including "50 Ways to Fight Gender Bias" and #IamRemarkable by Google. We have also enlisted team members to submit photos of their #EachforEqual pose, which you can see on our social media channels.

So here is my challenge: Today and every day, I encourage everyone—both at Signet and in the broader business community—to take a look at how you are supporting and cultivating an #EachforEqual mindset. You don't have to be a CEO to do your part. I strongly believe that, together, we can foster a culture built on equality for all. It's more than the right thing to do, it's a strategic imperative.

Digital platforms like YouTube also can prove to be not only an effective platform for posting videos but also an efficient channel to reach internal stakeholders. That's especially true for mobile, dispersed employees who may not have access to video channels that may be housed on servers inside the company's IT firewall. Frontline employees, in particular, may have YouTube as the primary video channel that enables access to the CEO. During the Covid-19 global pandemic, many CEOs used YouTube to efficiently reach their national or global populations.

Southwest Airlines CEO Gary Kelly used YouTube to update not only external stakeholders but also the airline's employees, on a number of Covid-19-related issues through a special video series on YouTube, called "Ask Gary." The program format featured asking the CEO questions that represented the needs of employees, customers and other stakeholders. From safety issues to how the company would use the multi-billion-dollar loan Southwest received from the U.S. government, the video was a more efficient way of reaching a mobile workforce during a crisis.

Blogging, through either internal or external channels, is yet another common channel that executive communicators will need to support and help navigate on behalf of the CEO. While many CEOs don't have the time to sit down and write a blog post, they have plenty to say. Executive communication leaders will find ways to tap into the CEO's experiences and thought processes to help craft an engaging blog post.

It might mean scheduling a "download" session when the CEO returns from an international trip or completing a series of customer or employee meetings. Or it may involve having the CEO record thoughts on a flight home and handing off the audio file. Some CEOs may even snap a photo or record a video of something they find that represents the culture or values they want to highlight. Others may find stories of innovation or customer service that they want to amplify. These are the kinds of content that successful executive communication professionals learn to sift through and support their CEOs in telling engaging, concise stories.

A cautionary note for any future executive communication leader: be sure to ensure that the CEO understands the expectations from stakeholders—particularly internal stakeholders—that come from introducing a blog or video program or social media feed with the CEO's name attached to it.

After a successful launch and a couple of engaging posts, employees quickly come to expect a fairly regular cadence of communications from their CEO. If the chief executive, after a few weeks or months of posting, decides to stop investing the time, employees may view the efforts as half-hearted or may equate a lack of new content with problems the CEO is encountering in the business. In other words, stopping or inconsistently delivering CEO internal communication through blogs, videos or other branded channels may lead to unintended consequences. The lesson learned by many executive communication leaders is this: make sure the CEO understands that when starting to use digital channels that there is a clear understanding of the time and effort it takes to be a legitimate, active participant.

Communicators and executives also should understand that employees and other stakeholders increasingly indicate that they expect their leaders to be active on social media. Advisory firm Brunswick, in its 2021 Connected Leadership report, asked readers of financial publications and employees of companies with more than 1,000 employees about their communication expectations of corporate leaders across 13 different countries and markets. From correcting misinformation to employee engagement to crisis response, the data are clear. Stakeholders expect executives to adapt to the changing circumstances they face. They expect a connected leader.

By a more than 5 to 1 ratio, employees prefer to work for a CEO who uses digital and social media. Nine out of 10 financial readers cited the importance of social media communication by CEOs during a crisis, while 60% of employees consider-ing joining a company will research a CEO's social media accounts. And there's a trust connection, too. By a margin of 9 to 1, financial readers trust a "connected leader" more than a CEO who does not use social media as part of their work.

Engaging with social media isn't something to be taken lightly with executive communication. The time and skills required for preparation, production, posting, follow up and measurement of CEO communication efforts are significant. Exec-utive communication professionals must support the CEO in setting the agenda, mining for content, aligning it with broader communication strategies and show-ing the impact of all those efforts.

And they must do it all while capturing the authentic "voice" of the CEO. That means they understand they must reflect the way a chief executive com-municates in "live" settings in what they help create for digital communication to the masses. Word choice, pacing, tone and style are all elements that internal audiences, consciously or subconsciously, learn from their experiences seeing and hearing a CEO or reading that chief executive's written words. When a new communication effort doesn't match what they see or know to be authentic, they come to believe the communication is not authentic, or that the CEO has been scripted and their real feelings about a topic are masked.

During crises, there are significant expectations from employees to hear from their CEOs with greater frequency. They are looking for straight talk and motiva-tion rolled into concise communications that reflect authenticity and compassion for the hardships the crisis creates. The Covid-19 global pandemic is a recent example for that need. Whether it was through emails or videos, CEOs were required to step up their communications with all stakeholders but particularly with employees. Executive communication professionals were tasked with helping set a communication agenda for their CEOs that thoughtfully considered when and what to say and how to deliver it.

Common metrics for CEO level communication for internal audiences often include items such as clarity of the CEO's communications, authenticity, trans-parency, belief in company strategy and commitment to supporting internal stakeholders, among others. Externally, metrics could include share of voice on a particular topic or within the competitive industry, reach of voice and digital "likes" and "shares," among others. Whichever metrics are selected, they should represent an alignment with the CEO and should complement other CEO-specific measurement efforts—such as those included in Organizational Health survey metrics (see Chapter 4 for more measurement concepts).

Expanding the Definition of Executive Communication

When executive communication includes support for additional members of the C-suite or officers of the company, the level of communication support provided to those leaders correlates to the communication resources available.

In some organizations, communication professionals are assigned, or embedded, in key corporate functions or assigned to executives running significant parts of the business. Many of the same tools and processes supporting CEO communication apply, with the added requirement of coordination with the CEO's executive communication agenda.

CEOs and CFOs, for example, often speak jointly to investor audiences, but alignment and coordination with other executives are central to managing a well-oiled executive communication agenda for the enterprise. This includes ensuring not only that communication professionals supporting different executives align calendars but also that they align on messaging.

Here's where corporate narratives and segmentation—covered in Chapter 7—play a critical role. A Chief People Officer's speaking agenda may be one that is tailored to very different audiences than a CFO, Business Unit President or Chief Digital Officer might be speaking to, but the core message that each executive should connect with remains the same. That's how individual executives amplify the corporate narrative that defines their companies' mission and vision and give it traction over time.

Many organizations will develop processes to vet communication opportunities for executives other than the CEO and coordinate content and venue reviews so that all executives understand who is saying what, to whom and when. Developing and using those processes to maintain a consistent message and voice, the executive communication leader may feel a bit like an air traffic controller at times and a United Nations negotiator at others, but the outcomes of alignment and coordination mitigate the risks that come from misaligned messaging.

That's equally important with employee communication. Understandably, functional and business unit leaders will want to communicate with their respective internal stakeholders. The role of executive communicators supporting those leaders is to set and help execute both function- or business-unit-specific agendas and still support enterprise-wide communication agendas as well.

An example of the need for that alignment comes from Wilmington, Delaware-based DuPont Company. In 2015, the company had envisioned a significant change agenda that it called "Next Generation DuPont." The business agenda included shedding a $6 billion chemicals business and focusing its resources in other materials and bioscience areas. To prepare its executive team to communicate the change agenda, the CEO and all senior executives attended an intensive training session on messaging. Central to the successful introduction of the change narrative was the ability of senior executives to take corporate messaging and tailor it to their respective businesses, functions or geographies. Executives left the training with a clear understanding of the story, expectations of them in communicating it and tools for them to share the change agenda with their teams.

Communication for People Leaders

Empowered managers in every organization are critical enablers of business success. When they're given the tools and latitude to manage their teams, they will take greater accountability for the decisions they make and the performance they deliver. The same is true with communication. When leaders across the enterprise are equipped with information, messaging and other tools to help them engage their teams around focused business priorities, they more often than not will use those tools and, as a result, see stronger engagement and results from their teams.

That's why many organizations will define executive communication to include not only the CEO and the executive team but also all managers and supervisors, or *people leaders* as they're often known. Essentially, that's everyone who has one or more team members reporting to them.

Unlike more comprehensive service levels for senior executives, support for hundreds or even thousands of supervisors, managers, directors and vice presidents means developing efficient tools and processes to reach them and empowering them with the right tools at the right time.

It means focusing on this segmented group of communication stakeholders as a discreet audience with specific needs. Big announcements coming from "corporate" and centralized sources—without advanced communication to managers—often result in a lack of support from people leaders. They understandably feel left out, even blindsided, by news or big announcements they know nothing about, and adopt an "us/them" mentality. That means they will not support news, especially if it's bad news, because they haven't been engaged in advance with the right tools and insights.

Effective executive communication functions routinely include broader management briefings with people managers so that those leaders understand—on the continuum—what issues the business is facing, and how, as managers of people, they can provide context and support for the decisions the organization makes. Often hosted by the CEO or top executive, these briefings—typically web-enabled or large-scale conference calls—feature some prepared content, followed by an open Q&A session. For people leaders unable to attend the live presentation, these events are recorded and made available for on-demand playback. And, not surprisingly, best practices would include sending a follow-up survey to attendees to assess the effectiveness of the briefing.

When there are bigger decisions, or news, to announce, similar events are scheduled. Timing, as the saying goes, is everything. Every effort should be made to pre-brief managers broadly when big, bold news is planned to be shared. In some cases, the news may be "material" to shareholders—meaning it could influence buying or selling stock of publicly traded companies. In those instances, it likely is not possible to pre-brief large numbers of people managers. In those cases, there should be efforts made to brief them as quickly as possible once external disclosures are made, and they should include the reason why people managers could not be pre-briefed.

One way to mitigate the potentially negative response from managers when they cannot be pre-briefed is to make digital assets available to them instantaneously when the company makes external disclosures. Given that people managers are likely dispersed across larger distances, digital tools are the most likely platform that executive communication professionals will use. Leaders portals—essentially dedicated intranet sites just for people managers—are effective platforms to share communication tools quickly and efficiently.

Those sites, which typically require authentication for people managers to identify them as such, include tools such as key message documents, Q&A series, videos, template presentations, recorded management briefings and searchable content that includes archived tools.

"Sequencing is so critical to keep leaders engaged in communications to their teams," one executive communication leader for a Fortune 500 science and technology company said.

> When they believe you've planned for them with big news, they feel better connected to the decisions and better empowered to support them with their local team(s). That's especially critical when the content of news may be more difficult to deliver.

Concurrent with sharing a press release externally, hitting the "send" button internally on an email to hundreds or thousands of people leaders, with a link that takes them to a prepared communication kit, shows inclusive and strategic communication planning. When it's routinely executed and sequenced in close timing to external closures, internal communication to managers allows them to quickly access, digest and share critical context with their teams.

While it might be easy to think of the discipline as one defined solely by supplying executives with speeches and presentation decks, it goes far deeper. It's about developing and delivering a combination of communication discipline and creativity to leaders who need to engage their teams. It demands not only communication skill sets but also coaching and counseling.

Clearly, the world of executive communication includes far more than tactical execution of executives' communication agendas. It demands strategic planning, research, skillful messaging, brilliant storytelling and logistical detailing. It only works when there is significant partnership and collaboration with other communication areas, other functional leaders and a range of subject matter experts.

Profile: Caryn Feeney

**Director, Internal Communication
Qurate Retail Group,
Suburban Philadelphia, PA, USA**

Career Bio

I began my career in media relations for a college athletic department. After quickly realizing PR wasn't for me, I pivoted to editorial work for a wire service, where I was able to hone my writing and managing skills while interacting with communication professionals from all industries. This led to my first internally focused role, where I quickly learned that internal communication was my passion. Since then, it's been a steady progression to my current leadership role, supporting senior executives for a global organization.

I lead our company's global Center of Excellence for Internal Communication. My team is responsible for our global internal communication programs, including our channels (video, intranet, email, town halls, etc.) and all internal communication efforts for our largest business unit. I also spend a significant amount of time providing strategic communication support to our CEO and other senior leaders; this includes communication planning, message development and execution.

Working With Executives to Communicate

It's not uncommon for leaders to feel less inhibited when speaking to internal audiences. This can not only be a good thing—as employees want to feel a connection to their leaders—but it can also be dangerous when they don't realize their every word is being diagnosed by the audience. I first experienced this quite early in my career when a business leader mentioned his belief that there are benefits to splitting companies apart. The information caused undue panic amongst employees and eventually was leaked externally, resulting in the need to issue a statement that no such plan was in the works for our organization.

In the immediate aftermath, we made sure there was a clarification email sent from the leader to the organization, and we armed our entire leadership team with appropriate talking points for conversations with their teams. From there, it was all about my go-forward approach: how I could better anticipate these potential situations and counsel my internal clients so that they understand where the sensitivities are?

From that point forward, my No. 1 rule of internal communication is that anything shared internally should be viewed as external—especially now, in the digital world where anything can be broadly distributed in a matter of moments. It's critical that I offer that counsel to anyone I'm supporting, from leadership on down through the company. But what I've also learned is that I will never be able to control it 100%. The most important thing, as a communicator, is to be as aware as possible up front, provide stakeholders with the tools that will help them stay on message (e.g., better scripting up-front, speaker training, FAQs, legal guidance), and be as ready as possible to react, as needed, after the fact.

In this specific instance, I had the benefit of the leader "learning the hard way," and, therefore, being more cautious and open to counsel going forward. More importantly, it had an impact on me, personally—giving me a critical learning that I have carried through my career. I'm now better equipped with my own "lesson learned" that I can share and leverage as I counsel leaders and help them avoid similar situations.

Communicators working with executives can't be afraid to speak up. This example was related to an earnings release, but it can happen with any number of topics and in many different internal venues. Leaders often will have good intentions and feel they owe their internal stakeholders' certain levels of information—it's our job to know when and where it's appropriate and to be willing to push back if needed. Most importantly, ALWAYS come to the table with an informed opinion and an alternate approach so that your client, whoever it might be, can feel fully prepared and comfortable not sharing something.

Case Study

GREATER BANK RE-CONSTRUCTS EXECUTIVE COMMUNICATION TO DRIVE STRATEGIC PLAN ENGAGEMENT

Situation

Australia's Greater Bank, a mutual bank with 60 branches spanning New South Wales and Queensland, has more than 750 employees, 260,000 customers and over $6 billion in assets. What it didn't have, however, was a fully functioning executive communication capability.

In early 2017, the bank had a significant set of changes at the most senior level of Greater Bank—70% to be specific. It was also the mid-point of a three-year business strategy the bank called Blueprint for Change. It was designed to prepare the business for future transformation.

At the time, formal executive communication was limited and ad hoc. The executive team had a low profile, employees lacked understanding of the business strategy and their role within it and felt underappreciated. When benchmarked against the mutual banking industry, key engagement factors were below competitors and trending downwards—particularly for awareness and clarity of purpose, mission and strategic priorities (15% lower and just over 50% employee awareness); organization pride (30% lower); and satisfaction with information received from senior leaders about what was happening in the business (10% lower).

With only 12 months to ready the business for significant transformational change and a new strategic plan, it was critical that the executive team build visibility and begin inspiring, informing and involving employees with its mission, vision and strategic direction to ensure employees would go the extra mile to deliver great outcomes for its customers—its defining feature and key competitive advantage.

Using data from multiple sources (including the 2017 Employee Engagement survey, sector benchmarking, internal focus groups, one-on-one meetings, Engaging for Success studies and informal "watercooler" employee feedback), the communication team reinforced the links between employee engagement, effective leadership communication and customer outcomes to the executive team and recommended a leadership communication framework designed to build four key engagement enablers.

Those included delivering a strong, inspiring strategic narrative; engaging leaders and managers to inform their teams; focusing on the employee voice; and ensuring "say-do" alignment that builds integrity. This was underpinned by a suite of fit-for-purpose communication channels and a 12-month program of activity for the executive team.

The team's overall goal was to introduce strong, long-term leadership communication to inspire, inform and involve employees—ultimately engaging employees to deliver great customer outcomes and support the final year of the Blueprint for Change business strategy. To deliver on that goal, communicators sought to improve awareness of company purpose, vision and strategic plan among employees at all levels of the bank so they could identify the roles they have in helping the bank achieve goals for the final year of the Blueprint for Change.

Another objective was to increase visibility and voice of the executive team by establishing a regular cadence of communications to build confidence in their leadership, improve employee perception of the team and inform and connect employees with what's happening in the business.

The team's final objective was to identify and leverage opportunities for the executive team to highlight employee behaviors that positively influenced customer satisfaction so that employees felt recognized and rewarded from the top for their hard work and felt proud to contribute to delivering the final year of the Blueprint for Change.

Campaign

The first stage of the communication team's solution included the development of a leadership communication and engagement framework to guide strategy and tactical implementation. Using the four engagement enablers the team identified, it started by educating the executive team on the potential business benefits of a structured leadership communication.

Accordingly, the team's focus for 2017/2018 was primarily on inspiring (strategic narrative) and informing (engaging leaders and managers) both the executive team and senior managers, given the considerable gaps that research identified for internal stakeholders in understanding the bank's strategic direction. The team developed a 12-month program of activity including key initiatives that it directly aligned with at least one of our four engagement enablers; it also introduced a number of new executive-led channels to support implementing the program.

The communication team consulted with executives and relevant stakeholders in developing each initiative throughout the year. A full communication plan was developed for each major initiative and, before executing initiatives, communicators sought 100% support at executive meetings; they formally presented measurement and evaluation data following each implementation to demonstrate the positive impacts of each initiative.

Circling back with executives gave the team license to push boundaries more each time. Given the limited exposure to strategic communication support, the team worked closely with each executive to identify communication strengths and preferences, then develop a tailored communication calendar. The team continuously coached and upskilled leaders to build confidence—leveraging the competitive nature of the group to encourage execution of the tactics. In 2018/2019, the program was refocused to more comprehensively address the employee voice and "say-do alignment" enablers. Clearly, that followed the "tone from the top" that was prioritized and more firmly established through the bank's most senior leaders in the first phase.

Results

Based on results of post-implementation surveys, the leadership communication and engagement approach delivered significant improvements—bringing Greater Bank in line with, or exceeding, mutual banking sector benchmarks. This provided the team with a strong mandate to continue building and evolving the framework to further cement the four engagement enablers and support the business to deliver great customer outcomes.

As for outcomes, 90% of employees believed executives effectively communicated the bank's strategic direction, with 83% saying their knowledge of Blueprint for Change had improved within the previous 12 months. Eighty percent also said that they understood their role in the strategy.

Leaders got what they needed, too; 86% of managers agree they had the communication material and information they needed to have an effective team strategy conversation and 93% of them reported having a good understanding of the bank's strategic priorities.

Finally, the employee view of top management also showed strength, with 98% of employees reporting positive impressions of the CEO and executive team, and 90% saying that they felt the frequency of communication from the top was "about right."

Source: IABC Gold Quill Awards (2019)

Bibliography

Brunswick. (2020). Connected leadership. *Brunswick Group*. Retrieved February 23, 2021, from www.brunswickgroup.com/perspectives/connected-leadership/.

Men, L. R., Yue, C. A., & Liu, Y. (2020). Vision, passion, and care: The impact of charismatic executive leadership communication on employee trust and support for organizational change. *Public Relations Review, 46*(3), 101927. https://doi.org/10.1016/j.pubrev.2020.101927.

10

CHANGE MANAGEMENT

The Emerging Internal Communication Expertise

To understand where, arguably, the most visible opportunities are for employee communicators to make an impact with business, look no further than 500 BCE. That's when Greek philosopher Heraclitus summed up what was, is, and will likely always be the constant denominator for where communication within organizations can make its biggest mark: change.

"Change is the only constant in life," Heraclitus wrote. And when we apply that to the business world today, it's a universal reality. If you find an enterprise that isn't going through change, it probably won't be around for long. It's the nature of the beast; in order for businesses to thrive, they must adapt to constant changes in, and around, them. Whether it's customer preferences, new competitors, disruptive technology forces or a host of other catalysts, the reality for employee communication professionals is that there is an endless supply of change influences that demand their engagement.

This is where change communication comes into play. *Change communication* is more than just a subset of internal or corporate communication. In the public relations literature, it's been described as "communication and behavioral management that is event-driven and close to processes and campaigns."

Here's both the problem and the opportunity: most employee communicators aren't educated or trained in the discipline of change communication. They're often given a single change or a series of independent changes to communicate. These more tactical executions of change communication may be effective in explaining what's changing, but, over time, they miss a much bigger opportunity to engage employees in longer term or more substantive, complex change. And increasingly, that's what organizations find themselves having to address.

DOI: 10.4324/9781003024118-10

In recent years, it has been the understanding of how to manage larger-scale and more complex change—and the corresponding demands it places on communication—that has created the biggest new opportunities for employee communicators. The scale and timing of change certainly can be different for every organization, but the ability to manage change successfully has a real and tangible impact on organizational performance. Communication is central to every effective change management.

Fundamentally, change for organizations is being driven from every direction. Stakeholder expectations are rising: customers want innovative, integrated solutions faster; employees want growth, meaningful work and a sense of belonging; and shareholders want faster growth and greater financial performance in responsible ways. In the midst of the ongoing trends and changes, organizations find themselves having to continuously adapt and evolve to position themselves more competitively.

Think about two organizations merging into one. Or two organizations merging into one, then breaking up into three companies. Or it could be companies implementing new technologies to put them on common platforms or to engage customers online in ever-improving ways. Human beings have no shortage of ideas leading to change but implementing change to support those ideas inevitably will create a working environment of both optimism and fear. Well-managed change tips the scale more toward optimism.

The positives associated with change can often get lost in employees' speculation about what's causing the change. They may be concerned about the impact on their jobs, such as whether those jobs will change or possibly be eliminated. Or it could be fear over how the organization will implement its changes, like if the change is fairly distributed, and the time frame is reasonable or too aggressive?

Well-run change management ensures the "people side of change" is considered each step along the way in the change process, from planning to implementing to reinforcing change. Essential to the change effort is a communication plan that reaches the hearts and heads of those affected by the change and helps get their buy-in.

The Bottom Line: Change Managed Poorly Costs

Research from McKinsey & Company reported in 2015 that 70% of change programs fail to achieve their goals, largely due to employee resistance and lack of management support. The firm also went on to say that when people are truly invested in change, it is 30% more likely to stick.

Poorly managed change can lead to millions of dollars in lost productivity, wasted resources, increased costs and rework. Additionally, it can impact employee morale and engagement. And even when some type of change management process is used, it is often implemented too late to be measurably effective.

Impact of change-related stress on performance

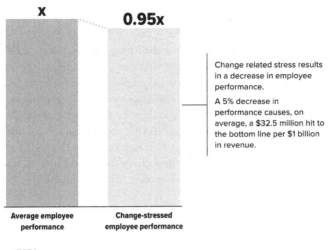

X **0.95x**

Change related stress results in a decrease in employee performance.

A 5% decrease in performance causes, on average, a $32.5 million hit to the bottom line per $1 billion in revenue.

Average employee performance

Change-stressed employee performance

n = 7,354
Source: CEB, 2015

FIGURE 10.1 CEB's 2015 Employee Change Survey illustrates the impact of change-related stress on financial performance.

The impact of change-related stress on performance is, however, measurable. Gartner reported in 2019 that 79% of employees have experienced a significant organizational change in the previous two years, such as mergers and acquisitions, a new company strategy or executive leadership turnover. Seventy-three percent of change-affected employees report moderate to high stress levels. That's important to understand because stressed employees impact business outcomes: change-stressed employees perform 5% worse than those who are not stressed. For the average company, this performance decline translates to a $32.5 million hit to the bottom line per $1 billion in revenue (see Figure 10.1).

The connection here for employee communicators is that change costs money, but change managed well generates significant positive returns on investment (ROI). Rather than being viewed as a cost center in financial terms, communication that supports change can be, and is, viewed as a central enabler of ROI for change efforts, and that almost always means a lot of money.

Clearly, managing the "human side of change" is important, and doing it well means understanding exactly how humans respond to change. One of the most widely accepted explanations of how people experience change is the *Kubler-Ross*

Change Curve. Psychiatrist Elisabeth Kubler-Ross initially articulated the change curve through extensive research on how humans experience death. She identified five stages of grief, which include denial, anger, bargaining, depression and acceptance. She introduced this five-stage model in 1969 in a book called *On Death and Dying.*

The model was widely accepted as a road map for processing grief, but over time, business professionals came to see that the model applied to how people, more generally, experience change. For example, in the early stages of denial, it's important to equip managers and employees with information to help them understand the rationale behind the change. As they move through the curve and get to anger and fear, communications that focus on listening and watching reactions are more appropriate. And, as stakeholders move through experimentation, providing communications that allow them to test and give them reasons to believe in the future state, often are well received (see Figure 10.2).

The Kübler-Ross change curve

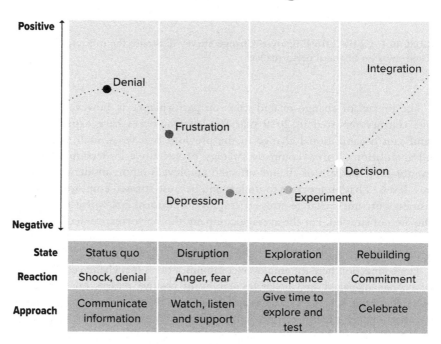

State	Status quo	Disruption	Exploration	Rebuilding
Reaction	Shock, denial	Anger, fear	Acceptance	Commitment
Approach	Communicate information	Watch, listen and support	Give time to explore and test	Celebrate

FIGURE 10.2 The Kubler-Ross Change Curves shows the range and sequence of emotions associated with change. Understanding this curve helps employee communicators develop strategies that best support change management efforts.

While humans experience the stages in different ways and to different degrees, the idea of identifying common stages gives change management, and change management communication professionals, specific insights to incorporate into their strategies for managing and communicating change. The easier it is for the employees to adapt to change, the faster and less painless it is for any organization to move through the change curve. So, the Kubler-Ross Change Curve is a powerful model to incorporate when assessing where employees are in their experience of change and informing decisions on communication strategies and content to help them.

Change Management Models

Experts in the field of change management emphasize that the most successful change initiatives are those that deploy a series of important steps requiring time, focus and planning to help achieve anticipated results.

Ultimately, successful change management involves getting people to commit to or own a change. Applying change management "best practices" in the change effort increases the likelihood that change takes hold. Importantly, change management increasingly is not viewed as a temporary or episodic need, but rather a constant, systemic discipline that every successful business enterprise must deploy.

Change management is an intentional, repeatable approach designed to guide employees to the desired future state. It ensures the "people side of change" is considered and addressed effectively and aims to empower employees at all levels to prepare for—and embrace—the change. Essentially, it takes the "chance out of change."

It's critical for communication professionals to understand that change management is not the same as project management. *Project management* is defined generally as a managed effort in pursuit of a specific goal, often with a focus on initiating, planning, executing and monitoring a project's activities and deliverables. It ensures a strong solution design backed up with detailed project plans. *Change management* prepares the organization for the project impact, manages the transition from "how things are done today" to "how things will be done tomorrow"—and puts special effort into reinforcing and anchoring the change to everyday work to help make change stick. In their book *Change Management*, Robert Paton and James McCalman describe successful change management as requiring "an understanding of the likely impact of the change on those systems most affected by it, and thereafter the development of a means of establishing a shared perception of the problem amongst all concerned. The visible commitment and involvement of those charged with managing the change and those affected by it are crucial to achieving successful transition management."

Just as important, change management is not independent of change management communication. Ideally, the change communication strategy is a result of a well-articulated change management plan. This is important to understand because many organizations do not have established or dedicated change management functions or do not have change management disciplines as embedded disciplines within their management ranks. This often leads to employee communicators being asked to develop change management communication without the benefit of having an articulated change management plan.

"It's a bit like the cart leading the horse," one change communicator with a global technology organization said.

> Just about everyone understands that successfully managing change demands effective communication strategies. What they don't always understand is that the best change management communication plan is designed—strategically—to drive the change management plan. And that requires that the organization actually have one.

Change management, as a discipline, isn't built overnight. In his article, *Blueprint for Building an Internal Change Management Capability*, Jesse Jacoby, the founder of the global consultancy Emergent, wrote that the discipline of change management has great value. However, he believes that organizations have not fully developed the capacity to implement change effectively. Jacoby's research found that change management needs to be "an essential organizational capability that cascades across and throughout the whole portfolio, program and project management." His findings also showed that organizations that invest in an internal change management capability differentiate themselves from their peers. Finally, Jacoby's research indicated that companies with a common standard in place for change management more quickly and easily adapt to the constantly changing business environment, adopt solutions, realize project ROI, and have a competitive advantage.

There are many models of change management that an organization can adopt, including the aforementioned Kubler-Ross Change Curve. Most of them require an assessment of systems and tools and clear articulation of the change from the current state to the future state. Several are more focused on the emotional nature of change. Ideally, an organization will thoroughly assess which one best fits its culture, resources and scale of change. But once that selection is made, communicators and general management should unite in creating a solid organizational discipline around managing, and communicating, change.

Choices in change management models range from those developed by business school professors to approaches designed by change management consultancies. Each has merit and should be fully considered. Some of the more widely circulated models are shown in Figure 10.3.

Models of change management

Lewin's change management model	McKinsey 7-S model	Nudge theory
A popular three-phase model that breaks down big changes into more manageable chunks.	Features seven elements that are not designed to be addressed in a specific order but instead by how they affect each other so that weaknesses can be identified and addressed.	Relies on subtle, indirect suggestions backed up by evidence so that employees will be "nudged" in the direction of the desired change.
Bridges' transition model	**The Satir change model**	**Kotter's theory**
Focuses on emotional reactions through three stages of transition.	Monitors the emotional progress of employees by tracking performance through five stages.	This model, developed by Harvard Business school professor John P. Kotter, divides change into eight stages.
Maurer's 3 levels of resistance and change model	**The Deming cycle, or PDCA**	
Focuses on three specific influences that cause change to fail.	Developed by Dr. Williams Edwards Deming, this model presents a framework on process improvement that is divided into four phases.	

FIGURE 10.3 While there is no universal change management model used by every organization, these change models can be used to better understand, plan for, and communicate change.

Perhaps the most widely used change management discipline is the *ADKAR model*, which is central to consultancy Prosci Change Management's approach. It is heavily focused on the people side of change where the acronym ADKAR defines the specific goals of change management (see Figure 10.4).

With significant focus placed on employees going through change, the ADKAR model is designed to limit resistance and speed implementation. Instead of going to employees with a mandate for change, ADKAR strategies require starting a conversation with them to create awareness of the need for change. Getting their early buy-in will engage them in participating in the change versus being dragged through it.

In this model, knowledge and ability goals are closely linked, but knowledge focuses more on understanding how the change can be made, while ability is about giving employees the tools, processes and confidence they need to change. This people-centric method ensures a higher success rate for sustained change compared to methods that do not actively involve the employees affected by the change.

For example, if an organization decides to bring all of its financial systems on to a common IT platform, change communicators would need to take a deep dive into understanding the changes it will require for employees to make. Using the ADKAR model, communicators would likely need to articulate a burning platform—the reason with a sense of urgency and purpose—for change. It might include illustrating how the current systems cost time and money. They might show how continued use of existing outdated systems would put the organization at a competitive disadvantage. Successfully engaging employees to create a desire to change would likely require team meetings that allowed meaningful dialogue among employees and leaders. It would be critical to help employees understand that implementing a new system would make existing financial reporting significantly faster, freeing up valuable time for employees to do more value-added work. That's an example of "What's in it for me?"

But implementing a significant change, like a new financial reporting system, can take months or years to complete. Communicators would be asked to develop a plan that ensured the organization moved to a state of readiness, that appropriate training was delivered at the right time, and that all stakeholders impacted by the new system understood what was happening, what they needed to do and why. That's where communications that support delivery of knowledge and ability would come into play. When the day comes to launch the new system, communicators would be responsible for developing plans to support not only the launch but also sustained communication that reinforces critical needs to make sure the change sticks.

While Prosci's approach to change management is summarized with the ADKAR model, there is much more to its methodology. It has specific, proprietary processes and tools that are designed to help change managers fully assess

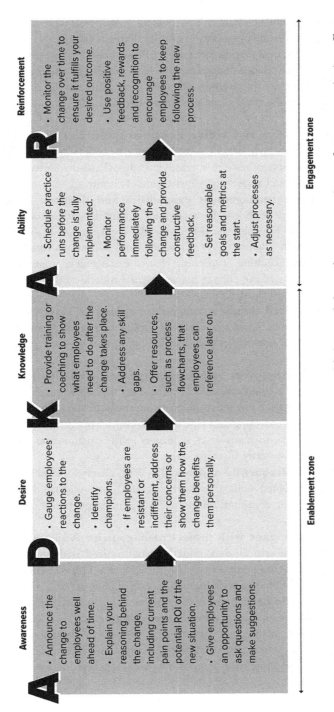

FIGURE 10.4 Prosci's ADKAR model is a change management model that can help employee communicators focus communication efforts through a clear and effective process.

the impact of change, the populations impacted by them, potential roadblocks and strategies best suited for the organization as it implements change.

In addition to its change management model, Prosci conducts extensive research on best practices in the change management field. Research participants identified these seven best practices that support not only success for change management but also significant enablers of communications success:

- **Mobilize an active and visible executive sponsor**. This is typically a high-level executive who has a C-suite presence, or a role close to it. This role often is used to secure resources, remove roadblocks and resolve significant strategic issues the change management team encounters.
- **Embed change management capabilities and dedicate resources**. Change management should be a constant discipline with resources dedicated to drive and deepen the skill across the enterprise. Whether this is a specific team with a dedicated set of resources and skills to manage change, or an investment in coaching or teaching change management more broadly to leaders, it's about making change management a muscle of the organization, versus a set of project management skills.
- **Apply a structured change management approach**. This includes identifying specific roles, teams and working groups with clear accountabilities, specific priorities, deliverables and deadlines and processes for reporting and resolving conflicts.
- **Engage with employees and encourage their participation**. Communication plays a significant role in providing channels to reach employees going through change, engaging them in conversations about change, soliciting feedback and analyzing and reporting the impact of communications on the change agenda. In many cases, managers in the organization need to be coached to develop active listening skills.
- **Communicate frequently and openly**. With channel and content strategies that are aligned with a well-articulated change management plan, a cadence of regular communications will keep attention focused on what's ahead.
- **Integrate and engage with project management**. While change management skills are critical, they must be synchronized with strong project management plans to ensure deliverables are achieved. This is about balancing the project side of change with the people side of change.
- **Engage with middle managers**. Engaged and empowered middle managers can make or break a change management effort. As covered in Chapter 7 on segmentation, creating and executing communication strategies for managers will enable people leaders to engage their teams with meaningful, relevant content and allow them to collect and assess inputs and feedback from their employees.

The Communicator's Contribution to Change Management

As we think about how communication can drive each of these goals, it isn't hard to see how content, channel and measurement strategies—covered in Chapters 2, 4 and 8, respectively—are central to creating awareness of the change, the desire to participate in it, the knowledge and ability to actually make the expected changes, and the reinforcement to help make change stick. Keeping employees informed of change progress is critical through every step of the change process, in fact, studies by global management consulting firm McKinsey & Company have found that continual communication is a leading factor in transformation success.

Communication is a key component of change management and is critical to the success of any change initiative. It's a thread that runs through the whole process of change management—especially helping employees gain awareness of the change and helping build desire to change (buy-in). Key components of effective change management communication plans include:

- Sharing information in more than a "tell" manner—using delivery channels that prompt them to react to what they have heard, discuss or internalize the impact the change may have on them and engage them in thinking through the implications.
- Providing employees opportunities to raise questions and get responses relatively quickly.
- Incorporating a focus on addressing "What's in it for me?" (WIIFM). When employees understand what's in it for them personally, they are far more likely to commit to and own the change. Failing to articulate WIIFM will only hinder change efforts.
- Building desire for the change while promoting continuous improvement and collecting data/employee feedback about their experiences in the change process. *Harvard Business Review* writer Morgan Galbraith reported that, in 2017, his client FMC Corporation was preparing to acquire a significant part of DuPont's Crop Protection business. The transaction would transform FMC into the fifth-largest crop protection company in the world. "In preparation for FMC's crop protection transaction with DuPont, more than 150 FMC employees were nominated by leaders to be part of the Change Champion Network. The group was established to engage their peers, answer questions and excite employees about the future of the company," he wrote. "The group was an essential resource for fellow employees and served as a channel for two-way feedback for leadership."
- Developing/updating a change transformation "story" (a master narrative) to better explain change. This is core to creating a clear vision of the future state that change will create. Using the example mentioned previously, FMC also

developed a unifying internal communication campaign called the "Nature of Next." It fully articulated the reasoning and vision for the acquisition.

- Illustrating transparency as an avenue to building trust with leadership. From the first communication about change, leaders must be equipped with, and coached, to deliver insights about change that are candid and compelling. Change is rarely pretty or perfect and leaders must find balance with change communication—motivating their teams while being realistic about the difficulties that come with change. This demands significant "live" communications throughout the change journey, enabling team members to ask questions, vet their concerns and seek clarity.
- Equipping leaders with communication tools, skills and content that empower them to lead the change. This includes the creation and consistent use of a master narrative that places the change, and discrete actions tied to it, in context of the "bigger picture" that the narrative presents. Major changes or transformations often require asking employees to adopt specific behaviors or skill sets in order to be successful. And when senior leaders model the behavior changes, transformations are five times more likely to be successful.

Obstacles to Effective Change Management

On the flip side of enablers to successfully managing change, Prosci also reported the most common obstacles to effective change management in its *Best Practices in Change Management*. Not surprisingly, they include:

- Ineffective change management sponsorship from senior leaders
- Resistance to change from employees
- Middle management resistance
- Poor communication

Each of these obstacles needs to be addressed within the change management plan, but research indicates the quality of communication during change is the most significant contributor to managing resistance.

Prosci highlights several specific benefits that well-executed change management and communication fields deliver, which reinforce why organizations need change management (see Table 10.1). These include:

An effective change management approach will help any organization enhance its portfolio change plans, increase the speed of change implementation and improve the probability of success for each future intended company. Supplying leaders with the communication tools and content to be champions of change, and helping them develop the skills to drive their change agendas, will be priorities for the company's overall change efforts. All of this must be done with an eye toward the "people side" of change.

TABLE 10.1 Many Organizational Change Efforts Fail, Costing Companies Time, Money and Lost Opportunities. Prosci's 2017 Summary of Why Change Management—and Communication—Matters, Clearly Articulates the Case for Investing in a Change Management Discipline.

Why Organizations Need Change Management	Highlights
Thriving in an ever-changing world	Applying change management enables organizations to deliver results on each change more effectively and build competencies that grow the organization's capacity to tackle more change at one time.
Delivering the people-dependent portion of project ROI	Change management focuses on helping people change how they do their jobs, also called the "adoption contribution."
Closing the gap between requirements and results	Change management enables the closing of this gap by effectively supporting and equipping those people impacted by a change to be successful in bringing it to life in their day-to-day work.
Increasing likelihood of project success	The data are clear. The better that organizations apply change management, the more likely they are to deliver on project objectives. Prosci's correlation data from over 2,000 data points and 10 years show that initiatives with excellent change management are six times more likely to meet objectives than those with poor change management.
Mitigating mission-critical risk	When the adoption and usage of a solution are ignored, and the focus is exclusively on meeting technical requirements, the result is excessive risk and cost. Change management is the discipline to help mitigate those mission-critical risks.
Taking the chance out of change	Change management removes the chance from change by providing employees with the preparation, support and skills they need to succeed in change.
Treating employees right	By proactively engaging and supporting people in times of change, organizations demonstrate in action that they value them.

Source: Prosci, "Why Change Management," 2018

Digital Transformation: The Biggest Force Behind Change Today

While there are many forces of change that influence employee communicators, the biggest and most global change force of the 21st century arguably is digital transformation. Holistically, we can think of this force as including digital technologies to create new or change existing business processes, culture and customer experiences. From sales to marketing and customer service, it's all about how organizations change to engage with customers.

Digital transformation most often includes changes to a business process or a business model, a move into new markets and cultural/organizational changes. Each type of digital change—in order to be successful—demands that communication with internal stakeholders be strategic and impactful. To illustrate just how big these opportunities are for communicators, consider what they include. Andrew Annacone, managing partner at TechNexus Venture Collaborative, articulates four kinds of digital transformation. He writes that process transformation features new ways to reinvent existing processes throughout the enterprise. The goals of this type of change could include lowering costs, reducing cycle times or increasing quality. For example, in 2015, Domino's Pizza completely re-imagined its food ordering process, using its AnyWare technology to let customers order from any device. In fact, this process change increased customer convenience so much that by 2017 it helped them overtake Pizza Hut in sales. Process transformation can also dramatically reduce costs for back-office functions such as accounting and legal.

While process transformation is focused on changing finite areas of the existing business, business model transformation more strategically focuses on how the enterprise delivers value. Netflix's reinvention of video distribution, Apple's reinvention of music delivery (iTunes) and Uber's reinvention of the ride-hailing industry are all examples of business model transformation. Insurance companies such as Allstate and Metromile are using data and analytics to un-bundle insurance contracts and charge customers by-the-mile—a wholesale change to the auto insurance business model. And there are numerous efforts underway to transform the business of mining to a wholly robotic exercise, where no humans travel below the surface.

Longer-term success for businesses isn't solely about staying in markets where they're successful today. Using new digital technologies to move into new markets is yet another form of digital transformation. Amazon moved into a new market in 2006 with the launch of Amazon Web Services (AWS), now the world's largest cloud computing/infrastructure service, in a domain formerly owned by the IT giants such as Microsoft and IBM. With Amazon's strong digital capabilities built for storage, its computing databases to support its core retail business and thousands of relationships with young, growing companies, all enabled its entry into cloud computing. AWS is a wholly different business in a fundamentally different market space and, as of 2020, it was reported that AWS represented nearly 60% of Amazon's annual profit.

Cultural and organizational transformation change is all about the people side of digital transformation. It's about developing and growing mindsets, processes, talent and capabilities for the digital world. The speed and complexity of working in digital transformation demand agile workflows, a mindset for testing and learning, decentralized decision-making and a significant understanding of how the business operates and what interdependencies exist. Experian, the consumer credit agency, has changed its organization by embedding agile development and collaboration into its workflows and by driving a fundamental shift in employee focus from equipment to data, company-wide. Similarly, Pitney Bowes, the 100-year-old postage equipment company, has made the successful transition to become a "technology company" by promoting a culture of innovation and by shifting company values to focus on customer-centricity. Neither of these transformations could be accomplished by just sending broadcast email messages. They required a thoughtful, sustained, strategic communication plan.

A Rapidly Evolving Industry

The variety of change management types and critical drivers, like digital transformation, have spawned significant needs and investment from organizations across the globe. The demand for change communicators, along with change management skills, will continue to grow as well. In fact, trade organizations have been created specifically to focus on these disciplines.

One of the world's most influential professional business trade organizations is the Conference Board, a global, independent business membership and research association working in the public interest. Its mission is to provide the world's leading organizations with the practical knowledge they need to improve their performance and better serve society. The Board's Change and Transformation Council exists to bring the best minds and practices from organizations across the globe together to focus on how best to manage change.

The Change and Transformation Council states:

> The rapid rate of change and increased complexity in markets, customers, products and services is making it almost impossible to keep up, let alone stay ahead, in business. Combined with the emergence of unimaginable competition, the frequency and pace of change required to thrive in the global marketplace has reached a point where it affects everything.
>
> We need to be able to change swiftly to solve new problems faster, accelerate innovation, and get our products and services to market faster. If we do this, we outperform the competition.

The Conference Board's stated mission is to advance the practice of change management by creating new thought leadership and developing capabilities for extraordinary performance. It focuses on change management challenges in business transformation and renewal, global reorganization and employee engagement. According to The Conference Board's website, these business needs drive its research, collaboration and application in the following areas:

- Change management assessment and strategy development, sponsorship and stakeholder alignment
- Change management programs for adoption and implementation of new business processes and practices, new leadership and workforce competencies and social technologies
- Coaching and facilitation of behavioral change

Riding the Change Wave, and Gaining Influence in the Process

One of the more common items on the wish lists of employee communicators is to be viewed as strategic contributors to the business. While there will always be value in communicating news of the day to employees, communicators in the more strategic position of driving organizational change are far more likely to find themselves with a "seat at the table," where some of the most important, long-term decisions about creating value are made.

Through creating and telling a compelling master narrative or story, by enabling and equipping committed leaders with communication and by creating a clear roadmap that enables transformation, business success clearly can be enabled, and measured, through change communication.

Beyond the business results, successful change communicators also can build influence and confidence for themselves and their function, too. With an understanding of how complex change is best managed, they can develop best-in-class employee communication that does far more than deliver understanding to employees. They can fully engage those internal stakeholders in executing and sustaining the change through strategic employee communication. And throughout that process, they'll gain greater influence as strategic advisors on the biggest of internal bets that organizations make.

Profile: Angeline Cheng

Global Head, Change and Transformation Communication, Corporate Affairs, Brand & Marketing Standard Chartered Singapore

Career Bio

I started out in human resources, but I decided to specialize in internal and change communication after being recruited for a change strategy and communications role with a local bank early in my career. Finding the sweet spot with people and communications, I have spent the last two decades in various regional and global internal/change communication roles, primarily in the technology and financial services sectors—including IBM, Nokia Siemens Networks and Visa.

I lead a fairly new and small team responsible for developing and delivering communication strategies for large and complex global transformation programs in the Bank. Focusing on the people side of change, we engage and equip our colleagues through thoughtful and timely communications. Working closely with the program teams, people leaders and other communication partners, we ensure that change is adopted and embedded successfully and in support of the Bank's strategy and purpose.

Engaging Employees Through Change Management Communication

One of our Control Functions was in the middle of a multi-year transformation program, where a specific project was looking at eliminating duplicate roles, streamlining processes and clarifying central contact points for the businesses. This meant that many of the existing roles would either fall away or be reshaped to fit the new target operating model.

As part of the communication strategy, we outlined the top-line team structure and ways of working and the business reasoning for doing so in simple, clear messaging. Employees were to approach their line managers if they had questions. However, decisions and discussions were restricted at the most senior levels of the function, and line managers received the news at the same time as everyone else and were not able to address the uncertainty and anxiety in their own teams.

Over the next several weeks, we researched and developed a set of resources and tools that our line managers could arm themselves with and use when they are expected to guide their teams through change. The Change Toolkit includes a 16-page guide to help them understand and manage change, communications checklists and suggested timelines, as well as two short videos that quickly bring to life the concepts in the guide. We also packaged the content into a short workshop that we conducted for the next set of people leaders affected by change.

We learned that line managers were usually not well prepared for, or did they have sufficient understanding of, such changes. They were not able to adequately respond to the questions from their teams or skills to manage the feedback from the ground. More broadly, it was assumed that they would understand what change means and their role in leading their teams through the change. That was not necessarily true, and we had to bridge the gap between the expectations and the reality of the situation—and do it quickly enough that it did not happen again with the next project or rollout.

We have observed smoother transitions in our change programs, with employees being more measurably engaged according to our annual employee survey.

This has also given us the opportunity to work at scale with our HR colleagues to strengthen the change capabilities in the organization. These materials are included in the learning curriculum for all line managers, and we have also conducted workshops for change managers as well as leaders keen on building these skills. This also reflects the natural curiosity that people have about change and effective communication when we point them to the relevant tools and concepts.

Employees usually identify their line managers as their most trusted source of news or comfort, especially when there is uncertainty or change affecting them directly. However, the role of the line manager is often understated and taken for granted. As change management communicators, we can help them play the critical role they have by equipping them with what they need to effect and manage successful change. As we have done, there should be constant education around the need and understanding for effective change management for the long-term growth of the Bank—putting people as the priority.

Case Study

ATB FINANCIAL ENGAGES EMPLOYEE COMMUNICATION TO LAUNCH NEW CUSTOMER ONBOARDING TOOL

Situation

ATB Financial is a full-service financial institution in Calgary, Alberta, with 5,400 employees. Three of the company's key priorities centered on its commitment to transform banking, make banking work for people and be the place to bank. The problem presented to employee communicators was that customers and bank employees needed 45 minutes, on average, to onboard a new customer. A new digital tool to reduce that time, and free employees to focus on customer relationships, needed significant communications leadership.

The existing onboarding process allowed little time for employees to listen and build relationships with clients. Research conducted by ATB's consumer research team highlighted customer complaints about the process taking too long, and showing the experience was painful. ATB delivered Onboarding Express—a digital onboarding tool that streamlined the process for employees and decreased the application data entry, to provide an opportunity for employees to deepen connections with customers.

This project had lots of visibility and attention from the ATB executive team, as it was the first big initiative to be developed in-house by ATB's Transformation department. It was also the first project to be deployed using the Agile methodology, where the company would release a minimal viable product (MVP) on a wide-scale, and the solution would see continual iterations or improvements over time.

Campaign

In April 2018, ATB's communication team was engaged to support the pilot expansion in the spring and summer, then the organization-wide launch in the fall and winter of 2018–2019. The team's employee communication needed to ensure the company's frontline Retail Financial Services (RFS) branch leadership and team members had a clear understanding of timelines; understood what steps they needed to take and where to direct questions and go for support; knew what the system could do and that it would continually be able to do more with added features and functionality; and had confidence and were excited to use the new technology and solution in front of customers.

The solution fully addressed project goals, which included reducing the time/increasing team member capacity to onboard a customer; mobilizing employees so that accounts could be opened anytime, anywhere; and increasing employee engagement by providing better tools to do their job.

Those translated into clear communication goals, which were to make it easy for team members to find and access the right information at the right time.

Before creating the communication plan, communications, organizational change management and training leads conducted needs assessments with initial pilot participants and leaders from various internal stakeholder groups. This resulted in a four-phased communication approach:

Phase 1 featured a Pilot (April–June): The pilot phase had three main priorities for communication: creating a set of core materials and tactics to leverage for the broader rollout; testing and refining any materials that didn't resonate or help achieve objectives; and identifying any gaps not defined in earlier assessments.

Phase 2 was about delivering awareness and understanding (June–July): Knowing direct leaders and RFS executives are crucial to communicating change and driving adoption, communication in this phase started by focusing on increasing RFS leaders' awareness and understanding in advance of sharing communication with their teams. It was also during this phase that communicators activated a Champions group. By focusing initial communications activities on these two groups, communicators were able to inform and excite leaders and champions, while providing them with the details they needed to lead the change at the local level.

Phase 3 was focused on Action (June–August): The action phase of communications focused on specific steps all frontline team members needed to complete in order to begin using Onboarding Express. This phase was particularly critical to the success of the project because the business made a significant investment in the purchase of iPads for all employees who needed to use the tool, so they could use them fully. Once the iPads were delivered, communicators needed to ensure they didn't sit on team members' desks or drawers to collect dust. The success of communication in this phase would link directly to the iPad activation and branch use objectives. If employees failed to take action in this phase, they would not meet their target of 80%. To increase engagement and have some fun with a process that could be tedious and boring (spending 30 minutes to 1 hour setting up an iPad), communicators encouraged teams to turn the action into an event—an Unboxing Party.

The fourth and final phase was centered on Adoption & Sustainment (September–on): The focus of the adoption and sustainment phase was to use many different channels and mediums, including intranet articles, community posts, newsletter updates, videos and live stream calls, to continue building on the momentum built during the awareness and understanding, and action phases of the rollout. This further supported developing team members' knowledge and increased use of the Onboarding Express tool. This phase also provided ongoing communication that addressed employee feedback, issues and concerns. It showed transparency about what the project team was working to resolve them and instilled confidence that their feedback had a direct impact on future development.

Results

The results were significant. In November 2018, Onboarding Express had a weighted adoption score of 77.25 (vs. a target of 75.00). The weighted adoption score is made up of a combination of behavior intent or intended use and perceived barriers of the tool, team member impact on work and satisfaction.

Eighty percent of the company's branches (158) used Onboarding Express to open accounts within the first three months of rollout, as measured with project team reporting data; 95% of branches (165 out of 174) used Onboarding Express to open at least one account from July 1 to September 30, 2018; and 100% of branches opened at least one account by October 31, 2019.

Getting to individual employee behaviors, 86% (vs. a target of 80%) of team members activated their iPads within the first three months of rollout, as measured by an IT activation report; 89% (vs. a target of 80%) of team members surveyed indicated they understood why the company launched Onboarding Express and were able to communicate the "why" in their own words.

Source: IABC Gold Quill Awards (2020)

Bibliography

Ackerman Anderson, L., & Anderson, D. (2014). Ten common mistakes in leading transformational change. *Being First, Inc.* Retrieved from http://changeleadersnetwork.com/free-resources/ten-common-mistakes-in-leading-transformation.

Aguirre, D., & Alpern, M. (2014). *10 Principles of Leading Change Management.* Retrieved November 24, 2018, from www.strategy-business.com/article/00255.

Alexander, M. (2016). *What's the Difference between Project Management and Change Management?* Retrieved November 23, 2018, from www.cio.com/article/3121685/project-management/what-s-difference-between-project-management-and-change-management.html.

Anderson, D., & Anderson, L. (2014, appeared in Change Leaders Network). *Ten Common Mistakes in Leading Transformational Change.* Retrieved November 23, 2018, from https://changeleadersnetwork.com/wp-content/uploads/2010/09/PC_TenCommonMistakes_v1_101006.pdf.

Annacone, A. (2019). The 4 types of digital transformation. *LinkedIn.com*, June 19, 2019. Retrieved from www.linkedin.com/pulse/4-types-digital-transformation-andrew-annacone/.

The Conference Board. (2021). Change & transformation council. *Conference-Board.com.* Retrieved from https://conference-board.org/councils/change-transformation.

Ewenstein, B., Smith, W., & Sologar, A. (2015). Changing change management. *McKinsey.com*, July 1, 2015. Retrieved from www.mckinsey.com/featured-insights/leadership/changing-change-management.

Galbraith, M. (2018). Don't just tell employees organization changes are coming—explain why. *Harvard Business Review*, October 5, 2018. Retrieved from https://hbr.org/2018/10/dont-just-tell-employees-organizational-changes-are-coming-explain-why.

Gartner. (2019). Change management communication. *Gartner.com.* Retrieved from www.gartner.com/en/corporate-communications/insights/change-communication.

Jacoby, J. (2014). *Blueprint for Building an Internal Change Management Capability.* Retrieved November 23, 2018, from http://blog.emergentconsultants.com/2014/04/16/blueprint-for-building-an-internal-change-management-capability/.

Kotter, J. (1995). *Leading Change: Why Transformation Efforts Fail*. Retrieved November 24, 2018, from https://oupub.etsu.edu/125/newbudgetprocess/documents/leading_change_why_transformation_efforts_fail.pdf.

Lies, J. (2012). Internal communication as power management in change processes: Study on the possibilities and the reality of change communications. *Public Relations Review*, *38*(2), 255–261. https://doi.org/10.1016/j.pubrev.2011.12.015.

McKinsey & Company. (2015). How to beat the transformation odds. *McKinsey.com*, April 1, 2015. Retrieved from www.mckinsey.com/business-functions/organization/our-insights/how-to-beat-the-transformation-odds.

Mind Tools. (2018). *Kotter's 8-Step Change Model: Implementing Change Powerfully and Successfully*. Retrieved November 23, 2018, from www.mindtools.com/pages/article/newPPM_82.htm.

Musselwhite, C., & Plouffe, T. (2010). *Four Ways to Know Whether You Are Ready for Change*. Retrieved November 23, 2018, from Harvard Business Review, https://hbr.org/2010/06/four-ways-to-know-whether-you.

Newell, C. (2018). *Change as an Opportunity: A Strategic Approach to Change Management*. Retrieved from www.forbes.com/sites/forbeshumanresourcescouncil/2018/07/20/change-as-an-opportunity-a-strategic-approach-to-change-management/#3ac7135f2241.

Paton, R. A., & McCalman, J. (2008). *Change Management: A Guide to Effective Implementation* (3rd ed.). Hoboken, NJ: SAGE Publications Ltd.

Pollack, J. (2007). The changing paradigms of project management. *International Journal of Project Management*, *25*(3), 266–274. https://doi.org/10.1016/j.ijproman.2006.08.002.

Prosci. (2018). Best practices in change management. *Prosci.com*. Retrieved November 23, 2018, from www.prosci.com/resources/articles/change-management-best-practices.

Prosci. (2018). Enterprise change management. *Prosci.com*. Retrieved November 23, 2018, from www.prosci.com/resources/articles/enterprise-change-management-overview.

Prosci. (2018). Why change management. *Prosci.com*. Retrieved November 23, 2018, from www.prosci.com/resources/articles/why-change-management.

Stebbins, S. (2017). *Change management methodology and strategic communication: An essential partnership*. Retrieved November 24, 2018, from www.forbes.com/sites/forbescoaches-council/2017/06/19/change-management-methodology-and-strategic-communication-an-essential-partnership/#483a67f27b32.

11

STORYTELLING

Engaging Hearts With Heads and Hands

Business, by design, is about making money. The importance of revenue growth, cost management, margin expansion and, in the case of publicly traded companies, shareholder returns drives a reliance on data, typically in the form of charts and graphs, all in the name of performance.

But charts and graphs depicting profits and losses don't engage or inspire most people who need to deliver those results that illustrate growth. And they certainly don't engage internal and external stakeholders in the essence of whatever brand(s) the organization is in business to grow.

As humans, we naturally crave meaning in our work, purpose in our efforts and a vision for a path that leads to a new and meaningful tomorrow. That's where the power of storytelling comes in. No matter what path we take to become professional communicators, one of the most fundamental skill sets needed is that of a storyteller. This skill remains central to the strategies we develop and the results they generate throughout a communicators career.

For the purposes of engaging employees through communication, it's critical to understand the connection between "*A* story" and "*The* Story." When we talk about "A story," we're talking about understanding, and applying, the successful components of a story to engage readers, viewers or listeners. When we talk about "The Story," we're talking about a master corporate or organizational narrative that clearly inspires employees to be a part of a quest, a mission or shared purpose. Each "A story" ideally should connect to "The Story" as a proof point or illustration of progress on that master narrative. We'll cover more of that later in this chapter.

DOI: 10.4324/9781003024118-11

Why a Story?

Before we get into some detail on either type of story, every communicator should understand why they're important. And part of the answer is based on science.

Research has shown that the daydream, defined as when your mind has nothing to do or occupy it cognitively, is the mind's default state. Each of these daydreams lasts an average of 14 seconds and the average person has about 2,000 daydreams each day, taking up about half of your waking hours. One way to stop someone from daydreaming is to present them with a compelling story. When this happens, people experience zero daydreams per hour as it lulls them into an altered state of consciousness where they are engaged in the story.

Science also tells us how our brains are wired to intake stories. Think about those biology classes we've taken, where we learned that our left brain is all about processing inputs with logic and reason. This is where we analyze, look objectively at things and examine independent or unique parts of the world around us.

Then there's the right brain, where we look at things more randomly, use our intuition, try to see things more holistically as we synthesize all those inputs. It's the part of our brain we use to look at things more subjectively, where we look at the whole, or big picture.

Our right brain interacts with the limbic or emotional brain. It's where those "aha" moments and gut reactions happen when we process a good story. Indeed, our brains are wired to make sense out of those independent pieces we're constantly getting. We are drowning in information but crave meaning.

Paul Zak is a well-known neuroeconomist who has written extensively on this topic based on his research with measuring brain activity of individuals experiencing stories. Zak's research has shown that character-driven stories cause the release of oxytocin in the human brain, which impacts how much people were willing to help others. Additionally, these types of character-driven stories result in people having a better understanding and recall of messages they hear, such as a CEO's message in a town hall or like setting, and that people are "substantially more motivated by their organization's transcendent purposes (how it improves lives) than by its transactional purpose (how it sells goods and services)."

In the simplest of communication, that emotional connection can make a substantial difference. For example, the introduction of a communication consultant can go from "ho-hum" to "aha" simply by telling a short story that makes sense of otherwise-disconnected facts. Consider this less-than-engaging version first:

Meet Stuart Hopkins

He's a communications consultant who previously worked for Carrefour for 17 years and spent an additional 10 years in the energy sector.

He started Imagine Consulting this year and has a graduate degree in Communication from University of Cambridge and a bachelor's degree from Purdue University.

He firmly believes that life's obstacles serve as learning experiences that enrich lives. He also sits on the boards of Boston College and Oxford communication schools. He had a full knee replacement a year ago and works out regularly now.

Re-written in more of a storytelling format, the introduction takes on a very different meaning:

Meet Stuart Hopkins

A year ago, Stuart Hopkins sat in a hospital bed for two weeks, watching an electric device automatically manipulate his newly replaced left knee. Staring at the swollen joint with 43 stitches and listening to the drone of that clicking machine, he came to a turning point.

A year later, he's lost 13.6 kg, he's bench pressing 136 kg and can traverse a mile in under five minutes.

Through love, science, attitude and lessons learned from life, he believes he's living proof that no challenge is too big, and that every story begins with the human desire to make a difference. That's where Imagine Consulting comes in.

Did the second version of the story connect with you in a different way? Perhaps it made it a bit more memorable or connected with something emotional in you? Did it make you want to learn a little more from, or about, Stuart Hopkins? Well, it turns out there's a reason or two behind that reaction.

Research psychologist Dr. Norman Holland, who retired from the University of Florida as a member of the English Department and the university's McKnight Brain Institute, said chemicals in our brains actually change when we are influenced by compelling narrative. Holland has a Ph.D. in English literature from Harvard and studies at the Boston Psychoanalytic Institute, and he said neurological evidence shows our brains organize experience in narrative sequence.

We respond emotionally and intellectually to narratives versus statements of fact. Holland wrote:

We have good psychological evidence that people believe stories momentarily, even when the stories cast doubt on something they know perfectly well is true. And we have neurological evidence that our brains organize experience in narrative sequences. We have every reason, therefore, to believe that we respond both emotionally and intellectually more to narratives than to mere statements of fact.

In the end, employee communicators want, and need, stories to drive action. So, when we think about storytelling in broad communication terms, a well-told story can spur sales, shape a news release that gets wide pickup and prompt stakeholders to comment, like and share through social channels.

For internal stakeholders, stories need to inspire and motivate employees to focus on priorities, behave in ways to support the intended culture and to deliver goods and services to their customers. But unlike a random story off the shelf, stories for employees must answer a fundamental question: "What's in it for them?" If the story answers that question in the right way, engaging hearts and hands gets much easier.

Fundamental Elements of "A story"

Like most things in life, there are different takes on what makes a good story, but few will dispute at least five core elements of a great tale.

The first is a main character, or *hero*—someone who shares similar traits and unfulfilled desires with the audience. It's the character who advances a story, or drives the action. The hero in some corporate narrative could be the company itself. Or the hero in another narrative could be one employee, or literally every employee working to drive the company to its vision.

The second element of every great story is the *catalyst*—a person or force that ultimately will transform the hero's situation. The catalyst in some stories could be a villain or condition that challenges our hero.

When a hero encounters a catalyst, *conflict* ensues—this is the third essential element of a well-constructed story. Our hero must navigate the conflict that the catalyst introduces.

Next, the fourth element is all about our hero reaching a *turning point* (or finish line)—the point in the story where the final transformation takes place.

Our fifth and final element is the *moral* of the story, or the lesson learned, where our hero is transformed, and both hero and audience learn a fundamental truth.

If we think about every memorable book we've read, every short story, or even commercial, these five elements just about always are present. If we applied these elements to a well-known Charles Dickens tale, A Christmas Carol, we can clearly see how these elements work together.

Ebenezer Scrooge clearly is the (albeit unpopular) hero in the story. He is the character who advances the story line. While his negative traits aren't those most of us would admit to sharing, the idea of a character seeking fulfillment through a happier life, and righting wrongs we've committed are among things with which we all can identify.

The catalyst(s) in this tale are the ghosts of Christmas Past, Present and Future— the trio of apparitions who take Scrooge on a journey that highlights what his life has been, what it is, and finally what it will be if he does not change.

Conflict ensues as Scrooge is forced to see his past and present behaviors, and the impact it has on those who surround him. The ghosts of Christmas Past, Present and Future give him no choice but confront the harsh realities of his words and deeds, leaving him to choose the path that will define his final earthly days.

The fourth element, the turning point, is clear in Scrooge's transformation, as he awakens Christmas morning a new man. By confronting his cold heart that has driven his prior actions of cruelty and selfishness, and by understanding the consequences for everyone from Tiny Tim to Bob Cratchit and himself, he has made the choice to change.

Of course, the moral or lesson learned is that each of us has but one life to live, and we are accountable for our time and our actions on Earth, and our impact on others. We all have a choice to make.

Applying Elements of Storytelling to Business

A Christmas Carol is a great example of how critical elements of a well-told story are knit together and can appeal to any reader.

But, when we think about how to apply the elements of storytelling to engaging employees, not just any story will work. It needs to contain all of those elements, while connecting to the organization's mission or purpose, amplifying its values and/or connecting to a specific organizational goal. And most importantly, it must connect to "The Story"—the master corporate narrative that serves as a North Star.

Even the most experienced communicators sometimes forget the importance of this connection. With tight deadlines and a focus on "getting things out the door," we sometimes forget what storytelling can do for us. We forget that the connection to a master narrative is what helps people remember it, and—better yet—tell it or share it again. And, in the age of social media, isn't that the very definition of being viral?

Stories come in all shapes and sizes for businesses, but at the end of the day, they engage employees. Even shorter stories can deliver a moral and connect to an organization's larger purpose. Frito-Lay, a division of global food and beverage giant PepsiCo, had a shared purpose around the empowerment of employees. A brief story used by executives in the company illustrated how senior leaders believed in that sense of empowerment. In this internal example, then-CEO Roger Enrico was used in a story to illustrate that very point.

Frito-Lay

In 1991, after Roger Enrico was put in charge of our Frito-Lay division, he launched a major effort to improve the quality of our snacks.

His goal was to get everyone in the organization to view product quality as their personal responsibility.

The phrase he used in speeches to our management was . . . Make Quality a Reality. It was a message he conveyed at every opportunity . . . in speeches . . . letters and a thousand conversations.

Well . . . a couple of years later, Steve Reinemund, PepsiCo's next CEO, was taking over the Frito-Lay business.

> And on a tour of a plant in Texas, he asked a woman who worked on the production line what she'd do if the quality of the product on that line wasn't up to standard. Without hesitating she said, "I'd shut it down."
>
> Steve was surprised. He asked her why she thought she could do that. And she said . . . "Roger Enrico told me I could." That might not seem remarkable, except that Roger had never been to that plant. He'd never seen that woman . . . or spoken to her. Yet the message he had communicated to the managers above her had gotten through . . . *and made a difference.*
>
> It wasn't just a matter of the right slogan. Roger realized how important it is to communicate in the right context, and in a personal way. He knew that you can't rally human beings solely with profit and volume targets. You need *a noble cause* . . . something that stirs human emotions.

Global financial services company Visa also has used storytelling to engage internal and external stakeholders with its products, and its brand, as the hero. In this short-format example, used for training communication professionals on the power of storytelling, the brand's zero-liability for fraudulent credit card activity, underscores the company's commitment to making financial services simple, fast and pain-free, using the voice of the customer.

Visa

> Opaqua Hrundilli, a 43-year-old bakery owner in Cameroon, had a BIG opportunity with a customer and intended to order 40 custom-made cake molds through an on-line supplier.
>
> But as she made her order, it was rejected—indicating she'd reached her credit limit.
>
> After calling VISA, Ms. Hrundilli learned of fraudulent activity on her account that took ALL her remaining credit.
>
> "I was overwhelmed and desperate to find a supplier who could deliver what I needed. Thankfully, VISA's zero-liability guarantee meant that I wasn't liable for the fraudulent purchases and my credit was restored immediately. And . . . I didn't have to spend any of my time sorting out the problem."
>
> Zero liability. Zero additional problems. Zero never felt so good.

With an understanding of the elements of what makes "A" great story, and why it needs to connect to "The Story," let's better understand what a master corporate narrative is and why we need it.

The Corporate Narrative: A North Star Story

The corporate narrative essentially is the big picture that explains the organizations' reason for being. A shared sense of purpose, told in a compelling story, will engage and inspire employees and all other stakeholders. And most importantly, it is the consistent connection point for every proof point—or "A story"—that will be told.

This kind of narrative puts the organization in the role of the hero, the catalyst is the condition or problem that the company exists to solve or defeat, or the value it creates for customers and other stakeholders. The conflicts can be market conditions, competitors, disruptive technologies, regulatory rulings, social discourse or a wide range of hurdles that the organization must address in advancing its purpose.

But what's different about the corporate narrative is that it doesn't have an ending. Employee communication leader Shel Holtz, in describing the attributes of the corporate narrative in his blog, *A new model for employee communication*, said it well. "Not that the strategic narrative is just any story. It requires skill to tell, especially considering that it has no end. It has a beginning (where we came from and how we got where we are) and a middle (where we are now, what we stand for, and more). Instead of an end, though, it has a vision of where we're headed and how we'll get there," he wrote.

The master narrative has many purposes, whether it's explaining change, grounding employees in a crisis or motivating them to tackle a new challenge. Whatever words are ultimately created to explain it, ideally, it will connect employee's heads and hearts with their hands and the work they do.

The narrative isn't a book, or a 10,000-word missive; it's a simple, relatively short story of a few hundred words built with insights from a range of stakeholders, and often aligned—sometimes with a fair amount of pain—with senior leaders, affinity groups and even focus groups of internal and external stakeholders. Why? How it "plays in Peoria" is important to understanding before it is widely circulated.

The story can, and likely will, change over time, so communicators must be mindful of changes that require adjustments in the narrative. Mergers and acquisitions can impact things such as customer focus, portfolio priorities and even articulated values—all of which typically factor into a corporate narrative.

In many cases, a corporate narrative may exist, but have little, if any, traction, largely reflecting the lack of use in ongoing communications. CEB Global Research (now Gartner) found that even when relatively small percentages of employees are aware that their corporate narrative exists, more than half do not choose to use it.

That's where employee communicators are needed; to amplify the volume and to tie "The Story" to every "A story." That includes every initiative, anecdote, change initiative, product or service launch or news story that they touch. It's not about cutting and pasting the narrative at the beginning or ending of every story. It's about artfully inserting common consistent language from the narrative in the communications we touch.

It's also about helping others learn how to do the same. CEB Global Research supported the idea of providing the big picture narrative, quantifying that its use increases 48% when it reflects the values and beliefs of the employees, connects with outcomes that matter to employees and is relevant to the work they do.

CEB concluded that one high-level version of a narrative doesn't deliver this kind of employee uptake. Leaders need tools, training and permission to make it their own, and their teams need the same.

Mining for Stories and Counseling Leaders on Using Them

In organizational communication, where do great stories come from? In short, the answer is everywhere. Employee communicators must develop an "ear" for finding them through conversations and sharp listening. Companies with customer, or consumer response functions have built-in story-collection capabilities. Sales organizations, in their connections with customers and clients about products and services, often are rich sources, too. And HR professionals often have great skills listening for, and sharing, great stories about employees, their work with teams and customers. The key is to be active in mining for stories that advance the company's vision and mission and connecting them to the corporate master narrative.

Leaders, in particular, benefit from understanding the value of short stories and learning how to share them. If they're not sharing stories about others in their organizations, they may want to tap their own personal experiences. That can work, but only if they're carefully guided about how personal stories best connect with employees.

Humility is essential for credibility. Leaders who highlight their personal accomplishments with one success after another quickly lose interest from their teams. Stories of their failures and the consequences are what broader groups of employees can identify with. People learn more from their executives' mistakes than from their successes. Admitting the negatives of life's lessons and how they overcame them is what brings real, identifiable emotion into the storytelling experience. Importantly, it brings a real authenticity to every executive who strives to become an effective storyteller.

Pittsburgh International Airport (2019)

Pittsburgh International Airport, part of the Allegheny County Airport Authority (ACAA) in Southwestern Pennsylvania, embarked in 2019 on a multi-year transformation initiative—the Terminal Modernization Program. A new, modernized terminal and parking facilities, when completed, will be the most visible sign of change to travelers, but the airport needed to bring its internal stakeholders on a change journey, too. Employees, contractors, vendors, police and fire employees on site all had to understand, and believe in, the corporate narrative. So, the communication team developed one, aligned it with senior leaders and provided storytelling training as they kicked off a clear and compelling narrative. They'd previously launched a five-year strategic plan they called "Smart Plan Forward." The narrative they used to incorporate their plan into an engaging story went like this:

> For the past five years, we've been transforming ACAA to restore our position as a leader in aviation and as a catalyst for economic growth in our region.
> We've come a long way, with smart people and targeted innovation. Now we need to go further, faster and with even more intelligence than before.
> That's why we announced our Smart Plan Forward, which is a five-year journey with innovative ways of working, inspiring people and a clear destination: A Smarter Airport.
> We are redefining what it means to be an airport. More than an airport operator, Smarter Airport encompasses everything and everyone that goes into delighting travelers, and getting aircraft into the air safely, on time, and to their destination. Smarter Airport means a modernized physical space, cutting-edge technology and stakeholders—ACAA employees, airlines, tenants and the local community—all working together to put our customers first.
> We're building our Smarter Airport now, and we will pioneer the next generation of aviation leadership in the process.

Applying the Narrative in Ongoing Communications

Employees at the airport were made aware of new training that impacted every internal stakeholder. As the airport launched its Customer Care pilot program, communications leveraged the master narrative yet again. Elements of the master narrative are used in day-to-day communications to employees; the examples below—with those elements shown in italicized type—illustrate how they did it.

Customer Care

> For the past four years, we have been transforming *the ACAA to restore our position as a leader in aviation and a driver of economic growth for our region.*
> *We've come a long way. But we need to go further, faster and with more intelligence.*
> *We need to redefine what it means to be an airport.*

That's why we announced our Smart Plan Forward: a five-year journey with innovation, inspired people and a *clear destination—A Smarter Airport.*

It's why we're *enabling, empowering and equipping our people to innovate* and collaborate in the name of change. And it's why we are taking a customer-first approach in everything we do.

With that in mind, Pittsburgh International Airport is beginning a pilot training program that's anchored in what we call social customer care. It's essentially a way of thinking—and acting—that takes our care for customers to an entirely new level—not just for our airport but also for our industry.

We will set the industry standard for customer care, and our expectation is that every ACAA employee will demonstrate this new way of thinking and acting. Over time, we'll ensure every ACAA employee receives customer care training and learns new ways to engage and help people coming to our airport for any reason.

We're working to develop this first-of-a-kind program that will help our employees deliver unprecedented levels of service to travelers. The multi-module training program, which trains employees to use effective communication techniques and specialized on-demand mobile and digital tools to care for customers, is unlike any other airport program in the United States.

This combination of new technology, processes and people skills is a perfect example of how a *Smarter Airport looks, feels and acts—enabled, empowered and equipped* people seeking out innovations to help ACAA win, teaming with others to turn problems into opportunities, and delivering an improved experience for airport stakeholders.

Another example of using a master narrative for ongoing communications came in the form of a template, which the airport used to invite select employees to a variety of training opportunities.

Training

Our commitment to creating the *Smarter Airport of the future is well under way,* and in tangible ways. We have change projects already launched, in the process of kicking off, or about to launch.

Managing each and every one of these change initiatives requires both existing and emerging skill sets—not just for current leaders but also for future leaders.

We're committed to empowering our teams to solve problems collaboratively and innovatively. And we need to equip employees at every level with critical skills and tools that help them grow as professionals and help ACAA ideate, design and implement change.

We've said that *enabled, empowered and equipped people seeking innovative change* will help ACAA win. So, we're acting on that belief with you.

We believe in your potential, and we want to invest in you. That's why we're asking you to participate in our upcoming course on _____(Course name).

You'll receive more information on the specifics of this training. But it's important to understand it's one of many ways we're empowering you to team with others to turn problems into opportunities and deliver an improved experience for airport stakeholders.

An HR Function Narrative in Practice: United Technologies (2018)

Some master narratives, while tying to a corporate narrative, may have more finite applications. Prior to its merger with Raytheon Corporation, United Technologies Corporation (UTC) in 2018 made the decision to transform its global HR function. The impact of creating a shared services organization, changing HR business professional roles and responsibilities, establishing call centers and driving new behaviors for HR services among employees, managers and HR professionals required a clear and compelling change narrative. The multi-year transformation benefitted from consistent language that tied each unique action to a consistent story.

UTC started the introduction of the change narrative by taking a step back, explaining why the narrative was needed and the value it would deliver for the company.

> *Every effective change initiative begins with a clear and compelling story: a narrative that serves as a guide for every decision and action. The reality is that UTC's HR function is already well into its story, but without the benefit of setting up its big-picture narrative. So that's what we're doing with this HR Transformation narrative.*
>
> *Think of this narrative as the story we want every UTC employee and leader to both understand and believe in. Telling this corporate story—in and of itself—won't deliver on that. But it's a critical part of the broader communication strategy.*
>
> *This broad story is THE story to which all other stories about UTC's HR transformation should connect. In written and spoken word, it is home base for any update, request or proof point that serves as evidence of HR's commitment to driving change.*
>
> *Our transformation story clearly connects to our business priorities. The world is changing FAST, and stakeholder expectations are rising. Customers want innovative, integrated solutions—faster. Employees want a workplace that gives them meaningful work; where they are treated with respect and expectations are clear; where they have the tools they need to make work easier; and where they have the opportunity for—and a clear path to—growth. Shareowners want greater growth, too. That's why we've organized ourselves differently and are transforming how we work. We own the tools and processes that identify, grow and unleash the full potential of our employees.*

> *Anyone communicating about HR's Transformation can, and should, lift from this story, and add to it with each future story. That's how we connect "A" story, to the "THE" story of HR change at UTC.*

The resulting narrative—while short—was supported with a clear message architecture that tied to its existing HR brand.

The World of Storytelling: More Than What We See on the Surface

Hearing, reading and seeing a great story isn't as simple, or as easy, as some believe. Directly behind the emotion that a great story evokes is very real discipline. Yes, storytelling is an art form, but communicators must put some discipline around it to ensure it engages its intended audience. There are a lot of different "models" for what constitutes a story. But most of them will agree that there's a hero, a catalyst (character or event), conflict or juxtaposition, resolution and a moral to the story. Every communicator should ask himself or herself, "Is there a story here? Does it have these elements in it? Do I care?"

It's about a mindset. With everything we write, review and/or approve, employee communicators must remind themselves that a real story embedded in otherwise drab content will increase the odds of employees engaging with it. It should have a clear, compelling point and—even better—an actionable response connected to it. Science shows that our brains are wired to re-engage when we hear/see the words, "I have a story for you." So, as we draft, edit and route content through approvals, we have to ask: Is there even a story in this work that can engage our employees? It can if it's simple, contains something unexpected, is concrete and credible and taps into emotions of the reader, listener or viewer.

In the business world, the ability to tell many stories to employees—and on the continuum—is critical. They're all part of one, big ongoing story. Each "A story" might ultimately be viewed as the next "chapter" of the master narrative.

Some communicators are just plain wired to be better storytellers than others. But that doesn't mean we all can't get better by re-framing our approach to the craft, applying discipline, exploring ways to tap into our creative capabilities and—yes—even playing around with it. The idea of play may be anathema to some of the more financially driven in the world of business, but unless a communicator plays with storytelling, the odds of getting any better at it are against them. We can "play" by reading a story we've written out loud, or sharing with a colleague. Ask them for feedback. Ask them what's missing or what didn't make sense? What was out of order? Remember that the best stories are those that cut through the noise, feel real as opposed to abstract concepts and capture employees on an emotional level. That's a story worth telling.

Profile: Daniel Pierce

Director of Global Commercial Vehicle Communications
Ford Motor Company
Detroit, MI, USA

Career Bio

From my first day working on the corporate side of communications (I started my career at an agency), I learned that no matter what PR role I played in a company, I always needed to speak with, or keep, our employees informed. That lesson stayed with me throughout my career. Whether I was launching Budweiser in foreign countries or working on autonomous vehicles, employees are a key audience that needs to be made aware of the work you are doing.

My job is to create awareness and excitement for Ford's plans to build and launch a self-driving service. A key part of this responsibility is educating people on why self-driving vehicles can be a safe, trusted means for transportation. When you look at the people/audiences I need to speak with, they include consumers in our launch markets, policy makers, investors, potential business partners and employees. My specific responsibilities would be to develop story ideas that help create awareness for our service, write messaging for the executive team to use internally and externally about our business and engage with the news media on a regular basis to pitch them stories.

Storytelling as a Strategic Tool for Engaging Employees

There is a lot of hype around self-driving vehicles being driven by many companies in this space who want to be perceived as leading in the development of this technology. This hype has resulted in some pretty lofty expectations from media and consumers about when the technology will launch and with what capabilities. Ford didn't want to be a part of contributing to the hype cycle when it came to launching self-driving vehicles but, at the same time, wanted to make sure our key audiences (employees, consumers, policy makers, investor and potential business partners) knew we had a plan and were taking a very strategic approach to building our self-driving business.

We solved the problem by developing a communications narrative that we stayed true to when developing story ideas. In researching Ford and competitors' plans for building a self-driving service, we recognized that Ford's plan to build a self-driving service was more holistic than others.

While some competitors were looking at developing just the technology, Ford was looking at the tech, vehicle integration, fleet operations and more when it came to launching a self-driving service. We developed a narrative that showed Ford was best positioned in the self-driving space because we were bringing all these pieces together. When we looked at stories to tell, if they didn't support positioning Ford as an orchestrator or convener of all the different parts needed for a self-driving service—we didn't tell the story.

I think I learned that staying true to a narrative will ultimately lead to successful communications, and that without a narrative, you are just creating stories for stories' sake. The narrative helped us tie everything together. Without that strong narrative we had stories we could tell, they just didn't seem to be as connected.

Results were more than just story placements. We saw that our narrative resonates both internally and externally. Our employees started thinking about what they were doing on a daily basis to help bring all the pieces of the self-driving future together. They would give us stories that they thought could help us. Externally, we saw media and policy makers start referring to Ford as best positioned to launch a self-driving service because we were taking a holistic approach.

My advice would be to identify a space you or your company can own and own it. Own it by developing messaging and stories that consistently support that space. Doing so will resonate both internally and externally as long as you stay true to that narrative.

Case Study

ASTELLAS PHARMA DRIVES INNOVATION STORY WITH STRATEGIC NARRATIVE

Situation

Japanese multinational pharmaceutical company Astellas needed a new way to tell its innovation story. The company's previous model of using only in-house development teams had become a thing of the past, and it needed to find a way to show how the company was looking outwards—for high-quality partnerships with academia and biotechnology companies, creating a new competitive frontier in the industry.

That's why the communication team developed the Astellas Scientific Innovation Narrative toolkit, a first of its kind initiative. It was developed to help Astellas leaders deliver powerful and compelling strategic communication, internally and externally. The narrative brought together a complex matrix of different innovation functions under one messaging platform, across geographies and languages, to describe scientific innovation at Astellas.

Astellas' leaders were not equipped with consistent, strategically aligned and engaging messaging to help them articulate, with one single voice and *global* story, the company's approach to scientific innovation and pipeline. As a result, before the Astellas Scientific Innovation Narrative, there was poor internal and external understanding of, and support for, the company's innovation approach, R&D strategy and pipeline. Key stakeholders reported that Astellas' R&D strategy and pipeline seemed disparate and non-strategic.

A single and compelling narrative was identified as a critical communications resource that could enable Astellas and its leaders to build a corporate scientific reputation for delivering value, differentiating themselves and shine in a fiercely competitive environment. Ultimately, a clear scientific narrative could help enhance the perception of Astellas as a "partner of choice" among potential innovation partners and a "company of choice" for prospective employees, engaging and uniting the organization behind a common purpose.

While the communication team identified both internal and external targets, this summary focuses on internal audiences. To be clear, external targets included existing and prospective biotechnology innovation partners, business analysts, trade/business and medical/scientific media.

Primary internal audiences include Astellas senior scientific leaders, communications heads and Investor Relations (IR) professionals. Within the Astellas organization, this includes stakeholders such as the chief executive officer (CEO), chief medical officer (CMO), heads of therapy areas and scientific functions, business development (BD) and IR teams, as well as corporate, regional and affiliate communication leads. These groups were all engaged in the development of this project and, after finalization, were equipped with the resources. This ensured both alignment with the value of the narrative's use across all internal and external communication touchpoints and, for the first time, the same company-wide compelling innovation story was being told.

The other primary internal audience included current and prospective employees. Retention and attracting talent is critical to a pharma company's success, with current and prospective employees expecting to maintain a clear, ongoing understanding of the progress and success of the company in its R&D endeavors. Those stakeholders also needed to understand the strategy behind the company direction and any organizational developments. A compelling narrative would connect current employees' responsibilities and daily activities to the company vision and strategy—key for driving employee engagement and loyalty. A narrative would also enable strong communications, through media, HR and other channels to attract new talent (employed by competitors/academia) into the Astellas innovation organization.

Campaign

With those insights in mind, the communication team set the goals of enabling Astellas to differentiate itself and shine in an extremely competitive and challenging external environment; build and maintain Astellas' corporate scientific brand; improve internal and external understanding of Astellas' R&D strategy and pipeline; enhance the perception of Astellas as "company of choice" among potential innovation partners and current or prospective employees; and connect Astellas employees, at all levels, to the corporate vision, strategy, activities and values.

The solution clearly pointed in the direction of a scientific innovation narrative—which the team designed to meet the challenges and opportunities of the new innovation landscape in which the company operates. It reflected a collaborative and inclusive development process, combining broad internal leader insights with in-depth secondary research to create a unique, differentiated corporate scientific identity and a core scientific story that is supported by fully referenceable supporting messages and proof points.

The narrative toolkit included a comprehensive set of multimedia tools, developed to suit a variety of communication opportunities and channels and provide leaders with the foundation to effectively and consistently communicate (see Figure 11.2).

The kit included a one-pager (summarizing Astellas' core scientific innovation story); a PowerPoint presentation (clearly and visually presenting the core story and pipeline); printed booklets (showcasing the narrative PowerPoint slides and core story); an animated video (bringing the core story to life, featuring the voices of Astellas leaders from across the globe); and a master message document (the core story alongside fully referenced supporting messages and proof points for in-depth and validated messaging). These tools were intended to be customizable, enabling leaders to select and tailor relevant messaging for their specific needs, audience and channel. Full guidance on how to use the tools is provided to leaders in an in-depth guidance and FAQ document.

Strategy and content for developing the narrative key messages included detailed internal and external environmental analysis, including in-depth competitor and stakeholder research of the external communication environment (scientific innovation teams, IR, biotech organizations, university technology transfer teams); internal interviews and research across the organization (early discovery, clinical development). Both sets of inputs ensured authentic voices formed the core of the messaging. The narrative describes, and demonstrates with tangible examples, how Astellas takes a collaborative, "Science First" approach to innovation to ensure it delivers value for patients. That also ensured a connection to the Astellas' corporate

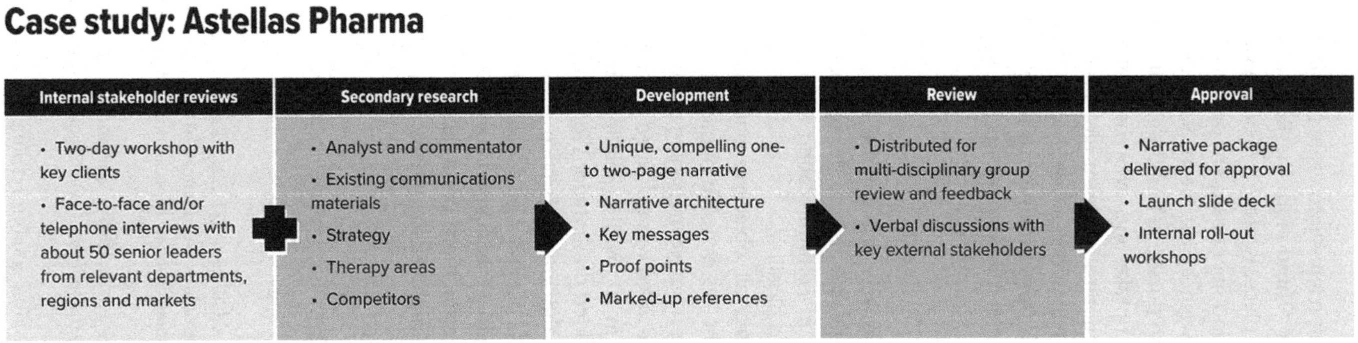

Case study: Astellas Pharma

Internal stakeholder reviews	Secondary research	Development	Review	Approval
• Two-day workshop with key clients • Face-to-face and/or telephone interviews with about 50 senior leaders from relevant departments, regions and markets	• Analyst and commentator • Existing communications materials • Strategy • Therapy areas • Competitors	• Unique, compelling one-to two-page narrative • Narrative architecture • Key messages • Proof points • Marked-up references	• Distributed for multi-disciplinary group review and feedback • Verbal discussions with key external stakeholders	• Narrative package delivered for approval • Launch slide deck • Internal roll-out workshops

FIGURE 11.2 The communications team at Astellas used a clearly defined process, from research to approvals, to develop a compelling narrative to tell its innovation story.

vision: "Turning innovative science into value for patients." Key messaging included content such as "Throughout the R&D process, from bench to clinic and into the marketplace, we take a 'Science First' approach to optimize the chances of creating new treatment options and value for patients with high unmet needs. Science First means we focus on the best science, empower the best talent to pursue it, and develop it at the best location."

To ensure maximum uptake and awareness of the narrative among Astellas leaders, the communication team globally launched the narrative toolkit in 2019. The launch included a CMO, company-wide email and URL to download the materials from the intranet, targeted "desk-drops" of the booklets and a series of leader rollout meetings across functions and regions.

Results

The results of the initiative were unparalleled across Astellas, and the narrative has become an invaluable asset to the company. Leaders report that they are more confident in communicating Astellas' corporate scientific position, R&D strategy and pipeline.

Communicators reported all objectives and targets were met and/or exceeded: page views of the kits materials numbered 2,192 from the intranet page (vs. a goal of 500). The narrative messaging also was incorporated in Astellas scientific job listings, and video was uploaded to the company's careers site.

The content was used in 10 Investor Relations presentations and scripts (vs. a goal of six) and included presentations for Astellas R&D Days, UBS disclosures and JPMorgan Healthcare Conferences. Externally, the narrative was used in 14 events (vs. a goal of eight world-leading events) and was featured prominently in four influential media interviews.

Internally, 10 leader presentations (vs. a goal of five) featured the narrative and included several employee town halls.

Source: IABC Gold Quill Awards (2020)

Bibliography

Gartner. (2017). *Gartner Executive Guidance Q1 2017 Edition.* Retrieved February 26, 2021, from www.gartner.com/en/executive-guidance/2017-q1-edition.

Gottschall, J. (2013). *The Storytelling Animal: How Stories Make Us Human* (1st ed.). Boston, MA: Mariner Books.

Holland, N. N. (2009). *Literature and the Brain.* Washington, DC: The PsyArt Foundation.

Holtz, P. (2020). *A New Model for Employee Communication.* Retrieved from https://holtz.com/blog.

Zak, P. (2014). Why your brain loves good storytelling. *Harvard Business Review*, October 28, 2014.

12

THE EVOLUTION OF EMPLOYEE COMMUNICATION TO EMPLOYEE ENGAGEMENT

Unlike the early days of employee communication—which generally featured one-directional media broadcasting the company's agenda—contemporary employee communicators have evolved to use far more dynamic and strategic models. Employee communication professionals today understand that connecting with employees demands multi-directional exchanges between employees, their peers, their leaders and a range of other stakeholders. Continuous feedback loops are used more than ever to understand how internal stakeholders are responding to content, and measurement has become commonplace. Communication that encourages employees to engage with content, respond to it and apply it, has become the standard.

As critical as it is for employees to engage with content, it's a means to another end that carries far more importance for business leaders. CEOs and other C-suite executives simply don't care about how many articles have been published in the company newsletter or how many team members attended the latest town hall.

What leaders care about is engagement with work, and that's where employee communicators increasingly are spending their time, energy and financial resources. This shift fundamentally illustrates how practitioners have moved from roles as writers and reporters to roles as connectors and engagement professionals.

Employee engagement has often been described in the corporate world as the special sauce that prompts "discretionary effort"—that extra effort any employee chooses to make in the work he or she does. Whether it's working extra hours, cleaning equipment or work surfaces when no one asks, or spending that extra moment connecting with a customer, engagement ideally reflects a deeper commitment from an employee to the organization's mission, vision and values.

There are as many definitions for engagement as there are organizations that strive to improve it. However, without a solid definition, organizations trying to

DOI: 10.4324/9781003024118-12

understand employee engagement through measurement are doomed to failure. In this case, *employee engagement* should be defined as using the following concepts as identified in a literature review of the concept by William H. Macey and Benjamin Schneider. In their article "The Meaning of Employee Engagement," the authors lay out several elements that traditionally make up the measurement of employee engagement, which include job satisfaction, organizational commitment, psychological empowerment and job involvement. Based on this historical examination, they come up with a definition of engagement as a state that involves "a strong affective tone connoting, at a minimum, high levels of involvement (passion and absorption) in the work and the organization (pride and identity) as well as affective energy (enthusiasm and alertness) and a sense of self-presence in the work."

In their article, Macey and Schneider created a framework for understanding employee engagement. Using that as a basis, we've expanded upon that to create a model around communicating about employee engagement (see Figure 12.1).

Employee engagement is viewed as a critical driver of business success in today's competitive marketplace. If employee engagement is done well, it can help companies retain employees and increase their production and inspire loyalty among customers.

It's neither easy nor common place to keep employees engaged with work. Every year over the last decade, global analytics and advisory company Gallup performed an employee engagement meta-analysis looking at employee engagement and performance data from more than 100,000 teams worldwide. Based on the analysis of this data, Gallup in 2019 reported that worldwide only 15% of employees are engaged. In the United States, just 35% of the workforce was engaged, which it defined as being involved in, enthusiastic about, and committed to their work and workplace. Gallup reports its analytics show that employee engagement drives business improvement, from lower turnover to higher customer engagement to higher profitability. Specifically, it reports higher employee engagement leads to:

- 41% lower absenteeism
- 24% lower turnover (high-turnover organizations)
- 59% lower turnover (low-turnover organizations)
- 28% less shrinkage
- 70% fewer employee safety incidents
- 58% fewer patient safety incidents
- 40% fewer quality incidents (defects)
- 10% higher customer metrics
- 17% higher productivity
- 20% higher sales
- 21% higher profitability

Creating and deploying tools with specific questions designed to assess engagement, most often in partnership with Human Resources.

Tie engagement assessment tools (e.g. Pulse Surveys and/or Organizational Health Surveys) with specific desired business outcomes (e.g. increased productivity or reduced voluntary attrition).

Assessing and influencing survey tools and intended business outcomes to determine where communications can be most impactful.

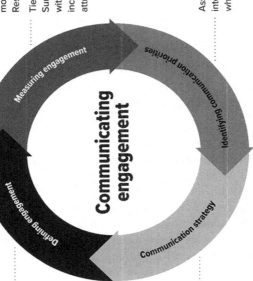

Trait: Employee positive views of life and work (proactive personality, autotelic personality, trait positive affect, conscientiousness)

State: Feelings of energy, absorption (satisfaction, involvement, commitment and empowerment)

Behavioral Extra-role behavior (organizational citizenship, proactive/personal initiative, role expansion, adaptive)

Communication strategy, objectives and tactics to include segmented employee targets, messaging/content, creative, cadence, sequencing, channel choices, measurement, analytics and reporting.

FIGURE 12.1 Communicating in ways that strengthen employee engagement is for any organization; demands a clear definition of what engagement is for any organization; defining how it will be measured; and articulating and how communication actions contribute to business outcomes. Together, these priorities will inform a clear engagement communication strategy.

To be clear, employee communication plays a significant role in influencing engagement. In the wake of the global pandemic and the murder of George Floyd in 2020, U.S. employee engagement spiked to an almost 20-year high of 38% in May, only to drop to 31% by July—the most significant drop in the Gallup's history of measuring employee engagement.

While initial communication and management attention to Covid-19 response increased employee engagement early on in 2020, Gallup offered three explanations for the rapid decline that followed. First, societal unrest following the killing of George Floyd made it more difficult for leaders to attend to performance-related engagement elements, with diversity, equity and inclusion challenges heightened like never before. Second, Gallup said employers had taken their focus off—or had been unclear in—their plans, as businesses within many states began to reopen in June 2020. And finally, previously laid-off employees returned to the workforce with slightly lower engagement than those who continued to be employed. All three of these reasons for decreasing engagement could be positively influenced by strategic employee communication.

Measuring Employee Engagement

Just as there are different definitions for employee engagement, there are different metrics for measuring it (see Chapter 4 for more information on measurement). More often than not, organizations use organizational health surveys, and/or pulse surveys (used more frequently, but with smaller samples—often between one- to two-year cycles for broader organizational health surveys) to assess employees engagement levels and which drivers are, and are not, working.

This is where differences in measurement begin to clearly emerge. HR functions typically hold responsibility for survey design and selecting specific items to measure that they believe best reflect engagement. For some companies, it's asking employees how happy they are in their jobs (job satisfaction). In others, it may be a combination of questions or metrics that assess understanding of the organization's mission, purpose and value, trust in leadership, belief in transparent communication or other items.

For employee communicators, it's critical to understand what metric, or set of metrics, are deemed critical for defining employee engagement in their organizations and then assessing how communications can best support improvement with any, and all.

For example, if transparency in communications is a component of an organization's definition of engagement, employee communicators should be looking at, and influencing, the clarity and truthfulness of communications. Or if metrics don't look good for understanding the company's purpose, mission and values, an employee communication strategy targeted to those content areas can yield important, measurable results.

The bottom line is that communicators need to know what their organizations value for assessing engagement and align communications and strategies to those priority areas. They need to be fully engaged in organizational health and pulse survey measurement efforts. Ideally, that includes inserting a question or two that is specific to communications that employees receive. Often, questions in those kinds of surveys are closely guarded by owners in other functions, so communicators must be clear, concise and persuasive in explaining why communication-specific questions must be included.

Beyond measurement and related communication strategy development driven directly by communication functions, there are many areas within most organizations that can be included in employee engagement communication efforts—many of them "owned" by other functions, especially HR.

Engageable Moments

Engageable moments, identified by Watson Wyatt's WorkUSA, include both formal and informal activities where employers can motivate and provide direction for employees through strategic communication. Formally, they include processes such as recruitment and onboarding, goal setting and performance reviews, training and senior leadership communication. We cover more on those types of employee communication in Chapter 13, where we delve into the world of HR.

Informal communication opportunities are those where middle- and front-line managers can have a considerable amount of influence. Coaching, mentoring, career development discussions and ongoing performance feedback represent critical interactions where communications can enable progress or, if done poorly, derail performance. These kinds of communication opportunities are significant and often time consuming as they require more one-on-one and small-group communication skill training and support. All too often, business people acquire these kinds of interpersonal communication skills through observation but don't receive concrete insights about how to do it well.

Communicators, working independently or in partnership with training and organization development professionals, can help close gaps with interpersonal skills needs through well-crafted tools that explain communication concepts and best practices, and apply them. Beyond introductory training, communicators can play a pivotal role in equipping management with ongoing tools, content and training that empower them to better lead their teams, manage change and coach individuals. This could also include communication around recognition programs, company social events or even personal crises.

As we covered in Chapter 9 on executive communication, employee communicators can play a significant role in supporting managers—and consequently engagement—through supporting leaders with communication skill development. Whether delivered directly by employee communicators or contracted with firms to do training, management can significantly improve its communication skills through training on topics such as:

- Writing for better communications;
- Understanding interpersonal communication and small group dynamics;
- Presentation training;
- Communicating to influence; and
- Storytelling, among others.

Typically, identifying communication training needs and selecting delivery models for that training is done in partnership with HR and its organizational development professionals.

Communication Methods Supporting Employee Engagement

Beyond training managers and delivering broad-scale communication channels, savvy employee communicators understand the power of both face-to-face and digital collaboration and feedback channels to prompt employee engagement. Often, these can take the following forms:

- Small group meetings, often weekly or every other week in frequency, allow for issues to be aired, ideas to be discussed or immediate feedback to be gathered. "Stand up meetings"—often used in manufacturing environments—might occur even more frequently, even daily before shifts start. Managers can use those live meetings to deliver information specific to the day's priorities, share more strategic priorities and recognize individual or team performance.
- Digital communication channels offer important capabilities that go well beyond disseminating news, information or insights about organizational priorities.
  - Employee listening platforms allow communicators to survey workers, gather comments and suggestions and enable HR professionals to conduct exit interviews.
  - Social media and mobile application tools can prompt employees to discuss issues, share ideas, conduct surveys and vote on issues. Increasingly, many organizations use social media platforms, such as Facebook and Twitter, to crowd-source employee preferences on topics items, like critical employee questions, and vote on them for inclusion in live town hall Q&As with CEOs and other executives. Thus, employees can influence content and shape agendas for communication events planned for them.
  - Video blogs (vlogs) and blogs can engage employees on both internal priorities and external (customer) trends and feedback that can be used to improve business performance.

- The global pandemic of 2020 dramatically accelerated the use of video-conferencing and internal social media platforms that prompted more remote collaboration and engagement. While the live/in-person experience is most widely preferred, employee communicators were put on a steep learning curve during the global pandemic to create more inclusive experiences for CEO global town halls—held remotely.

What's important to understand is that, just like all other employee communication agendas, strategic solutions that support employee engagement demand thoughtful planning, clear messaging and a range of internal channel solutions.

Connecting Employee Engagement to the Employee Value Proposition and Employee Experience

With a general understanding of what employee engagement is and how communications can influence it, communicators are better prepared to support their organizations with two specific communication agendas that directly tie to it.

The *employee value proposition* (EVP) and the *employee experience* (EE or EX) have become increasingly important topics that management, HR, IT, Legal, Corporate Affairs and Communications each can influence in significant ways. Further, they set the agenda for, and assess the impact of, efforts to attract, retain and grow talent.

According to Global HR consulting firm Mercer, in order to attract and retain a workforce for the future, employers must create a meaningful EVP that delivers a compelling employee experience and meets the full range of their employees' needs.

While compensation and benefits remain critical contributors to an employer's EVP, Mercer maintains those elements are easily replicated in a competitive environment and expensive to change. Mercer's research says employees want more.

- 79% of adults trust employers to give advice on planning, saving and investing.
- 78% of employees would work on a contract basis, and 51% want more flexible work options.
- 51% of employees want more equity in pay and promotion decisions.

A more holistic view of EVP should include focus on career development, total well-being, purpose and belonging. All are highly correlated with employee outcomes, including motivation, advocacy, commitment and intent to stay with their employers, according to Mercer.

When communicators are engaged in efforts to drive awareness and understanding for anything from ethics and compliance training to philanthropy to corporate social reputation (CSR), they are, in fact, influencing the EVP.

To new or prospective employees, the EVP often is used as an "employer brand"—meaning it represents an organization's promise in its effort to recruit new talent. That promise ideally is something that is both real (we'll get to that later in this chapter related to employee experience) and aspirational, meaning it illustrates standards or principles the organization holds itself accountable to delivering. Done well, it delivers a compelling answer to the question "Why should I work for your company?"

Consider Nike's answer to that question:

Nike

When you join NIKE, Inc., you're part of the family. To inspire greatness inside and outside work, we invest in our culture and offer employees competitive health, financial, security and work-life benefits. From opportunities for career development to personalized benefit options, we want all who join our team to realize their full potential.

Since employee communicators often are engaged with developing EVPs, we can deconstruct what's actually in them. Ideally, an EVP includes content on five core topics: compensation, benefits, career growth, work environment and culture. Each of these elements covers a broad range of choices that every employer makes to be competitive. From flexible work hours and location to valued management skills, articulated values and culture (What's it *really* like to work here?), saying something meaningful, and doing it and concisely, can be a significant task.

A well-crafted EVP begins with solid research on what the organization currently offers its employees, and how employees feel about their experience with the company. It also includes a clear picture of that "perfect employee"—including their values, skills and motivation, along with what would drive that ideal candidate's decision to work for the company. That naturally would lead to the creation of a customized expression of the EVP that is unique to the company and includes the components mentioned earlier.

The ongoing use of an EVP presents communicators and recruiters with an infinite number of ways to further customize its use. For example, recruiting for roles that come with remote-work options, communicators might adjust the messaging to focus more on that offering than, say, compensation. Just as there are master narratives and supporting stories for corporations, the EVP can originate from a single master story but be customized for specific uses (see Chapter 11 on storytelling for a refresher).

While there are five core elements for EVPs, some companies may choose not to include them all. Consider Google's EVP, which makes no mention of compensation and benefits. Rather, its focus is on diverse talent and "big thinkers."

Google

There's no one kind of Googler, so we're always looking for people who can bring new perspectives and life experiences to our teams. If you're looking for a place that values your curiosity, passion, and desire to learn, if you're seeking colleagues who are big thinkers eager to take on fresh challenges as a team, then you're a future Googler.

Employee Experience

If the EVP is the face of any organization to new, prospective employees, we can think of the employee experience as the reality for current employees—how that value proposition plays out after employees are hired. Said another way, EVP can be viewed as marketing an organization's promise, while the employee experience is the product.

Increasingly, organizations are taking far deeper, sustained and integrated looks at how the experience of current employees matches up to words on the website.

Employee communicators can, and do, influence significant components of the employee experience. Communication around value and culture, for example, can influence how employees experience behaviors from their colleagues. Executive and global employee communication content can influence employee perceptions and experiences of priorities such as organizational transparency and ethical behavior.

One particular area where communication can influence the employee experience is digital communication. For example, company intranets have been notoriously oblivious when it comes to the employee experience. From the number of clicks required to find a colleague's phone number or email address to multiple sign-on requirements needed to gain access to applications that live "behind the firewall"—every extra click and drag required by an employee can influence their perception of the organization's commitment to efficiency and providing employees with critical tools. That, in turn, can either enhance or sour the employee experience.

Continuing with the example of intranets, employee communicators seeking to improve employee engagement should view intranets as gateways to working for employees, not repositories for information. That means they need to not only host information about the organization's business. An intranet needs to be a tool that employees use to get their work done. From filling out expense reports to processing invoices and a host of other business processes, these digital gateways have to serve many purposes, but the most important is that of doing work.

And even with sharing information, intranets increasingly are becoming more relevant to employees by recognizing who they are, where they work and what interests them. Artificial intelligence used behind the scenes is used to customize news feeds that meet the unique needs and interests of individual employees. In fact, the "external experience" employees have using non-work-related technology is the standard they expect for company-sponsored digital tools (we'll examine the use of AI in employee communication in Chapter 14).

Employee communicators should be closely involved with, if not responsible for, assessing how intranets and other communication tools enhance the employee experience. Social digital platforms, for example, are new, emerging priorities that companies are deploying to enhance the employee experience. In particular, the rapid explosion of remote-work options has made social platforms that enable collaboration, such as Slack and Microsoft Teams, an important capability. Whether it's the selection of the application, its introduction and training on how to use it, or providing continuous content, employee communication has a big role to play.

When digital tools like employee intranets are not well designed, maintained and continuously enhanced, the employee experience can take a significant hit. When employees can't find what they need to work, don't have access to the right tools to make them efficient, or don't trust information they're receiving from their companies, there are significant opportunities for employee communicators to be a part of the solution. Whether it's working with IT to remove multiple sign-on requirements for employee intranets, or developing strategic content that shows what employees are doing to reflect organizational values, the need is real and significant in scope. When these tasks are done well, they can make employee communicators highly valuable strategic business partners.

Disengaged employees cost employers a lot of money. According to Gallup, disengaged employees have 37% higher absenteeism, 18% lower productivity and 15% lower profitability. When that translates into (U.S.) dollars, you're looking at the cost of 34% of a disengaged employee's annual salary, or $3,400 for every $10,000 they make. Whether the number is exactly that across the world or not, we can assume that a disengaged employee costs substantial money, regardless of where they work.

Building an Employee Engagement Communication Plan

Like any effective plan, building a communication program to drive improvement with employee engagement starts with two critical ingredients—partnership and data.

A partnership with HR, Organizational Development and IT is a great place to start, though other functions may be important to include as well. Understanding what's important to the organization for engagement, and how it defines and measures it, is critical to understanding how employee communication can help. HR, in particular, should fully understand the touchpoints of the employee lifecycle from hiring to leaving the organization and can map all work-related interactions. Partners also can help better interpret the data, so that there is greater clarity as to where communications can help. Armed with insights about those touchpoints, definitions and measurement, employee communicators can then assess how future communication strategies can support improvement in specific areas.

Communication strategies should be aligned with owners of the measurement process, and, where appropriate, communications metrics should be added or adjusted so that future surveys can reflect the impact of communication actions. It's critical to align on where and how communications can move the needle on employee engagement efforts, and that's done with direct and transparent conversations with senior leaders who have accountability for driving engagement improvement.

If, for example, an employee engagement strategy is ensuring 100% of managers conduct meetings with team members to review engagement survey results, communication professionals can't be held accountable for forcing managers to have meetings with their teams. They can, however, be accountable for delivering clear, concise and relevant communication tools on how to conduct those meetings, and managers can provide feedback on the usefulness of those communication tools.

Best practices for engagement communication strategies typically begin with reporting the results of a formal survey, or pulse surveys, used to measure engagement. Broad themes can be well articulated and framed through employee communicators and their writing skills. Importantly, results need to be transparent, with both the good and bad news, and offer more specific, granular insights to team leaders, along with guidance on how to best communicate those more local results to their teams. Here again, employee communicators can support the process with tools and discussion guides that management can use to customize the delivery of their teams' results.

Beyond delivering the results, employee communicators play a pivotal role in bringing broader visibility to the process and the broader results. This can include strategies like putting the CEO, and other senior leader voices behind the importance of participating in the surveys, attending meetings to review local team results and engaging in prioritizing team solutions and tracking implementation. In other words, beyond talking about survey results, managers need to engage their employees with action items, and senior leadership needs to hold managers accountable for taking those actions. Companies that follow this practice of putting action behind words are using tried-and-true strategies that improve engagement and can directly measure communication effectiveness in the process.

Broader communication strategies that go beyond engagement survey results are important to develop and execute longer term. For example, a thoughtful full-year communication agenda that reinforces critical engagement topics—whether it's values, ethics, compliance or culture—often is central to sustained internal communication efforts that deliver meaningful engagement change.

Engagement and Change

In the previous chapters, we've discussed how employee communicators are asked to drive or support sustained internal communication efforts that spur awareness, deeper understanding and belief in values and culture. We also know that they're increasingly asked to help drive change management through communications. The reality is that all roads lead to, and through, employee communication.

Disengaged employees are far less likely to fully participate in significant change initiatives because they fundamentally are uninvested in the company, its purpose, their manager or a host of other issues.

When communicators understand what's driving disengagement—and have strategic business partners working with them—they can better support change and strengthen employee engagement. Without strong, strategic employee communication, those efforts would undoubtedly falter. Clearly, the employee communicator could not be better positioned to influence more critical business results.

Profile: Christina Ali

Senior Manager—Internal and Executive Communication
PepsiCo Beverages North America
White Plains, NY, USA

Career Bio

I started out my career planning to join the U.S. Foreign Service, but thanks to a job opportunity involving politics early in my career, I learned that it was not something I wanted to spend my life doing! It was while doing that political job that I "discovered" public and media relations. When I moved on from that position, it was to a new career path and a communication job in New York City, working for a nonprofit organization that dealt with U.S.-based companies doing business within the Americas. It was there that I had my first real opportunity to work with the press, work on annual reports, and learned about website creation and upkeep.

After a few years, I moved to a role in media relations at another non-profit, this time at a global humanitarian organization. When the opportunity to join PepsiCo's Corporate Communication team came up, I took it for a variety of reasons, including being able to round out my experience by adding corporate communication knowledge to my government and non-profit experiences. I started out in a public relations role, but was drawn to the internal side of communications, and have been able to work for both the corporate team and several sector teams—moving through a variety of roles over the years.

Currently, my role consists primarily of sector and executive content creation (both written and video) and event communication. Everything I work on is to help build the understanding of my sector's business strategy with associates and to help instill an ongoing sense of pride in being part of our business. It is also a priority for me to demonstrate a clear link between the work that our associates are doing and how the business performs.

The Influence of IT on Employee Communication

I faced an issue once during a project to upgrade our intranet. The project managers on the IT side—who were a series of contractors—changed a few times. That affected continuity. To make a long story short, we were getting close to the "go live" day, and during a regularly scheduled update meeting, the newest project manager told me that something that had been discussed and agreed to early in the process was no longer possible.

This change would ultimately make the deliverable much less desirable in terms of the end-user experience. There was a bit of back and forth between us, and when the IT team said it couldn't deliver—I knew they could but did not have the technical know-how to explain how it had originally been planned for execution.

In order to keep the project moving forward—and with the right outcome in mind—I instant messaged an IT colleague, who I'd partnered with on many past projects, to run the problem by him. Despite having nothing to do with that specific project, and having his own job duties to take care of, he not only agreed with me that the originally planned deliverable was possible but also volunteered to come down to the meeting and discuss with the broader project team. It took him five minutes in "IT speak" to convince the contractors that it was not only a possible action, but also actually a quick and easy thing to do from the technical side.

Ultimately, I helped deliver a product that was easy to find and navigate for our employees—increasing the value of the website and the overall engagement. Sometimes you may not be able to sway the outcome in your favor, but it is worth asking a few extra questions and pushing for it. I am very passionate about making the communications that I manage both easy and effective for employees to find, understand and use. That's why I always fight the extra fight to make things right for them!

Case Study

PSP INVESTMENTS DRIVES INCREASED EMPLOYEE ENGAGEMENT THROUGH CHANGE

Situation

PSP Investments ("PSP")—a Canadian Crown corporation established to invest funds for the pension plans of federal government employees—hired a new CEO in 2015, and he brought with him an ambitious change plan that required a fully engaged workforce.

For a decade and a half, PSP maintained a low profile—something that changed dramatically when a new president and CEO reinforced the corporation's growth strategy. It led to the opening of New York and London offices, the creation of a new asset class, fostered a stronger focus on worldwide partnerships and led to hiring more than 200 new employees in 18 months, representing close to a quarter of the company's existing staff.

An initial employee survey indicated that 42% of employees felt they were not receiving sufficient information regarding change, or sufficient communication from PSP Investments' leadership. An internal review of practices showed employee communication consisted mostly of traditional tools and a few intranet posts per week.

The approach was top–down, and on a strict need-to-know basis, leading communicators to set three specific goals, which included delivering an internal communication framework by increasing employee engagement by a minimum of 10%; leveraging the company's internal communication tools by increasing communication output by 25%; and leveraging and improving existing PSP employee programs by increasing participation by at least 10%—all in an effort to mobilize employees and encourage and strengthen collaboration.

Campaign

Communication efforts started with the company's 2017 launch of One Workplace, PSP's new work environment focusing on openness, collaboration, innovation and technology, at its primary business offices in Montréal. To complete the new environment, PSP relocated closed-door offices into various configurations of open, collaborative spaces in phases between April 2017 and June 2019. Employees received a welcome kit that included practical items to help them adjust to up-close neighbors; those kits included items, such as friendly neighborhood guidelines, ear plugs, sunglasses and granola mix, to encourage mobility and wellness.

In addition to its new, open-concept office spaces, One Workplace also included several common areas that focused on flexible functionality. A bistro café, an outdoor patio, The Studio—a space for ideation and collaboration, and a Zone Zen, a quieter space for those who want to focus or work individually, also were used for special employee events. The Studio, for example, was the site for PSP's first Inclusion & Diversity (I&D) forum.

Communicators also placed significant focus on ensuring strong dialogue and transparency with employees, mainly through improved and increased content on the company's intranet, ZOOM, and through employee town hall modifications. They introduced "like" and "share" buttons in 2016 to encourage interactivity and horizontal communication across the organization. In

2017, the number of likes and shares increased considerably over the course of the year, as the team continued to promote open dialogue with employees and improved the quality and frequency of its content. It worked on revamping key pages and improving navigation. Taking advantage of "One Workplace" and the popularity of its new bistro area, communicators installed a giant media wall to leverage key moments to reach employees through dynamic animations, videos, powerful images and engaging slide shows. The team also pushed important messages to employees by changing the backgrounds of their computer screens when necessary.

Finally, the team leveraged and improved existing PSP programs by increasing participation by at least 10%, to mobilize employees as they encouraged and strengthened collaboration.

To support PSP's five-year strategic plan, Vision 2021, employees across the organization were asked to commit to implementing numerous key initiatives that went above and beyond their regular work. As these initiatives were of high importance, communicators sought to maintain the momentum and employees' motivation. The team focused efforts on building Espresso à 2, events that brought random employees together for a coffee and integrated over 100 interns into the program. The team included the PSP Gives Back program into employees' scorecards to encourage volunteering. Additionally, communicators made significant improvements to the company's annual Employee Town Hall meetings—revamping content and format, and putting employees at the forefront instead of senior management, which led to a significant increase in attendance and participation.

Results

Measurement efforts showed increased engagement during this period of significant change. A follow-up survey, conducted five months after the baseline survey, indicated that employees recognized that the organization was managing change in a more effective manner. A September 2016 survey showed a 21-point improvement in communications. Moreover, PSP saw a dramatic increase in employee survey participation, from 67% to 84%—indicating it was making progress with an engaging cultural shift.

A third and final survey in June 2017 showed the employee response rate reached 85%, making it the highest participation rate in the measurement process. Communications greatly improved at PSP, representing the highest increase since Phase 2—an increase of 16%.

Output from the communication team during the campaign increased 25%, as the team generated more content on its intranet site. Employees were more engaged with that content—with an 87% increase in stories "liked."

Communication efforts also generated measurable improvements in employee participation in PSP programs. The company's PSP Gives Back Program quickly gained momentum, with more than 500 employees participating in volunteering initiatives, representing participation from over 63% of its permanent global team. PSP employees donated over 4,500 hours of their time to important causes, and local charity contributions from employees increased by 20%, and included an increase of 11% for United Way. Specific events focused on supporting change also registered increasing engagement: the company's Espresso à 2 program participation increased by 20%.

Employee town halls also became more dynamic, interactive and inclusive of all employees, in line with the One PSP culture. At the final town hall of 2017, 32% of employees attended the event and generated a 25% increase in questions asked, supporting the team's goal of increased engagement.

Source: PRSA Silver Anvil Awards (2018)

Bibliography

Borysenko, K. (2019). How much are your disengaged employees costing you? *Forbes.* Retrieved from www.forbes.com/sites/karlynborysenko/2019/05/02/how-much-are-your-disengaged-employees-costing-you/?sh=11e3deb43437.

De La Haye, S. (2019). The best employee value proposition examples for 2020. *Pinpoint.* Retrieved from www.pinpointhq.com/insights/employee-value-proposition-examples/#evp-example-1-hubspot-s-employee-value-proposition.

Harter, J. (2020). Historic drop in employee engagement follows record rise. *Gallup.* Retrieved from www.gallup.com/workplace/313313/historic-drop-employee-engagement-follows-record-rise.aspx.

Harter, J., & Rubenstein, K. (2020). The 38 most engaged workplaces in the world put people first. *Gallup.* Retrieved from www.gallup.com/workplace/290573/engaged-workplaces-world-put-people-first.aspx.

Hastings, R. R. (2009). The 'what' and 'why' of employee engagement. *SHRM.org.* Retrieved from www.shrm.org/resourcesandtools/hr-topics/employee-relations/pages/whatand-why.aspx.

Macey, W. H., & Schneider, B. (2008). The meaning of employee engagement. *Industrial and OrganizationalPsychology,1*(1),3–30. https://doi.org/10.1111/j.1754-9434.2007.0002.x.

Mercer. (2020). Expand the view of total rewards to strengthen the employee value proposition. *Mercer.* Retrieved from www.mercer.us/what-we-do/workforce-and-careers/total-rewards-and-employee-value-proposition.html.

13

BEYOND CHANGE

Other Employee Communication Roles

One size does not fit all for employee communicators. The size, needs and priorities of each organization drive the unique roles internal communication must play. While many organizations centralize employee communication as a corporate level function, others deploy internal communicators to work directly within business units or specialized staff functions. Depending on the size of the enterprise, communicators may be assigned to support multiple staff functions, for example, Finance and IT, or assigned to a single staff function.

While the skills and tools used for broader employee communication teams and initiatives are every bit as relevant and practical for these specialized internal communication roles, the focus areas themselves require deeper understanding, nuanced messaging and correspondingly customized strategies.

Larger global organizations, which have correspondingly larger staff functions, may employ dedicated employee communicators who report directly to the senior functional executive, like a chief human resources officer (CHRO), or may share dual-reporting responsibilities to both the function leader and a global communication head.

These roles exist to further the priorities and mission of the function, in line with the culture and values of the enterprise as a whole. Communicators in these spaces may be asked to focus on driving change within the function, planning and executing communications from the function to the rest of the organization, or both. The work ranges from tactical, practical support of regular functional processes, to more sweeping outcomes when staff groups are driving major transformation across their companies.

HR communicators, for example, are often accountable for communicating cyclical rollouts of benefits, compensation and other programs and policies, both by helping the program team communicate with HR business partners and then

DOI: 10.4324/9781003024118-13

sharing the end-user version of those changes directly with employees. But these same communicators also play a key role in managing people-related crises and the delivery of more strategic culture shifts, such as changes to an organization's employee value proposition, their external profile as an employer of choice or other issues relating to the employee–employer relationship.

In this chapter, we explore two specialized employee communicator roles, both connected to HR; we look at Finance and IT communication; and finally, we explore a ubiquitous role that every employee communicator must fill: the consultant.

Within HR organizations, communicators can be hired or deployed from global communication teams to support the CHRO, for a range of internal communication needs. The second role is connected to a rapidly growing area of focus: Diversity, Equity and Inclusion communication, which often resides within the HR function as well.

Whether a communicator chooses to work within HR for a few years, or ultimately spend a career going deeper into HR communication, learning the business agenda for people is never a bad idea. The interdependence of the HR agenda and the broader employee communication agenda is indisputable. Each requires a full understanding of the other.

HR Communication

Employee communicators hired or deployed to drive HR communication—as one senior IBM HR communication executive puts it—"ultimately influence how people feel about their jobs." It's not surprising that how employees perceive the fairness of the "deal"—the return they receive for the work they do—dramatically influences employee engagement, which is covered in Chapter 12.

As a result, the HR communicator's tasks will range as broadly as the HR leaders they support. One executive, assigned to the CHRO of a global Fortune 50 company, shared that a typical week included drafting a communication plan to introduce a new learning program, reviewing an outside ad agency's proposed recruiting campaign, providing feedback for the HR section of the company's redesigned intranet, reviewing an executive compensation presentation for the Board of Directors, staffing the final plan design review for that year's healthcare decisions, finalizing a speech the CHRO was delivering the following week and facilitating a half-day workshop for field HR teams on brand and values. This communicator also organized timing for key announcements with her communication peers in other parts of the business, so they could try to manage the potential for employee overload.

What's unique about the work is the degree to which the HR communicator must learn, understand and—sometimes—challenge the issues at play in an organization's labor costs, hiring plans, benefit costs, total rewards and other HR issues, while never losing sight of the larger culture, values and business priorities for the organization.

Consider, for example, *benefit communication*. HR communicators are often asked to help launch new programs or communicate repeating cycles. While that can seem transactional and administrative—and often is—it is also an opportunity to help the HR team deliver employee experiences in line with the values and culture their organization is trying to drive. Annual benefits enrollment in the United States, for example, is not a simple exercise in information dissemination. From dental care to vision and general health care, the choices are increasingly vast and correspondingly complex. Adding to the challenges of communicating what those choices are, the news isn't always good. Rising healthcare costs for companies can translate into higher premiums for employees, fewer choices and more involved processes for receiving medical benefits or prescriptions.

Rather than simply sharing headlines about increased costs or elimination of some benefits, communicators are charged with educating employees about how the benefit costs may be affecting the organization's competitiveness in the market. They may also partner with the benefits team to help employees become smarter healthcare consumers to make the most of their healthcare benefits money. From choosing a healthcare plan based on unique employee and family needs to explaining benefits that are increasing or decreasing—and why—the communicator is tasked with finding the right way to deliver messaging that both is clear and shows emotional intelligence about how that message will be received.

As often as not, there are firms specializing in benefits communications that deliver useful explanations of complex or technical components of benefits, which in many parts of the world are guided by law and regulatory requirements. But insights, context and perspective from internal communication professionals—who know the history of the enterprise, understand current business challenges and can identify any "hot buttons" that can influence employee perceptions—will generate more strategic and impactful communication that helps the organization.

Beyond choices, conditions demand HR communicators understand industry standards for benefits, marketplace dynamics from competitors and customers, and, of course, how all of those forces impact costs for the organization. Strong partnerships with benefits professionals in the HR organization, and participation in early, advanced conversations about proposed benefits changes, can dramatically and positively influence messaging and delivery of benefits changes.

Compensation-related communication is another significant area of focus for HR communicators. Organizations with bonus programs, longer-term incentive plans with elements such as stock options and restricted stock, and companies with merit increase programs—used to reward non-management and management employees for annual performance—can be complex and challenging.

For example, the decision to eliminate or postpone merit increases, as many companies did during the 2020 global pandemic, posed a number of challenges for companies to communicate. As organizations closed facilities and/or eliminated roles on larger scales, those who remained not only absorbed much of the work of their terminated peers, but also received the news that there would be no salary and/or bonus reward or increase during that period or that it would be deferred for months to years. Even in a depressed employment market, organizations still were concerned about retaining their best and brightest employees.

Someone needs to communicate those kinds of messages in ways that are thoughtful, direct and with emotional intelligence. That's where employee communicators in HR can provide high-value counsel and skills. From briefings for managers to CEO-level communications that go directly to employees, HR communicators should be key influencers for strategy, delivery and measurement of that messaging.

As many organizations began to pull back on their contributions to employee pensions, or eliminate them completely, employees across the globe were, and are, faced with new challenges to plan for their retirement. As each company has made the decision to stop contributing to employee pension plans, some have replaced that benefit with contributions to 401(k) plans or similar retirement planning funds. Others have partnered with financial planners to develop new retirement forecasting and investment tools to help employees make more informed decisions about how to plan for retirement. Regardless of what, if anything, replaced pension plans, HR communicators have had the responsibility for explaining the changes, giving perspective about what other companies and competitors were doing and highlighting what new options were created for employees and future retirees.

In 2012, global food and beverage giant PepsiCo told its salaried employees that it would no longer continue to match employee contributions to their 401(k) retirement plans. In the following example, the company provided context around fluctuating financial markets, annual reviews of programming and competitiveness of the total market competitiveness of the benefit plan, even minus the company match. The tone is straightforward from the company's CHRO and further offers a new Roth Individual Retirement Account (IRA) option that was to be introduced several months after this communication.

Dear Salaried Employee,

PepsiCo has long prided itself on the competitiveness of our retirement benefits. We provide all salaried employees with a Company-funded retirement benefit. Some of you earn this benefit through a traditional defined benefit pension plan, while others receive a retirement benefit through the Automatic Retirement Contribution (ARC), which is deposited into the 401(k).

We review our programs annually to ensure that we are providing market competitive benefits—from both the employee and Company perspective. Fluctuating financial markets continue to have an impact on retirement programs like our defined benefit pension plan. While we remain committed to our goal of helping associates prepare for a financially secure retirement, we do need to make an important change to continue to deliver a competitive retirement benefit. Beginning in late January 2012:

- **Salaried exempt and overtime eligible employees currently earning a benefit under a defined benefit pension plan** will no longer be eligible for the Company match on their 401(k) contributions. When compared to the market, retirement benefits for this group remain above average, even without the 401(k) match, due to the competitiveness of PepsiCo's defined benefit pension plan. **This change does *not* impact hourly, commissioned or OTR employees.**
- If you are impacted by this change, **your final Company match will be made for the 401(k) contributions deducted from your January 27 paycheck.**

Please Note: If you receive the ARC, this change does *not* apply to you. You will continue to receive matching contributions to your 401(k) since the Company match *plus* ARC is designed to provide you with a market competitive benefit. Also, as noted earlier, this change does not impact hourly, commissioned and OTR employees.

> For those impacted by the change, depending on your other investments, assets and resources, it may still be important for you to contribute to the 401(k) to supplement your retirement income. You'll have more choices for the saving in the plan when we introduce a Roth 401(k) feature this spring. Look for more information in April to learn how this new feature offers increased flexibility for tax and estate planning. In the meantime, to ensure you stay on track for retirement, use the online tools on NetBenefits at www.netbenefits.com. You can also call a Healthy Money financial counselor at xxx-xxx-xxxx to discuss how to prepare for your financial needs in retirement.
>
> If you have any questions relating to your pension benefit or 401(k), please call the PepsiCo Savings and Retirement Center at Fidelity at 800-xxx-xxxx.

Beyond compensation and benefits, HR communicators also find themselves in the middle of some of the more difficult situations that, for lack of a better phrase, "put them on the front lines of ugly situations," one HR communicator said.

Whether it's planned events, such as workforce downsizings, or crisis communication for response to events such as litigation or protests, they must exercise "emotional intelligence" to drive communication around established company protocols and processes. While there should always be clear protocols for notifying employees, family members and other stakeholders about things such as workplace accidents or violence, a communicator working with other HR professionals and operating managers must be a beacon of reason and appropriate tone in how those events, and the organization's responses, are communicated.

When events happen that claim employee or contractor lives and destroy property, most of us see only the media coverage of the news event. Behind the scenes, there are intense moments of decision-making on what, and how, to communicate to stakeholders who want to know what happened and why. Here again, HR communicators can be deployed to partner with managers, HR business partners and corporate PR professionals who all must be aligned with the response, the sequence in which it will be delivered, who will be the communicator and how the response to the communication is assessed.

To be clear, all of these areas handled by HR communicators require the same disciplines covered in previous chapters. Strategic messaging (Chapter 2), storytelling (Chapter 11), executive communication (Chapter 9) and change management (Chapter 10), just to name a few, are all critical skill sets that will serve the HR communicator well. And, as with broader employee communicator efforts, segmentation (Chapter 7) is a vital tool in the chest.

Specifically, HR communicators must view HR business partners (HR managers embedded across most enterprises) as a discrete set of internal stakeholders. These HR professionals have direct contact with management and broader employee populations and must be empowered to communicate effectively and in timely ways. Before any compensation or benefit change can be communicated to employees, or deployed across an organization, HR business partners should be fully briefed on the details and how their roles will need to support the change. That typically requires carefully sequenced, targeted communication messaging, tools and strategies to achieve.

It would be easier for communication professionals early in their careers to think of HR communication as process-driven or transaction-based. While some of that certainly would be a part of an HR communicator's role, it should not be all, or even most, of what the role should be in order to add value.

The flip side of transaction-based communication for HR is the ever-present need to strategically communicate the soul of an enterprise, and that's where HR communication should be a driver. The challenge of this particular responsibility for communicators is that it requires time and experience to get it right. To add further challenge to doing it well, HR communicators tend to move into those roles earlier in their careers. The positive is that a steep learning curve will drive quick learning. The downside is that the ability to influence and drive can be limited early on—simply as a function of being a more junior communicator. Whether communicators are hired into HR functions directly, or deployed from centralized Corporate/Employee Communication teams, the need to learn quickly and become an influencer is significant but manageable.

When there is a centralized Corporate or Employee Communication function, it's critical for an HR communicator to stay connected to that centralized function. That usually means reaching out, and ensuring they remain on the "radar" for broader communications development and advancement. While some organizations are better than others at ensuring strong connectivity between functional communicators in areas like HR, others can create more siloed ways of operating. This can lead to functional communicators feeling disenfranchised or pigeon-holed in a more defined area of employee communication. "It can be a tough place for more junior communicators to cut their teeth," one senior HR communicator said. The key to ensuring connectivity is to be proactive in managing relationships with colleagues and leaders in the centralized communication function.

As with any communication role, the ability to influence—to get a "seat at the table" where decisions are made—means HR communicators need to think and behave more than task communicators. They must dive deeper into what's being asked, understand why, and assess how communications can influence the desired result. This is particularly important with IT-related changes that connect to HR communication. Too often, technologies deployed through

HR—for compensation- and benefits-related activities—are not consumable for employees. Whether it's too many "clicks" to get what employees want or navigation flaws that do not align with HR process changes, having an HR communicator engaged early and often can help deliver a better product, and a better experience for employees.

Every employee can experience a company in a different way. But HR communicators, perhaps more than any other communicator, will have a front-row seat for seeing, and potentially influencing, how the company's initiatives reflect its values and, ultimately, attract and retain engaged employees.

Diversity, Equity and Inclusion Communication

The 2020 murders of George Floyd, Breonna Taylor and Ahmaud Arbery in the United States, and the resulting protests across the country, drew more attention to the Black Lives Matter (BLM) movement and refueled many organizations' commitments to diversity, equity and inclusion (DEI). Over the last two decades, companies have come to understand that more diverse workforces can deliver greater innovation and insights into the markets and customers they serve. When added to the #MeToo movement—a social movement against sexual abuse and harassment against women by typically powerful and prominent men—BLM sparked a dynamic new wave of energy targeted at supporting diversity and inclusion efforts.

In fact, the impact of more diverse workforces is measurable. Global management consulting firm McKinsey has found that gender diversity on executive teams shows the strongest correlation between diversity and profitability. They report that having gender diversity on executive teams is consistently positively correlated with higher profitability across geographies.

In the firm's original research in 2014, diversity data showed that companies in the top quartile for gender diversity on their executive teams were 15% more likely to experience above-average profitability than companies in the fourth quartile. Its 2017 data set showed the number rose to 21% and continued to be statistically significant. For ethnic and cultural diversity, the 2014 finding showed a 35% likelihood to outperform, comparable to the 2017 finding of a 33% likelihood to outperform.

These correlations show why improving representation of diverse employees by gender and race in employment and leadership roles has become a staple goal for modern-day, diverse organizations in about every industry. Adding inclusion to the mix—driving behaviors that make employees feel they can bring all of their unique attributes to the workplace—soon followed efforts to recruit, retain and advance more diverse workforces.

But the BLM movement's acceleration in 2020 added something new to the mix: equity and equality. Equal treatment of all employees and the recognition of unconscious biases in day-to-day interactions with people of color have become far more commonplace in the wake of 2020's social and civil unrest. Organizations have come to realize that ensuring equity—in pay, promotion and influence—for people of all colors and genders, isn't just a good thing to do; it's the right thing to do for their businesses. Today, the longstanding "diversity and inclusion" (D&I) plank in many organization mission statements began to transform to something bigger and broader, now often referred to as DEI.

It's no surprise, then, that companies everywhere are looking for employee communicators to help them articulate DEI strategy, support training efforts, showcase stories of success and challenges and measure the impact of communication efforts. As often as not, communicators will be embedded in the organization's HR function and focused specifically on this rapidly emerging communication priority area.

Effectiveness as a DEI communicator demands deeper skills and understanding of the strategies the organization selects to drive greater performance in this area. Professional organizations, such as PRSA and IABC, have created toolkits and offered workshops and other information to help provide a deeper understanding to communicators.

These organizations, and others, highlight topics for communicators such as:

- Global trends around the workforce of the future
- Unconscious bias training
- Talking and walking the diversity and inclusion mandate: What to do about DEI in the workplace
- Best practices in equity, inclusion and diversity and planning for the future
- Ways to incorporate relevant takeaways into your integrated communication strategy

From change management to storytelling and measurement, many of the competencies that exist for general employee communicators apply to HR communication as well. It's getting into the specifics of recruiting and retention practices, working with *Employee Resource Groups* (ERGs)—which bring together employees based on gender, race, sexual orientation or other affiliations—and getting into the specifics of racial and gender bias that distinguishes this focus area for internal communication.

Role descriptions for DEI communicators show just how important it is to connect these specialized communication efforts to employee branding, broader employee communication and even PR efforts. At the end of the day, DEI communication should fully drive employee engagement efforts across the enterprise and help shape its CSR story on people.

Consider this role description Amazon used in 2020 to recruit a communications leader for its DEI efforts:

Amazon Diversity Equity and Inclusion Communications Leader

Come share your passion, innovative ideas, and creativity while helping Worldwide Operations (WWOps) Diversity Equity & Inclusion (DEI) team enable an inclusive workforce. In this role, you will build and drive the organizational DEI marketing and communication strategy to achieve measurable improvements in understanding, engagement and inclusion indicators. You will design both high-touch engagement solutions and cross-platform campaigns, in close collaboration with Amazon's Public Relations, Employer Brand, and Internal Communications teams.

You will engage employees by highlighting authentic stories and communicating the unique backgrounds and perspectives that will amplify our position and investment in DEI across employee touchpoints (internal website, digital newsletter, eSeries, internal campaigns, etc.). You will be responsible for creating and implementing a plan to more effectively engage employees in building an inclusive environment on their teams and at their sites. In doing so, you will nurture a network of our employees and bring their unique backgrounds and perspectives to amplify our employer brand across a variety of touchpoints.

Successful applicants will have experience designing and delivering innovative DEI marketing and communications programs, assessing performance, and communicating results. You should not only be passionate about delivering world-class DEI campaigns, but obsessed with driving meaningful results that ultimately impact our customers and elevate inclusivity within Amazon Worldwide Operations.

Note the focus on using storytelling to deliver awareness and understanding of the company's DEI investment and the comprehensive nature of building many employee touchpoints into the strategy. This is evidence of the need to connect this work to the employee experience (covered in Chapter 12) as well. The advertisement for the right Amazon candidate goes on to highlight more specific job duties.

In this role, you will:

- Design and execute the organizational marketing and communication strategy in close collaboration with the Public Relations, Brand, Legal and Internal Communication teams.
- Define key messages, talking points and branding based upon the WWOps DEI three-year plan.
- Define organizational key performance indicators (KPIs) to measure success and effectiveness of the marketing and communication strategy.
- Act as a DEI subject matter advisor to integrate DEI content across WWOps' internal and external marketing and communication materials.

- Build a scalable strategy for high touch communication/engagement mechanisms (e.g., eSeries, digital newsletter).
- Project manage and influence cross functional working teams, including PR, Legal and Internal Communication partners, to launch on-time, effective content.
- Define and report on marketing and communication outcomes as a result of the programs you are driving.
- Bring a high energy, results-oriented and resourceful mindset and quickly take control of your responsibilities.
- Influence others and be proactive in identifying risks/issues, providing solutions, resolving risks/issues and overcoming hurdles to drive results.

A Case Study in DEI Communication: City Year

At City Year, an education nonprofit that brings together young adults to serve as volunteers in the United States, the United Kingdom and South Africa to support student and school success, communicators overhauled their organizational core messaging to better fit its DEI agenda. Based on feedback from AmeriCorps members, staff and stakeholders, they learned that the language they were using did not honor their AmeriCorps members' experiences serving in schools. It also didn't reflect the strengths and contributions of their students, the schools they were partnering with or the communities in which they worked.

With this feedback, Tina Chong, vice president of Communications at City Year, and Colleen Flynn, former senior director of External Affairs at City Year Boston, worked with a third party to create new messaging with input through focus groups and interviews from a wide range of staff and volunteers across departments, levels and locations to ensure that their language was authentic.

From there, they recognized other communication opportunities to make their events, particularly fundraising events, more inclusive. This included making accessibility assistance explicit in their event invitations, a description of those accommodations in its social media posts; training and staff to be proactive about creating an inclusive guest experience. They made it a priority to ensure that event spaces include gender-neutral bathrooms and prayer spaces and they communicated that availability widely to those in attendance.

Based on what they learned through research, they also worked more diligently to prepare speakers for their events, to diversify host committees and to apply greater DEI capabilities with storytelling. Their advice:

> When assessing your communications vehicles, think critically about who you are including and potentially excluding. Are all members of your community able to participate or engage with your work? Who is represented in your stories? Who gets to tell your stories? How are you requesting feedback to gauge your progress?

Financial and IT Communication

While HR communication tends to get the bulk of "deployed" internal communication support because of its internal focus on people, employee communicators also may be assigned to Finance and IT functions, particularly in larger, global organizations.

Internal communication for Finance functions often includes supporting the CFO and related internal and external agendas. For employees across the enterprise, the CFO may be the voice most closely connected to quarterly earnings reporting. In other organizations, a combination of the CFO and CEO voices is featured in financial performance communications. Working with either or both of those senior executives, employee communicators must have, and develop, a deep understanding of financial drivers of the business and the strategies deployed to drive financial performance.

They must be able to translate how business actions drive revenue, cut costs, increased margins, or profits, and ultimately deliver greater earnings for shareholders in publicly held companies. In not-for-profit organizations, financial reporting to donors revolves around where and why income is spent, and what results it generated.

More than reporting financial performance to employees, communicators must help the CFO and senior Finance leadership thread a clear, compelling story about where the business is going. Consequently, the financial story inside an enterprise must mirror the external financial story to investors, while concurrently delivering a more action-focused narrative to enterprise employees.

Finance functions often find themselves in need of communication support within the function, too. As they look to become more efficient, and as digital technologies change internal processes substantially, employees within the Finance function may need considerable internal communication support to drive change and align activities. For example, as companies work to harmonize financial systems that range from payroll to accounts payable, taxes, inventory controls and others, they often undertake multi-year IT change efforts that demand internal change communication. This is particularly common in organizations that complete acquisitions and mergers, and work to integrate financial reporting systems.

IT employee communication, as well, touches virtually every line of business, every function and every individual employee. As organizations increasingly move to, and through, digital transformation, IT functions are moving at warp speed to drive everything from new HR systems that drive manager and employee self-service to customer facing/e-commerce initiatives.

Behind every chief technology or chief information officer (CTO/CIO) and their leadership team is a substantial need for employee communication support within the function, from the function across the enterprise, and from the function to external stakeholders such as customers, suppliers and even investors on what the technology story is for the enterprise.

The Consultant Role—A Ubiquitous Requirement for Employee Communicators

Regardless of where an organization places an employee communicator, there is a conceptual employee communication role that is common across every role and in all operating parts of an enterprise: that of a consultant.

The ability to serve as a trusted communication advisor—a consultant—to business people could be defined as a competency itself. It demands a range of skills that is technical and unique to communication and a wide range of research, project management and execution capabilities.

When an employee communicator is equipped with the ability to create a consultative relationship with his or her management "clients," there is no communication challenge that cannot be solved.

Developing those kinds of relationships cannot be done by simply saying "yes" to every request. On the contrary, delivering only tactical, responsive solutions to requests like "Will you produce a video for our employee recruiting efforts?" can often be as poor a communication solution as it is a career-limiting behavior. Put simply, every employee communicator should be a consultant.

Being consultative begins with understanding that employee communicators initiate proactive strategies as often, or more than, they respond to requests from business people who—with all good intentions—may believe that tactical communication solutions work best.

Proactive employee communicators will identify ways to drive broader corporate strategy through communication. These could be solutions to issues such as growth in emerging markets, enabling innovation, improving safety performance or reducing costs—bigger, broader challenges for the business. In each and every case, it demands understanding what the business strategies are, what enables them and what obstacles exist that communication strategies can address.

Reactive employee communicators, however, are equally important. There may be requests from business leaders to deliver a tactical response or a strategic solution to specific needs they've identified for the business. For example, more tactical requests to write press releases, or produce videos or posters are frequently identified by business managers because they may view them as simple, efficient or "the way we've always done things."

A consultative employee communicator will begin with the question, "Why do you believe you need a video?" or a press release, or any other tactical communication deliverable. And communicators won't stop asking "Why?" or saying "Tell me more" until there's a deep, clear understanding of what the communication objective truly is. Creating a video to create awareness of a safety program probably won't change behaviors of employees who need to follow established safety protocols. Creating a communication response that makes employees believe those safety protocols will save their lives, and those of their colleagues, will likely be more effective and it may or may not include a video.

Filling the role of a consultant, the employee communicator will seek a deeper understanding of what a business colleague is trying to achieve, why it's important and who needs to be included in the communication solution.

Providing a strategic response to more tactical requests is every bit as important as driving for proactive communication. In fact, some of the most important communication solutions are those delivered to business managers who are not looking for a particular tactical solution, but rather want a communication answer to a business problem they've identified.

Think of a business manager asking for a strategic communication solution to a safety problem they were experiencing, not a video or a poster. Broader strategic needs, such as improving employee engagement scores or driving more cost-conscious employee behaviors, could fall into the category of reactive or responsive asks of the employee communicator. However, the solutions can be every bit as strategic, and impactful, to the business.

In any scenario—proactive or reactive, tactical or strategic—the ability for the employee communicator to clarify the problem that needs solving, and identifying the root cause of the problem is where everything must start. The communication solutions will come from developing metrics that will define success and strategies that incorporate potential and real obstacles. Then it's up to that communicator to execute, measure and report.

It may seem easy enough to read, but delivering consistent, effective employee communication strategies, and results, is the foundation to becoming the trusted advisor to a business that every communicator should seek to be.

The behaviors of the consultant—from asking questions to gain deeper understanding to illustrating how communication solutions address obstacles and enable a defined result—should define the role every successful employee communicator strives to fill.

Every Internal-Facing Role Builds a Better Communicator

Where employee communicators reside within any organization will influence their work. While centralized employee communicator roles may include project work, or focus on supporting function communication within HR, Finance or IT, companies may also choose to have dedicated, embedded employee communication support in specific parts of the organization, and/or connected to specific strategic priorities like DEI communication. Each and every one of these roles and experiences should be viewed as building blocks for a broader, deeper portfolio of employee communication capabilities. Whether communicators start their careers in these specialty areas, are asked to take them as development opportunities or choose to build longer-term careers in these areas, they serve critical needs for the enterprise and can deliver significant knowledge and new capabilities for the employee communicator.

Profile: Vivian Bialski

Communications Director, Latin America
Corteva Agriscience
Sao Paulo, Brazil

Career Bio

I have been working in corporate and marketing communication roles for more than 20 years, and my first connection with employee communication was in early years of my career, when I worked for advertising agencies as a writer. During this period, I had contact with companies from different sectors and realities and was able to learn that—regardless of the industry—the work of connecting with employees was crucial and vital for any company's success.

I have a background in communications, with post-graduate education in PR and an MBA in Marketing, and lectured in these areas for 16 years at ESPM (the largest Marketing and Communications University in Brazil). I have always told my students that one of the biggest mistakes a company can make is to not consider employees their primary and most important stakeholders.

Partnering With HR, IT and Other Functions to Drive Employee Communication Through Covid-19

When Covid-19 hit us, we immediately changed the way that 21,000 employees from all continents operated and organized them in two groups: non-site essentials (those whose scope would allow them to work remotely) and on-site essentials (employees who need to be at a site location to execute their work). This unprecedented and sudden change imposed several challenges for employee communication worldwide, including Latin America, where we employ almost 5,000 people.

The critical questions and needs we had to immediately address were: keeping our leaders visible with employees in a completely new environment; adapting our existing communication channels to the new reality and immediately embracing new tools that we had not used before; educating employees and getting them engaged with new rigid protocols for prevention inside and outside our physical facilities; managing employees' anxieties, expectations and uncertainties during pandemic times that had no end date; and supporting our field (customer-facing) employees during times of social distance.

Our ultimate goal included keeping our people healthy and supporting the continuity of our business in a completely different environment. One unique thing about the agriculture industry is that it is essential for the global supply chain. The world must be fed, regardless of the circumstances. We needed to keep operating to support millions of farmers around the globe who depend on products and technologies that allow them to do their jobs.

There was not a simple solution, and we had steep learning curves. But one of the first things we did was to immediately partner with IT to figure out new, and easy, ways to communicate with our people.

Once we had the tools in place, we increased our town hall meetings' frequency from a quarterly to monthly in Latin America. The primary focus of these meetings before the pandemic was to review our financial results from the quarter. We changed the focus and adopted a much more personal and human dialogue, putting health and recognition of employees and teams that went above and beyond to help the company reach its goals during these difficult times as core focus areas on our agenda.

Besides the town hall meetings, we recorded regular videos with senior leaders working from their homes, showing their kids, pets, homes, and their challenges, difficulties and learnings. These videos demonstrated empathy that humanized our leadership and, consequently, helped increase employee engagement.

Recognition has also been a key element of our communications during the pandemic, and it has never been as important as it is now. We visibly and publicly thanked and recognized individuals who were working from home, from a site location and from the field to make our company successful.

We created and implemented an internal campaign that was subsequently leveraged by several regions, called "It Depends on Me" (everybody's health). It focused on Covid-19 prevention and on each individual's responsibility to keep the virus under control.

Latin culture is more "emotional" and, therefore, our goal was to create communications that could connect not only with employees' brains (rational) but also with their hearts (emotions).

"It Depends on Me" was launched in early months of the pandemic. Assets created included many variations of posters with very emotional appeal, a video in a cartoon format (no words, just images, creating an universal language), and a virtual book called "Heroes of Prevention," which included drawings from employees' kids, who expressed what their parents/families were doing to protect them and others from Covid-19.

We also established a solid partnership with IHS (Integrated Health Services) at Corteva to conduct regular health pauses with employees who are working from home (webinars) and from site locations (in person). Topics for these pauses vary according to employees' suggestions and feedback and include topics such as stress management, myths and reality on Covid, anxiety and work relationships in times of distance.

Adopting new technologies, providing employee recognition, delivering relevant information (with a rational and emotional appeal), all combined, have positioned our Covid-19 communications right where we wanted it to be.

I learned that sometimes we can definitely do more and better with less. Effective employee communication is not about how much money you invest; it is about the quality and impact of your message. If someone told me a year ago that I would need to engage thousands of employees remotely for a year or more, and I'd need to generate higher impact with fewer (or the same) resources, I would have said it was impossible. Do not underestimate your potential or ability to reinvent and recreate your work. Finally, I learned that employee communication has interdependencies. We do not usually succeed without establishing great collaboration with other areas such as HR, IT and, in this particular case, Medical Services.

Surveys conducted in all regions showed that employees in Latin America were very satisfied with the way we have been communicating with them during the pandemic. Great work has been done in all the regions where we operate, but the emotional appeal we used in Latin America made a difference, as it strongly connects with our people's culture and behavior.

My advice is to know your audience. Connect with them authentically. Use empathy. Use images. Go beyond the obvious and take some risks. Finally, put your brain and your heart to work together, and you will be surprised with the results.

Case Study

KERRY "KEEPS" TALENT THROUGH STRATEGIC EMPLOYEE COMMUNICATION CAMPAIGN

Situation

Global taste and nutrition company Kerry had a retention issue at its Beloit, Wisconsin, North American headquarters, and its employee communication team developed an innovative strategic solution to address the challenge.

Kerry employs some of the top talent in their respective fields—professionals who thrive in its demanding, high-pressure culture. So, in 2015, when leaders saw a 30% increase in employees choosing to leave its

North America headquarters versus the prior year, it became cause for serious concern. Located in the small town of Beloit, the Kerry Center (North America headquarters) is located about an hour from three large cities where other companies compete for talent and where most of Kerry's employees live. Communicators knew Kerry needed to deliver more than just rewarding work for its colleagues to keep them engaged and committed to the company.

The solution centered on Kerry's leadership priorities, which included "Advancing Talent Management" and "Creating a Winning Workplace Environment." Kerry's Employee Communications & Engagement team (EC&E) recognized the need to increase employee engagement to retain top talent and support these priorities. They needed to help position Kerry as a place to connect with colleagues, build relationships, give back to the community and gain enriching, personal experiences at work through effective programming and engaging internal communication.

Research indicated that voluntary attrition was increasing year over year, and that competitors were propositioning the company's talent. Communicators also learned that most Kerry employees preferred to participate in events and activities near their homes versus the small-town offerings of Beloit. And while Kerry offered some social events, it lacked a structured program, with focused, measurable objectives and employee input. Finally, they acknowledged employee communication at Kerry was well executed but not always measurable.

Campaign

These insights led to the development of the Kerry Employee Engagement Program (KEEP). Its mission: help employees connect with colleagues, build relationships, give back to the community and enrich their personal experiences working at the company.

The communication team developed a comprehensive plan, identifying the target audience as Kerry employees in the Kerry Center (population, 850). Less than a year later, they launched the program across all North American facilities (population, 5,292).

The team articulated six KEEP objectives, which included empowering colleagues to help create a more fun, collaborative, caring work environment; improve internal communication effectiveness to increase awareness of Kerry's commitment to its people, workplace, environment and community and the events and activities available; increasing participation in employee-led activities by 25%, achieving 75% of its North American facilities adopting KEEP; and reducing the rates of voluntary attrition from the

Kerry Center and in North America overall. A seventh objective was later added: ensuring KEEP was aligned to support Kerry's global sustainability program.

Communicators measured success through employee participation tracking; email and e-newsletter open rates; intranet views, likes and shares; and voluntary attrition rates (year-over-year change).

In March 2015, communicators surveyed the target audience to gauge interest, raise awareness and choose a name. From there, the team developed four KEEP focus areas: Active, Social, Caring and Green. The team then solicited volunteers to lead each focus area. Volunteer teams developed a motto, objectives and charters. Kerry allocated a yearly budget per KEEP team, and the communication team provided guidance, filled vacancies and encouraged participation. It invested in measurable communications tools (Newsweaver) and made use of the employee social intranet and networked digital TV screens. The program kicked off in July 2015 with a launch party and became further established in 2016.

Results

In January 2016, the team rolled out the program to 44 facilities in North America inviting facility "site champions" to the Kerry Center. There, they shared the KEEP mission, objectives and a Getting Started Guide. They exchanged ideas for localized KEEP success in dynamic brainstorming sessions. Communications then followed up with monthly touchpoints and promotions to encourage steady activity. In July 2016, EC&E team members organized a North America-wide KEEP event, the KEEP Families Fed food drive.

With more than 250 employee volunteers empowered to run North America KEEP groups and activities, the communication campaign increased colleagues' awareness of Kerry's commitment to employees, the workplace, environment and community with over 100,000 impressions through email, intranet, digital TV screens and newsletter promotions in 2016. Average KEEP email open rates were 72%.

Importantly, the efforts decreased the number of employees voluntarily leaving the Kerry Center in Wisconsin by 30%, and across North America by 25% versus the prior year. The communication team exceeded its target for the number of facilities to adopt the KEEP program (90% vs. 75% goal).

Employee participation increased in activities that enrich personal experiences at work. Fifty-seven KEEP groups/events and 176 activities at the Kerry Center headquarters in 2016, vastly outpaced just 20 in the prior year.

The team also exceeded targets set for participation across all KEEP focus areas. KEEP social activities average about 1/3 of the company's Kerry Center population versus 1/8 before launching KEEP. Further, KEEP Families Fed raised over 21,000 pounds of food and items versus its 9,876 pounds goal. And KEEP Green eliminated plastic cups, resulting in 23 pounds-per-person reduced waste to landfill annually.

Source: PRSA Silver Anvil Awards (2017)

Bibliography

Chong, T., & Flynn, C. (2019). How to make your communications team a catalyst for diversity, equity, and inclusion. *Big Duck*. Retrieved from https://bigduck.com/insights/nonprofit-teams-dei/.

D&I Chapter Toolkit. (2020). *PRSA*. Retrieved from www.prsa.org/docs/default-source/about/diversity/prsa-2020-d-i-toolkit-saved-7-27_2020.pdf?sfvrsn=233ad52a_0.

Edwards, J. (2012). Read the memo from Pepsi's HR department cutting 401(k) benefits. *Business Insider*, February 13, 2012.

Hunt, V., Yee, L., Prince, S., & Dixon-Fyle, S. (2018). Delivering through diversity. *McKinsey & Company*. Retrieved from www.mckinsey.com/business-functions/organization/our-insights/delivering-through-diversity#.

14

CURRENT AND FUTURE FORCES SHAPING EMPLOYEE COMMUNICATION

While there is an infinite number of potential influences on what employee communicators will be required to address in the years ahead, the largest among them already are making their mark on the discipline.

In this chapter, we'll examine three of the biggest forces that will demand time, energy, focus and strategic assessment for employee communicators: technology, the rising voice of the employee and the influence of distance (with more remote workers) on how communications to employees are conceived and executed. Each of these influences exists in today's marketplace and will continue to grow in scale and importance.

Technology

It's no secret that technology is the ultimate modern-day disrupter in just about any industry, but for employee communicators, the implications of new technologies—both communication-focused and not—are arguably even more significant. We must learn to use them efficiently with the practice of communicating and/or understanding how their introduction into the work environment will shape the strategies and tools we use.

Cloud computing has been the single biggest enabler for organizations to adopt new communication technologies. With on-demand availability of computer system resources, especially data storage and computing power typically requiring no direct active management by the user, the Cloud has become a game changer. As organizations grow in confidence with the security of cloud-enabled technologies, one of the biggest previous hurdles for employee communicators to clear—the security firewall—is significantly smaller.

DOI: 10.4324/9781003024118-14

These technologies have direct implications for not only how employee communicators will reach their stakeholders, but also how they will reshape the organizations themselves. Those that, for example, result in fewer total employees, more employees working remotely or lead to more contract, or "Gig," employees, will have profound implications on everything from the channels we choose, to the content we select and the emphasis we place on issues such as culture and values.

New communication technologies that focus on content distribution versus more traditional content creation on the part of employee communicators will drive new definitions for our roles. With the growing, and continued evolution of employee-generated content, communicators' roles inside organizations may well become closer to an orchestrator than a craftsperson of content. From self-made training videos to employee-generated documents on best practices, smartphones have equipped employees with new tools that place unprecedented power to communicate in their hands.

As the technologies take greater hold, they will prompt a continuous evolution versus more dramatic change for employee communication. Running parallel to digital transformation efforts across enterprises, the common denominator is that data increasingly are being put in the hands of all employees simultaneously; it's being done in ways that are easier and more intuitive for them to use. While this represents a big culture change for many organizations as they empower employees to make better decisions based on good data, it also demands increasing trust on the part of the enterprise and deeper analytical skills on the part of employees.

More broadly in the world of technology, there are two forces that are shaping, and will continue to shape, the workforce: artificial intelligence and blockchain.

We'll start with *artificial intelligence* (AI), which has been around as a concept for decades. Given that history, it's not surprising that the definition of what AI is varies by discipline. For example, as encapsulated in the *Journal of Advertising*'s 2021 themed issue on AI, in the world of marketing, AI refers to the "broad idea that computers, through the use of software and algorithms, can think and perform tasks like humans." This definition differs a bit from the definition from the world of business and management that paints AI as "the theory and development of computer systems able to perform tasks normally requiring human intelligence, such as visual perception, speech recognition, decision-making, and translation between languages."

In advertising, AI was defined as "a set of disruptive technologies which simulate human intelligence and realize machine intelligence." Finally, in the communication discipline, artificial intelligence-mediated communication (AI-MC) was defined as interpersonal communication in which an intelligent agent operates on behalf of a communicator by modifying, augmenting, or generating messages to accomplish communication goals.

The commonality among all of these definitions, as explained by Shelly Rodgers in the *Journal of Advertising*, is that AI is data driven for the purpose of making intelligent decisions. For our purposes in employee communication, it's about technology learning as it operates, getting smarter along the way and solving problems or needs in the process. Imagine feeding financial results from a quarterly earnings spreadsheet into an AI-enabled tool and having it write its own, new quarterly earnings news release.

While it may take a while for AI to replace the nuanced work of storytelling away from the communicator, it most certainly will play a more immediate role in giving communicators a bit of a head start in redefining how they prepare earnings releases. That, in turn, will free communicators to spend their energies on more strategic endeavors, like that nuanced storytelling.

AI already is running in full gear with functions such as HR and recruiting. It's already being used to review resumes, evaluate video interviews and even score potential inside candidates for a promotion, assessing who is most likely to succeed in a new position.

For the employee communication professional, the opportunities to make better decisions with AI are seemingly limitless. From which headline on an intranet story is more likely to attract readership to which photo is more likely to be liked or shared, AI will have a profound influence on content that communicators will use, where to use it and when to publish it. Pulling data from intranet sites, click-throughs on email newsletters and other technologies, it will inform communicators in ways that have never before been possible. It will deliver predictive analytics.

Technologies specifically for the communicator are rapidly evolving, too. Gone are the days when interviewing a CEO or subject matter expert and waiting for a transcript took days. Tools like Otter transcribe voice to text immediately, enabling instant choices for writing, editing and production. Video editing, using tools like Descript, can be done in a fraction of the time of previous editing, as the tool automatically deletes or inserts recorded content based on edits made to the transcript.

Virtual reality (VR) and augmented reality (AR) also are rapidly emerging forces. While early applications of this technology have been synonymous with gaming, the technology also lends itself to business environments, enabling collaboration and ideation. Spatial, for example, lets colleagues create virtual work rooms with 3-D images of themselves to share digital assets from the internet, their PCs and smartphones, among other sources.

"It's like taking Zoom and making it feel more like you're in a room with your colleagues," said Shel Holtz, director of Internal Communication at Webcor, a San Francisco-based commercial contractor. Responsible for employee and executive communication, as well as social media, he has spent more than 40 years in corporate roles and consulting on communications and technology. "From new hire orientations to virtual tools to training, virtual and augmented reality technologies are very much a future game changer for employee communication," he said.

The second significant technology that will continue to influence employee communication is *blockchain*. In the article "Blockchain and Communication," Peter A. Chow-White and his co-authors define blockchain as "an emerging technology that . . . is a protocol for a decentralized, digital ledger that facilitates peer-to-peer value transfers of all sorts." Although blockchain technology is relatively new, emerging in 2009 with the introduction of Bitcoin, it has moved beyond just digital currency to "smart contracts and social applications" that don't require other entities such as governments, banks or lawyers.

Using blockchain technology, virtually anything can be tracked and traded on a network, reducing risks and cutting costs.

Businesses increasingly are recognizing that the faster information is received and the more accurate it is, the better it is for performance. Blockchain's ability to deliver immediate, shared and transparent information stored on an immutable ledger, one that can be accessed only by permissioned network members, is a game changer in the business world. From tracking orders and payments to servicing accounts and monitoring production, members share a single view and all details of all transactions end to end. They're more efficient, too, as transactions are recorded only once, eliminating the duplication of effort that's common in many traditional business networks.

To speed transactions, a set of rules—called a smart contract—is stored on the blockchain and executed automatically. A smart contract can define conditions for corporate bond transfers, include terms for travel insurance to be paid, and digitize many more common processes.

For the employee communicator, blockchain is a disruptor. As more block-chain technologies are executed, work will be outsourced and transaction-based processes will become far more automated. As those technologies increase, the number of employees is expected to decrease. Blockchains build trust into the processes they enable through added transparency and commonly applied rules. "Why have an in-house product design team when I can enter into a smart contract through blockchain and hire gig workers, agencies and/or independent contractors?" said Holtz. "In fact, gig work could become a big part of companies, replacing in-house teams."

With all this expected change, the definition of what an "employee" is will most assuredly change. The implications of having fewer employees, more gig and contract workers, and more smart contracts means everything from values to culture to ethics and compliance will need renewed focus, and more strategic communication solutions for workers of all identities.

When it comes to technologies that support enterprise-wide employee communication, the number of choices increases substantially year upon year. Each has a set of unique value propositions that cover a range of costs and capabilities. Just as there is no "one-size-fits-all" employee communication strategy that fits complex organizational needs, the technology fit for each organization requires significant exploration and partnership with IT professionals.

While most employee communication applications highlight functions that clearly deliver value for employees, an equally significant issue is how—or whether—they will work with the IT systems in place for any organization. Firewall/security issues, data bandwidth and IT security policies can limit and prohibit some functionality in employee communication apps, or create so many hurdles for employees to use them that the people they're intended to help reject them. Consider a great employee communication app that, because of security and sign-on requirements, demands that employees click three or four times to gain access to them. It's a deal breaker.

When deciding on the right solution, Holtz says technology should do one or more of three things. "It should solve a problem, improve an existing process or allow you to do something that wasn't possible before," he said. Using those guidelines helps communication professionals avoid the "shiny object syndrome," meaning they're drawn to a technology because of what it promises, not necessarily how it can deliver in their environments.

One thing that most of them have is the ability to publish content on multiple digital platforms, including mobile. With more remote employees and fewer employees sitting at desks all day, mobile is a must-have for most organizations.

New players in the digital employee communication platform industry are emerging, and they're squarely focused on building new capabilities that solve challenges posed by increasingly mobile workforces with greater needs for more relevant content. Communicators must evaluate any potential digital solution against the unique needs of their organizations. Whether it's delivering flawless live streaming or creating digital break-out rooms, integrating with other existing digital platforms or distributing content by role, location or affiliation, these and other performance drivers often factor into the decision for what will work best.

Regardless of what solution is the right one in a given environment, communicators first need to learn how to develop a requirements document with their IT partners. Done well, it will specify what the technology should solve for and include more robust details about how the right solution will fit within the IT environment and culture of the organization.

Equally important, once the solution is chosen, is that its implementation should come with a thorough change management plan. Technologies rarely, if ever, are efficiently adopted without a significant investment in change communication. As intuitive as many solutions may be, the human ability to reject anything "new" can be remarkable. Applying the discipline of change management will greatly improve the potential adoption of the technology, and an acceptable return on the sizable financial investment the company will undoubtedly make.

The Rising Voice of the Employee

Over the last several decades, strategic employee communicators have learned to listen to the voices of employees. Understanding what they are thinking, how they're feeling and what they need have become "must-haves" in creating and cultivating continuous feedback cycles.

But there is a new force coming from employees that goes far beyond continuous feedback loops: *employee activism*. Employee activism is defined by global business journalism site Quartz at Work to include:

> actions taken by workers to speak out for or against their employers on controversial issues that impact society. Employee activists focus on campaigning to change their company's policies, with a focus on social activism—actions performed intentionally to generate social change.

This kind of activism isn't limited to only employees. CEOs and other C-suite executives are speaking—and acting—out on social issues as well, and it is big business. Global consultancy firm Gartner predicted that by 2022, 1/3 of crisis communication budgets will be allocated to address the growing needs of organizations working with employee activists. It is also noted that executives cited employee activism among their top 15 concerns for 2020.

AndThenComms president Sharon McIntosh, an employee communication consultant with corporate experience at PepsiCo, Sears and Waste Management, has deep expertise with the rise of employee activist voices and says it's a reflection of the convergence of three forces: the employee's comfort with visibility, value-based employees feeling the need to take action and the growing ease of organizing and sharing the employee voice. She believes the "three Vs"—visibility, value-based action and voice—are re-shaping the future of employee communication.

"In the past, when employees commented on company or social issues, they were more likely to do so anonymously. We're seeing now that they're more than willing to be identified, to talk with the media, and to be visible," McIntosh said. She added:

> Their passion for their values is empowering them to get involved with social and environmental issues. And they've learned that, collectively, they can be quite loud. Even small numbers of employee activists can be vocal and hard to ignore. They are willing, and know how, to get the attention.

Emily Cunningham, a former Amazon employee, did exactly that when and several of her colleagues stood at the company's annual shareholders meeting in 2020 and delivered their concerns to Amazon CEO Jeff Bezos. Among the concerns raised by Cunningham were how Amazon was addressing global climate change and working conditions in the company's warehouses facilities during the global pandemic. A part of the employee group called Amazon Employees for Climate Justice, she and two other members of the group were fired by Amazon for "repeatedly violating internal policies." Cunningham told *The Washington Post*, "Because of how effective we've been in getting Amazon to take leadership in the climate crisis, they've wanted me gone for a while." So, while employees' voices may be rising, they're taking a cautionary tale from Amazon in exactly how, and where, those voices can be raised without consequence of termination. As employee activism continues to grow, challenges to existing social media policies may be fair game for revision by management and protest by employees.

Amazon is hardly alone. On November 1, 2018, more than 20,000 employees walked out of Google offices in a sign of protest to the company's long history of protecting executives accused of sexual harassment. The walkout was sparked by a report in *The New York Times* that Google gave a $90 million exit payment to an executive, after he was accused of coercing a woman to perform oral sex in a hotel room (a charge that he denied, but that the company found credible).

Claire Stapleton, a marketing manager at YouTube—which is owned by Google—created an internal discussion forum used by organizers to plan the walkout in a week's time. Using Google's own collaborative tools and its open company culture, Stapleton and her colleagues reportedly created a significant employee movement. Their demands reflected the comments and suggestions of more than 1,000 employees who participated in internal conversations about the walkout.

"Our discussions expanded very quickly," Stapleton told *The New York Times*. "What is it that we want the company to be, and what should we do with the power that we very quickly see we are harnessing? Is Google for good? Do we think that technology is toxic? Are we navigating through a host of complex issues online in a positive way?"

In late June 2019, approximately 500 employees at home goods company Wayfair walked off the job at the company's Boston headquarters—protesting news that Wayfair had been profiting off of selling beds to the detention centers along the southern U.S. border. The protesters asked Wayfair to cease doing business with BCFS, a government contractor that manages the camps, and to establish a code of ethics.

In a meeting with Wayfair employees, website *The Cut* reported that co-founder Steve Conine told employees, "The level of your citizenship as citizens is really the appropriate channel to try and attack an issue like this. To pull a business into it—we're not a political entity. We're not trying to take a political side."

The resolutions to both the Google and Wayfair walkouts appear to have sparked ongoing conversations between management and employees, with more tangible actions less clear. But what is clear is that leaders cannot separate their businesses completely from political issues, or issues that challenge the values of their employees or their culture. Also, as companies use social media policies to control what employees say in external media channels, they face the ever-present challenge of unions forming. That, in turn, could provide an avenue of protection for employees who use social media to air their grievances in new ways.

"Employees increasingly are aligning their personal values with their employers' values," McIntosh said. She added:

> We're seeing several forces converging. First, as the political landscape is becoming more divisive, employees are becoming more divisive, and more vocal. In fact, research suggests that as many as 1 in 5 employees reports having had experience in activism. Second, the global workforce of millennials is a generation that is looking for activism. They've grown up on it, and they expect a lot more from their companies. They believe that the entity they're spending the most time with—their companies—should be responsible. And third, the expansion of internal social platforms has provided them with the tools to organize, and put volume behind their voices.

Millennials also are entering the C-suite, and they're not shy about being activists on causes they care about. Apple CEO Tim Cook has been recognized for taking a public stand on issues that include LGBTQ+ rights, the environment and standing up against racism. In 2017, pharma giant Merck's CEO Ken Frazier took a stance on violence and racism when he quit a presidential business advisory panel in the wake of President Trump's initial response to racially generated violence in Charlottesville, Virginia.

Not all employee activism is seen as a negative thing. In fact, some organizations are asking their workers to be actively engaged in social and environmental issues. Outdoor apparel retailer Patagonia not only has an external activist program for customers and external stakeholders, but it also advocates for employee activism on climate-related issues, as well as a part of its talent management strategy.

Patagonia's activist web page says simply, "We aim to use the resources we have—our voice, our business and our community—to do something about our climate crisis." The company places significant emphasis on volunteer work, reporting where employees donate their time to various environmental groups. It gives money to causes focused on grassroots efforts where their employees get into the trenches as part of their philanthropy. Employees plant trees, clean shorelines and nominate environmental groups that deliver exceptional work for grants through its Miracle Grants program.

What Can Employee Communicators Do?

Patagonia's practice of aligning its own corporate values with the interests and values of its employees is a fundamental principle that all organizational communicators would be wise to follow. Just as employees should carefully examine the stated values of their prospective employers, leaders within organizations—including communication leaders—would be wise to look at how their policies reflect those values. When decisions, particularly tough ones, are aligned with stated corporate values, the clarity of what an organization stands for is reinforced. While employees still may not like the decision, their bigger question then becomes whether they support the values the organization upholds.

Listening is the second critical practice that employee communicators should enact, but not in the same ways they've been doing it. Just as communication functions have invested dollars and time in robust external social media monitoring, the onus on employee communication to have similar capabilities on internal social platforms will be increasingly critical.

Beyond just listening, it's about engaging those employees quickly and meaningfully. They want to be acknowledged, heard and have their concerns addressed with action. When they're ignored, the issue moves quickly to both larger internal importance and greater awareness with external stakeholders.

In fact, McIntosh said that in almost every case of large groups staging company protests, employees attempted to take their concerns first to internal management and were ignored. That's when they organized and took their story externally.

Listening on social channels is one important way to understand what's driving internal discourse. So, too, are more formal survey approaches. But more traditional organizational health surveys, which can have gaps up to two years between them, won't cut it. Smaller samples, with far more frequent intervals, will prevail as a means for employee communicators to better keep their finger on the pulses of their respective organizations (see Chapter 4 for more about measurement).

A third capability that employee communicators can help develop in their organizations is the ability to have difficult conversations between management and employees. It's a skill set that organizations need help in developing. Through training, and through content selections for internal communication channels, communicators can help managers and broader employee populations develop the skills, enable the culture to develop the mindset and the communication function to further develop internal channels that reinforce desired behaviors. When organizations have that mindset, it makes for less ground to cover when the company, the communities it serves, or the world, encounters social unrest.

Retail giant Target CEO Brian Cornell and his communication team exhibited that mindset, and real emotional intelligence, when Cornell communicated to Target employees and communities in the wake of the George Floyd, Ahhmaud Arbery and Breonna Taylor murders in 2020. Here's what he wrote.

> We are a community in pain. That pain is not unique to the Twin Cities— it extends across America. The murder of *George Floyd* has unleashed the pent-up pain of years, as have the killings of *Ahmaud Arbery* and *Breonna Taylor*. We say their names and hold a too-long list of others in our hearts. As a Target team, we've huddled, we've consoled, we've witnessed horrific scenes similar to what's playing out now and wept that not enough is changing. And as a team we've vowed to face pain with purpose.
>
> Every day, our team wakes up ready to help all families—and on the hardest days we cling even more dearly to that purpose. As I write this, our merchant and distribution teams are preparing truckloads of first aid equipment and medicine, bottled water, baby formula, diapers and other essentials, to help ensure that no one within the areas of heaviest damage and demonstration is cut off from needed supplies.
>
> Our store and HR teams are working with all of our displaced team members, including the more than 200 team members from our Lake Street store in Minneapolis. We will make sure they have their full pay and benefits in the coming weeks, as well as access to other resources and opportunities within Target. We'll continue to invest in this vibrant crossroads of the Seward, Longfellow, Phillips and Powderhorn communities, preserving jobs and economic opportunity by rebuilding and bringing back the store that has served as a community resource since 1976. In any of our other locations that are damaged or at risk, the safety and wellbeing of our team, guests and the surrounding community will continue to be our paramount priority.
>
> It's hard to see now, but the day will come for healing—and our team will join our hearts, hands and resources in that journey. Even now, Target leaders are assembling community members, partners and local officials to help identify what more we can do together and what resources are required to help families, starting right here in Minnesota.
>
> Since we opened our doors, Target has operated with love and opportunity for all. And in that spirit, we commit to contributing to a city and

community that will turn the pain we're all experiencing into better days for everyone.

Rather than communicating anger in response to Target stores being destroyed by protestors, the Minneapolis-headquartered retailer responded with empathy for the victims of racial injustice and its employees.

Akron-based Signet Jewelers, the world's largest retailer of diamonds, responded to the social justice movements with a series of special town halls led by its CEO, Gina Drosos. "Signet Speaks Out" was designed in response to the racial injustice that sparked widespread protests as a way for the company to have the "difficult conversation" about race. Its first Signet Speaks Out event on racism and social justice happened in June 2020. Titled, "Owning It: Let's Talk about Race/ism," its goals were to encourage honest dialogue and action to fight racism and to lead by creating safe and inclusive working environments.

Employees of color at all levels of the company spoke about their experiences, their wishes and their needs. After thoughtful discussion, the company formed a new Black Enterprise Network (BEN) employee resource group and created a new mentoring program for minority employees. The BEN group funded a program that encouraged employees to vote in the 2020 elections in the United States and created a new company-paid holiday, Dr. Martin Luther King's birthday, in 2021.

The most important lesson here is that employee communicators—more than ever—will need to be advocates of listening internally, proponents of engaging leadership with substantive employee concerns and aligners of values with decisions and communication activities.

It's a tall order, but one that places greater responsibility and accountability with professionals who are uniquely tasked with connecting leaders and employees to the most consequential of social and environmental priorities that any organization must navigate. Opting out of engaging in these kinds of issues, even when they come with political overtones, is not an option at all. Organizations that turn a blind eye to the plight of the planet risk significant losses in the war for talent, the priority of engaging workers and the ability to positively influence customers, suppliers and communities they serve.

Distance: Remote Workers Changing the Game for Employee Communicators

In the wake of the 2020 global pandemic, a looming wave of change bigger than any other is coming for business—and it's bigger, faster and more complex than anything we've seen before.

It's not just about adjusting to a "new normal," reducing a real estate footprint or phased re-opening of facilities in the wake of a global pandemic, but it's also about transforming how employees work, think and behave in ways that protect people and business from risk and drive performance. We can call it the "Third Wave" of the pandemic's impact on business.

The First Wave of change forced communicators to address a global pandemic in immediate terms. Employee communicators worked feverishly in the first weeks of the pandemic to support shuttered operations to protect employees and customers as Covid-19 spread and found ways of creating some measure of continuity in their communications to internal stakeholders.

The Second Wave featured planning for, and executing, phases of re-opening. Depending on whose estimate we believe, anywhere from 25% to 40% of employees working from an office before the pandemic was not expected to return—at least full time—to an office. Communicators began creating hybrid solutions for employees working from many more locations longer term, examining policies and planning for issues that range from real estate contraction to digital collaboration.

But it turns out that remote workers are here to stay. Facebook CEO Mark Zuckerberg in 2020 announced his plans to allow some employees to work from home permanently and his organization began aggressively recruiting talent in remote locations. He projected that 50% of Facebook employees will be remote between 2025 and 2030.

But there is a looming *Third Wave* that is much bigger and more complex for employee communicators. This Third Wave—one of cultural transformation—has speed and power behind it unlike any wave that has preceded it. The global quest for racial equality—seen in organizations such as Black Lives Matter—is driving every organization on the planet to take meaningful action at a time when they are literally and physically less tied together than at any point in modern history.

It's about diversity and inclusion, but it's also about equity. How can organizations drive new cultural norms with workforces that increasingly are not located together? How can employees who don't have a choice to work from home feel they are equal to those who have the "luxury" of that choice?

Behind the long-term solutions for Covid-19 and racial justice are even more fundamental questions for businesses that are screaming for attention. How do companies drive behaviors, instill cultural norms, support employee brand ambassadors and ensure compliance with legal and regulatory requirements in this new world?

Answers to all of these questions will take the shape of new communication strategies for driving culture, new leadership behaviors, new communication channels for employees and new tools. And it starts with taking a hard look at how each organization is prepared for The Third Wave.

Communicators who can help their organizations maintain a strong culture during this seismic shift will be heroes in the business world. Entrepreneur.com reports that trust will be the tie that binds. "The companies doing well have strong cultures built on trust and are trading on the relationship capital they've earned over time. *Trust has economic value*," wrote Jocelyn Kung, CEO of The Kung Group. "It creates the foundation for honest dialogue, alignment and accountability whether someone is looking or not. [American Consumer Electronics Company] Tile is an example of a Bay Area company that made a conscious effort with this. They wanted to create an environment where you could be yourself and where you could grow. The CEO and Chief People Officer set out to define their core values and expectations, then trained all managers to embody and implement common practices. Consequently, they are reporting very high levels of engagement and uninterrupted productivity."

Kung went on to say that with the loss of physical interactions, companies need to find more innovative ways to institutionalize trust. They must commit to relationship building and ongoing communication that invites the whole person to work, wherever they are located.

Looking broadly at the implications of more remote workers highlights many significant issues that strategic employee communicators will be challenged to address. Brand citizenship will be tested externally and internally. Work-life integration—an organization's ability to be agile with not just work from home demands but a wide range of employee needs—will absolutely be a make-or-break capability. Strategic digital integration—pulling together the tools and systems that may have been thrown into place by the first two waves—will need to be examined and deployed in ways that create true, long-term value. Culture, values and ethics and compliance will need far more attention to cultivate and curate than ever before.

On that point, consider risks associated with ethics and compliance issues. Increased violations of an existing Code of Conduct can increase as new social norms evolve—often with bad behaviors—unintentionally. Collaboration and innovation efforts can slow, or suffer. Brand ambassadorship erosion—in the form of employee understanding of, believing in, and living—through day-to-day interactions with stakeholders—is likely. Voluntary attrition rates can increase. Each and every one of these risks, if not addressed, can lead to fines, lawsuits, reputation risk and/or underleveraged human capital supporting brand(s) and innovation.

But the good news for employee communicators with this Third Wave is that it brings opportunity to make a very big difference. Every business has choices to make when faced with a big, powerful, fast wave of change: feel its crushing power or ride it like a boss. Strategic employee communicators who understand what's happening have the systems in place to support solid decision-making and the skills to execute compelling communications inevitably will win the heads, hands and hearts of their employees. The full complement of these three forces—combined with the core employee communication needs of driving day-to-day business priorities—puts employee communicators in the driver's seat to influence the most critical of business decisions, and more importantly, performance.

Profile: Sharon McIntosh

**President and Founder
And Then Communications
Norwalk, CT, USA**

Career Bio

Employee communication chose me. It was the last thing I wanted to do, but I was told it would help round out my career. My first internal communication role was dedicated to manager communications—quite innovative at the time. From there, I built Sears' first intranet and then tried my hand at e-commerce and marketing for several years. That's when I realized how much I missed employee communication and took an internal communication role at PepsiCo. Eventually, I was promoted to vice president of Global Internal Communications there, overseeing the company's efforts to connect with its more than 270,000 employees worldwide. Today, I run my own firm, And Then Communications—a boutique employee communication consulting firm, specializing in change management communication, executive communication, career coaching, employee engagement and internal channel and content strategy.

Embracing Employee Activism

I've spent a great deal of time and energy researching the dramatic rise of employee activism. Here's my prediction—employee activism will only grow. And it's not a matter of if, but when. Now is the time to prepare. I've collected some sound, strategic advice from those who have experienced employee activism, and it includes these recommendations:

> **Listen.** As communicators, it's what we do best—keeping our ear to the ground to listen to what employees are saying. We need to be in constant contact with our employees, much more than through annual employee engagement surveys. We need to understand employees' questions and concerns to be able to respond before the issue escalates. That means formal listening—such as establishing an employee panel as a sounding board—and informal listening, having more casual conversations so you can quickly tap into the employee water cooler.
>
> **Revisit your vision, purpose and values**. How often are you discussing your values with your employees? Dust them off and ask yourself if leadership's actions match their words. Are you willing to

sacrifice short-term gain in the name of long-term purpose? If your answers are a resounding yes, good for you. If not, it's time to rectify that imbalance.

Don't play whack-a-mole with communications. You know what happens when you shut down communications? It becomes a whack-a-mole game where the issue inevitably pops up elsewhere. It's every company's first instinct—just tell employees "no" or remove that intranet article receiving the negative feedback. In Amazon's case, they sent employee activists the policy, reminding them that they could be fired. What did the employees do? They produced and shared a video on Twitter featuring employees holding signs saying, "We will not be silenced."

Prepare for the worst; involve your best. Don't wait until a crisis hits. Gather your communication, HR and legal teams to decide in advance how you'll handle any difficult conversations. Meanwhile, identify your most engaged employees who could help you in a crisis—especially an internal one—by building trust with them through listening, recognition and authentic conversation.

Case Study

DENTSPLY SIRONA DRIVES EMPLOYEE ENGAGEMENT 24 HOURS OF LIVE VIDEO STREAM TOWN HALLS

Situation

In the wake of low employee engagement scores, American dental equipment manufacturer and consumables producer Dentsply Sirona needed to reach its 15,000 employees in 90 locations across the globe to reinforce the company's culture and purpose. To foster employee engagement and a one-team mindset across a culturally diverse and geographically dispersed enterprise, communicators executed a technology-driven strategy like no other.

Over a 24-hour span on November 20–21, 2019, CEO Don Casey and his management team hosted an all-company event that promoted the company's culture and purpose. In 24, one-hour time slots, executive leaders addressed employees in all 90 of its global locations via live video stream with simultaneous translation in 10 languages. In each session, tailored specifically for each region, employees spoke directly to senior leadership and asked location-specific questions.

The reason for the laser focus on culture and purpose arose from change. In 2016, Dentsply Sirona was formed from the merger of DENTSPLY and Sirona and had since undergone significant change. In the first 19 months, the CEO had introduced a new operating model and launched a company-wide transformation aimed at returning the company to growth. This over-arching effort—called Project Växa, the Swedish word for growth—encom-passed the redesign and simplification of the company's entire value chain, including its structure and processes.

In addition, a clearly defined culture—bolstered by a shared purpose, mission and operating principles had been fortified across the company in an internal rallying cry, #OwnOurFuture. However, communicators learned through the company's employee engagement survey that its employees had low overall engagement, and a noteworthy number of them were actively disengaged. It also revealed weak cascading of key messages by leaders to various levels across the organization.

The survey revealed—because of ineffective leadership communica-tion about its mission and purpose—employees struggled to make a con-nection between their role and the ultimate impact of their work. That presented communicators with a clear opportunity: driving a stronger penetration of the purpose, mission, vision and operating principles; and reinforcing that focus through its top management team. They reasoned that the importance of a shared commitment to company culture would be evident and the opportunity to address local concerns could be taken into account with middle management activated to participate and lead by example.

Research also included feedback from the company's top 70 lead-ers on the communication of the company's priorities as well as engage-ment survey results. Insights showed that the relationship between man-ager and employee has a strong effect on engagement (including a +13-percentage-point increase in engaged employees when a manager was engaged). So while employees were identified as the primary audience, communicators focused on line managers as the secondary target.

Fifty-six percent of employees were non-desk workers, and almost 40% of them did not work in the offices but served as sales representatives on the road to serve Dentsply Sirona customers. As a consequence, many employ-ees did not have regular personal contact with their line managers and had no constant access to a computer to connect to the company's intranet or email. Employees reported that they did not feel key messages and critical information were being cascaded to them. Finally, the language barrier was a significant issue for many, since global town halls and CEO letters often were not translated into all local languages.

Communication team objectives included reaching at least 50% of employees directly (live) and 80% indirectly via various channels; activating middle management and employees to engage in a dialogue with the management team and have the management team address site/region-specific questions and concerns; and significantly increasing the overall employee engagement as measured in the company's 2020 engagement survey.

Campaign

Several principles guided communicators in developing their solutions, beginning with a focus on company culture. To achieve a globally shared understanding of, and commitment to, the company's culture, the event should be focused on engaging employees in a dialogue about Mission, Purpose, Vision and Operating Principles, what they mean for all employees and how they can help deliver on them. Secondly, communicators wanted to make it memorable. They wanted not only to create a memorable event but also to create buzz across the organization and ensure the enthusiasm generated from a focused discussion about culture would last well beyond the event. Thirdly, they sought to address local concerns. The solution should consider specific cultural contexts (sites/countries/regions). It had to be in the local language so that all employees would feel they were being addressed directly and individually. For that reason, communications knew holding one global town hall for all employees would not be effective. Finally, team members were committed to avoiding information delay. The solution had to be executed in a way that engaged all employees in a relatively short time frame to prevent an information lag across locations.

The solution was a "local" town hall in the local language at all sites over the world (almost) simultaneously. Town halls were broadcast via video livestream and with simultaneous translation—in 10 languages. Organizers bundled 90 of the company's largest locations into 24 slots—segmenting language needs and time zones and allocating one hour for each town hall. This resulted in naming the event DS24hours.

The structure for each one-hour included 15–20 minutes for the management team to talk about Mission, Purpose, Vision and Operating Principles and their implications for daily work. It was followed by addressing specific needs and issues from the region raised through the engagement survey and pre-submitted questions. The remaining 40–45 minutes addressed questions from employees—either those submitted in advance or those asked in the sessions. Employees during the sessions were invited to upload pictures showing company purpose. Communicator ensured there was a livestream available to all employees so that they could watch any and all sessions through a website.

Results

The event(s) reached close to 66% employees taking part in the live sessions at the sites (vs. a goal of 50%), and more than 13,000 employees (almost 90%) were engaged in the event indirectly through other channels (vs. a goal of 80%). The team was successful in activating middle management and employees to engage in an active dialogue with the management team. Approximately 700 questions were submitted by employees around the world in advance of the event. And employees uploaded hundreds of pictures showing the company's purpose, as regional leaders organized local events allowing as many employees as possible to take part at their sites. Local managers held follow-up meetings to answer additional site-specific questions.

Engagement levels were scheduled to be measured through the company's survey later in 2020.

Source: IABC Gold Quill Awards (2019)

Bibliography

Chatterji, A. K., & Toffel, M. W. (2019). The New CEO Activists. *Harvard Business Review's* 10 Must Reads 2019, pp. 47–65. Boston, MA: Harvard Business Review Press.

Chow-White, P., Mentanko, J., Adams, P., & Frizzo-Barker, J. (2020). *Blockchain and Communication*. Oxford: Oxford University Press.

Gaines-Ross, L. (2019). 4 in 10 American workers consider themselves activists. *Quartz at Work*, September 20, 2019. Retrieved from https://qz.com/work/1712492/how-employee-activists-are-changing-the-workplace/#:~:text=The%20report%20defines%20employee%20activism,controversial%20issues%20that%20affect%20society.%E2%80%9D.

Greene, J. (2020). Amazon fires two tech workers who criticized the company's warehouse workplace conditions. *The Washington Post*, April 14, 2020.

Hancock, J. T., Naaman, M., & Levy, K. (2020). AI-mediated communication: Definition, research agenda, and ethical considerations. *Journal of Computer-Mediated Communication*, 25(1), 89–100. https://doi.org/10.1093/jcmc/zmz022.

Kumar, V., Rajan, B., Venkatesan, R., & Lecinski, J. (2019). Understanding the role of artificial intelligence in personalized engagement marketing. *California Management Review*, 61(4), 135–155. https://doi.org/10.1177/0008125619859317.

Kung, J. (2020). Survey reveals 4 transformational remote work trends. *Entrepreneurship*, June 9, 2020.

Neel, M. (2020). 5 employee communications software companies making it easier for staff to stay connected with leadership and each other in the new remote world. *Business Insider*, December 1, 2020.

Patagonia. (2020). Activism. *Patagonia.com*. Retrieved February 28, 2021, from www.patagonia.com/activism/.

PRWire. (2020). Gartner unveils top marketing predictions for 2021 and beyond. *PR Wire*. Retrieved from https://prwire.com.au/pr/93671/gartner-unveils-top-marketing-predictions-for-2021-and-beyond.

Qin, X., & Jiang, Z. (2019). The impact of AI on the advertising process: The Chinese experience. *Journal of Advertising*, *48*(4), 338–346. https://doi.org/10.1080/00913367.2019.1652122.

Ransbotham, S., Kiron, D., Gerbert, P., & Reeves, M. (2017). Reshaping business with artificial intelligence: Closing the gap between ambition and action. *MIT Sloan Management Review*, *59*(1), 1–17.

Rodgers, S. (2021). Themed issue introduction: Promises and perils of artificial intelligence and advertising. *Journal of Advertising*, *50*(1), 1–10. https://doi.org/10.1080/00913367.2020.1868233.

Spellings, S. (2019). What happens after the wayfair walkout. *The Cut*, June 27, 2019.

Target. (2020). A note from Brian Cornell to our teams and communities in the twin cities and beyond. *Target.com*, May 29, 2020. Retrieved from https://corporate.target.com/article/2020/05/supporting-communities-minnesota-beyond.

Wakabayshi, D., & Benner, K. (2019). How Google protected Andy Rubin, the 'Father of Android'. *The New York Times*, October 25, 2018.

INDEX

Note: Page numbers in *italics* indicate a figure and page numbers in **bold** indicate a table on the corresponding page.

Printed in the United States
by Baker & Taylor Publisher Services